Beginning ASP.NET MVC 4

José Rolando Guay Paz

Apress·

Beginning ASP.NET MVC 4

ISBN-13 (pbk): 978-1-4302-5752-3

ISBN-13 (electronic): 978-1-4302-5753-0

President and Publisher: Paul Manning
Lead Editor: Ewan Buckingham
Technical Reviewer: Andy Olsen
Editorial Board: Steve Anglin, Mark Beckner, Ewan Buckingham, Gary Cornell, Louise Corrigan, Morgan Ertel,
    Jonathan Gennick, Jonathan Hassell, Robert Hutchinson, Michelle Lowman, James Markham,
    Matthew Moodie, Jeff Olson, Jeffrey Pepper, Douglas Pundick, Ben Renow-Clarke, Dominic Shakeshaft,
    Gwenan Spearing, Matt Wade, Tom Welsh
Coordinating Editor: Anamika Panchoo
Copy Editor: William McManus
Compositor: SPi Global
Indexer: SPi Global
Artist: SPi Global
Cover Designer: Anna Ishchenko

Distributed to the book trade worldwide by Springer Science+Business Media New York, 233 Spring Street, 6th Floor, New York, NY 10013. Phone 1-800-SPRINGER, fax (201) 348-4505, e-mail orders-ny@springer-sbm.com, or visit www.springeronline.com. Apress Media, LLC is a California LLC and the sole member (owner) is Springer Science + Business Media Finance Inc (SSBM Finance Inc). SSBM Finance Inc is a Delaware corporation.

For information on translations, please e-mail rights@apress.com, or visit www.apress.com.

Apress and friends of ED books may be purchased in bulk for academic, corporate, or promotional use. eBook versions and licenses are also available for most titles. For more information, reference our Special Bulk Sales–eBook Licensing web page at www.apress.com/bulk-sales.

Any source code or other supplementary materials referenced by the author in this text is available to readers at www.apress.com. For detailed information about how to locate your book's source code, go to www.apress.com/source-code/.

To Jesus Christ, my Lord.

To my wife Karina and my wonderful daughters Sara and Samantha. I love you.

To my brother Juan Manuel (RIP). I miss you so much!

Contents at a Glance

Contents

About the Author

José Rolando Guay Paz has over 18 years of experience in the field of software development. He has developed software for different types of companies such as retailers, banks, manufacturers, and many more. He holds a degree in computer science from the University of San Carlos of Guatemala and a master's degree in finance from the Carlos III University of Madrid. He's a Microsoft Certified Solutions Developer and has some certifiactions on SQL Server.

About the Technical Reviewer

Andy Olsen is a freelance consultant and instructor based in the UK. Andy has been working with .NET since the early Betas and spends a lot of time these days working with ASP.NET MVC4, Azure cloud solutions, and general web development using HTML5, CSS3, and various fun JavaScript libraries. Andy lives by the sea in Swansea, South Wales and enjoys running (with plenty of coffee stops), skiing, and watching the Swans! You can reach Andy at andyo@olsensoft.com.

Acknowledgments

I want to thank the wonderful team at Apress for helping me to complete this book. I especially want to thank Andy Olsen for his valuable help. He worked very hard reviewing the manuscript and providing feedback that greatly enhanced the concepts and examples in the book. Also thanks to Ewan Buckingham, Anamika Panchoo, William McManus, Kumar Dhaneesh, and the rest of the team that made this book a reality.

Introduction

With the introduction of ASP.NET MVC in 2009, Microsoft offered developers a new approach to building web applications based on the Microsoft stack. By combining the power and maturity of ASP.NET and the .NET Framework with the advantages of the MVC pattern, ASP.NET MVC offers web application developers important features, such as testability, full control over the generated HTML, and great support for large teams working on the same project by separating the application into the model, the view, and the controller.

The purpose of this book is to introduce you to the latest version of ASP.NET MVC, version 4. To ground the book in the real world of developing web applications, the concepts presented in all the chapters are examined in the context of a sample web application.

The book is basically divided into three parts. The first part, comprising Chapters 1 through 3, starts with a brief introduction to ASP.NET and discusses where MVC fits into the whole ASP.NET framework. Chapter 2 describes the software requirements and the different options for installing ASP.NET MVC 4. Chapter 3 explains the sample application you are going to build and the tools that you need to build it, and then steps you through the actual creation and configuration of the sample application.

The second part, Chapters 4 through 6, explains the three core components of the MVC pattern. Chapter 4 examines controllers, including how controllers handle user requests through action methods and how results are produced. Controllers is the first concept as that's where it all beings, handling a request from the user. Chapter 5 explains views and how HTML is generated. It shows how to process server-side code with the new Razor view engine and how to produce appropriate output for desktop and mobile devices. Generating a response to the user is the second concept as is normally what happens after the request is processed. Finally, Chapter 6 examines models. It defines the domain model of the application by showing how to create the data model using Entity Framework and the business models using C# classes. It also examines what view models are and how to use them effectively to produce the final HTML in the browser.

The third part, Chapters 7–12, examines different aspects of the ASP.NET MVC framework, such as data validation (Chapter 7), security (Chapter 9), and routing (Chapter 10). Chapter 8 shows you how to work with client-side code using jQuery and Ajax, and Chapter 11 demonstrates how to test the different aspects of your application using unit testing. Finally, Chapter 12 explains how to deploy the application to servers you control and to Windows Azure.

I hope that this book gives you a great foundation upon which to start building web applications using ASP.NET MVC 4.

We will be using Visual Studio 2012 for the examples in the book. You can use any of the paid versions (Professional, Premium or Ultimate) or the fee Express version. Also, some of the images you will see are based on modifications made to Visual Studio in update 2, so you will need to install that update as well. You can download Visual Studio 2012 and update 2 from `http://bit.ly/VS2012Download`.

CHAPTER 1

■ ■ ■

Introducing ASP.NET MVC 4

When Microsoft first introduced ASP.NET in 2002, it had a single programming model called Web Forms that allowed developers to quickly build web applications in a way that was familiar (to those who built applications with Visual Studio) and intuitive. At the time, the Web Forms model was a breakthrough. Although in many ways the model was a black box, it definitely moved the state of web development forward.

In Web Forms, web pages are (normally) represented by two files, one with extension .aspx that defines the user interface, and another with extension aspx.cs or aspx.vb (depending on the server language, C# or VB.NET) that is used to write code to implement event handlers (e.g., button clicks, list-item selection, etc.) and other functionality. Also, the applications usually have a page called Default.aspx that represents the home page for the website.

The inherent problems that this black box produced (poor separation of concerns, extremely difficult automated testing, minimal control on server controls rendered HTML, etc.) have been criticized over the years, and that opened the door to new development patterns and technologies. While MVC is not a new concept, it brought a fresh breath of life to ASP.NET along with capabilities that were extremely difficult, if not impossible, in Web Forms.

This chapter introduces ASP.NET in general, the Web Forms programming model, the ASP.NET Web Pages model, and ASP.NET MVC itself, including the MVC pattern and the ASP.NET MVC 4 history, benefits, features, and architecture.

What Is ASP.NET?

There are three technologies for building web applications in ASP.NET:

- ASP.NET Web Forms (the original programming model)
- ASP.NET Web Pages
- ASP.NET MVC

We'll look at each of these three technologies in turn in the following sections, but first let's discuss the ASP.NET platform—that is, the substrate technology upon which all ASP.NET applications run.

According to Microsoft's documentation (http://bit.ly/ASPNETOverview):

> ASP.NET is a Web platform that provides all the services that you require to build enterprise-class server-based Web applications. ASP.NET is built on the .NET Framework, so all .NET Framework features are available to ASP.NET applications. Your applications can be written in any language that is compatible with the common language runtime (CLR), including Visual Basic and C#.

> To create ASP.NET Web applications, you can use Visual Studio. The tools and options in Visual Studio that are designed for creating Web applications are referred to collectively as Visual Web Developer. In addition, a free standalone product—Visual Web Developer Express—is available that includes the core set of Web-design features from Visual Studio.

ASP.NET includes the following features:

- A page and controls framework

- The ASP.NET compiler

- Security infrastructure

- State-management facilities

- Application configuration

- Health monitoring and performance features

- Debugging support

- An XML web services framework, which was later superseded by Windows Communication Foundation (WCF)

- An extensible hosting environment and application lifecycle management

- An extensible designer environment

So, we have a rich and powerful environment in which we can build our web applications by using the language of our choice—and it's free. In this environment, we can build applications even with Notepad, but a more sophisticated tool would increase our productivity by doing a lot of work for us; yes, I'm talking about Microsoft Visual Studio. There are paid versions of Visual Studio, but if money is a problem, then you can use the free Visual Web Developer Express.

One of the major benefits of ASP.NET is the change from interpreted code, previously used for Classic ASP (the programming model before ASP.NET), to compiled code, allowing web applications to have better performance. When our code in the application is first compiled by the high-level language (C#, VB.NET, etc.) compiler, it generates Common Intermediate Language (CIL), which is commonly referred as Microsoft Intermediate Language (MSIL) code (an assembly language supercharged with lots of vitamins and minerals). The MSIL code is later taken by the .NET runtime to generate native machine code.

Web applications created with ASP.NET are executed by the .NET Framework, not the operating system. This makes our applications type-safe and has the advantage of automatic memory garbage collection. Additionally, the .NET Framework provides structured error handling and multithreading support. Finally, information about classes, members, and all of our code in general is stored as metadata in the assemblies generated at compile time. To deploy ASP.NET applications, you can use one of the different techniques available, such as Web Deploy or, the simplest method, a file copy to the server. Deploying ASP.NET applications is a fairly simple process considering that normally the .NET Framework is already installed on the server (and if not, it can be bundled with our applications). After our applications are in the server, we need to setup Microsoft's web server, Internet Information Services (IIS), which will host all ASP.NET applications and serve the applications to end users.

It is important to note that ASP.NET is fully object-oriented (OO), meaning that not only the code we write but also the code supporting ASP.NET is OO. Your code will have full access to all objects in the .NET Framework, and you can also implement all the goodies of an OO environment (inheritance, polymorphism, and encapsulation).

ASP.NET and the .NET Framework have come a long way since ASP.NET's first release, version 1.0, and the minor update release 1.1. Version 2.0, released in 2005, added richer functionality with new controls, master pages, themes and skins, web parts, full pre-compilation, and many more features. A year later, version 3.0 added Windows Communication Foundation (WCF), Windows Presentation Foundation (WPF), Windows Workflow Foundation (WF), and Windows CardSpace. In .NET 3.5 Microsoft added even more controls and ASP.NET AJAX was already built into the framework, WCF added support for RSS, JSON, POX and partial trust. .NET 3.5 Service Pack 1 introduced Dynamic Data along with improvements for AJAX, JavaScript combining and new namespaces. Version 4.0, released in 2010, added a new set of features, such as extensible output caching, jQuery as the default JavaScript library, routing in the framework, a much better ViewState control, and a lot of improvements to existing functionality. Finally, the latest version, 4.5, released in August 2012, includes asynchronous operations on HTTP requests, responses, modules, and handlers, strongly typed data controls, model binding, unobtrusive validation, and HTML5, among other features.

ASP.NET Web Forms

ASP.NET Web Forms allows you to create web applications in the same way you would create a traditional Windows Forms application. This means that you have a control-based interface and the following two files for each page:

- *A user interface (UI) file*: Includes the markup and is where you design how your page will look and which controls it will use. This file has the extension .aspx.

- *A code-behind file*: Includes the code that handles events and interactions of all the objects in the page (this code could be included on the preceding .aspx page, but normally is in a separate file). This file has an extension associated with the programming language, either aspx.cs for C# or aspx.vb for VB.NET.

Whenever ASP.NET processes a page, the page passes through several stages, each of which raises different events to handle the processing of the page and its controls. You write code to handle these events and thus respond to various actions related to the processing of a page. For example, you might write code that gets called when the user clicks a button. When a page is first requested, you often have to initialize data and controls. However, when the page posts back, you don't need to run this code.

A *postback* happens when a control on the page raises an event that must be handled by the server. *View state* is the information about the page control's status. After each postback, the page view state is modified with the new statuses of all the controls in the page. As a default, the page view state is stored in a hidden field inside each page (see Figure 1-1), and its scope and lifetime are limited to the page it belongs to.

```
<input type="hidden" name="__EVENTTARGET" id="__EVENTTARGET" value="" />
<input type="hidden" name="__EVENTARGUMENT" id="__EVENTARGUMENT" value="" />
<input type="hidden" name="__VIEWSTATE" id="__VIEWSTATE" value="/wEPDwUKLTM3MTE0ODc1Mg9kFgICAw9kFgQCBw9kFgJmDxQr
</div>
```

Figure 1-1. *The view state's hidden field*

The main use of view state is to preserve form information across postbacks. View state is turned on by default and normally serializes the data in every control on the page regardless of whether it is actually used during a postback. This behavior can be modified, however, as view state can be disabled on a per-control, per-page, or server-wide basis. Also, as a security measure, no sensitive information should be stored in view state because the serialized string can be easily deserialized.

To work effectively with Web Forms, it is very important to understand the page life-cycle events and how they are processed. Table 1-1 lists these events and the effect they have on the page and its controls.

Table 1-1. *Page Life-cycle Events*

Event	Description
PreInit	This is the first real event you might handle for a page. You typically use this event only if you need to dynamically (from code) set values such as master page or theme. This event is also useful when you are working with dynamically created controls for a page. You want to create the controls inside this event.
Init	This event fires after each control has been initialized. You can use this event to change initialization values for controls.
InitComplete	This event is raised after all initializations of the page and its controls have been completed.
PreLoad	This event fires before view state has been loaded for the page and its controls and before postback processing.

(continued)

Table 1-1. (*continued*)

Event	Description
Load	The page is stable at this time; it has been initialized and its state has been reconstructed. Code inside the page load event typically checks for PostBack and then sets control properties appropriately. The page's load event is called first, followed by the load event for all the controls on the web page.
Control (PostBack) event(s)	ASP.NET now calls any events on the page or its controls that caused the postback to occur. This might be a button's click event, for example.
LoadComplete	This event occurs after all postback data and view state data is loaded into the page and after the Load method has been called for all controls on the page.
PreRender	Use this event to perform any updates before the server controls are rendered to the page. Since all server controls know how to render themselves, this event fires just before that so you can modify any default behavior.
Render	This is a method of the page object and its controls (and not an event). At this point, ASP.NET calls this method on each of the page's controls. The Render method generates the client-side HTML, Dynamic HTML (DHTML), and script that are necessary to properly display a control at the browser. This method is useful if you are writing your own custom control. You can override this method to influence the HTML generated for the control.
UnLoad	This event is used for cleanup code. You use it to release any managed resources in this stage. *Managed resources* are resources that are handled by the runtime, such as instances of classes created by the .NET CLR.

An ASP.NET web application contains several types of files, and each type serves a specific purpose within the application. Table 1-2 lists and describes the most important files in an ASP.NET web application.

Table 1-2. *ASP.NET File Types*

File Type	Description
.aspx	This ASP.NET Web Forms file contains the markup (or UI) of the web page and, optionally, the underlying application code.
aspx.cs or aspx.vb	These are the code-behind files.
.cs or .vb	These are files for general code classes.
web.config	This is the application's general configuration file. It is an XML file that contains all settings for customizing the connection strings, application settings, security, external assemblies, memory, state management, and so on.
global.asax	In this file, you can add code for event handlers at the application level. Events are those for when the application starts or ends or when an error is thrown. You can also define Session State events for when a session starts or ends.
.ascx	These are user control files. In these files, you can create small pieces of UI real state (e.g. a reusable address panel) the same way as with a full .aspx page, but the difference is that they cannot be accessed directly and must be hosted inside .aspx pages. You can reuse these user controls in any page of your applications.

(*continued*)

Table 1-2. (*continued*)

File Type	Description
`.asmx`or `.svc`	ASMX files are ASP.NET web services, introduce in .NET 2.0. These files provide services for pages in the application or any other program that can access them. ASMX web services are now being replaced by Windows Communication Foundation (WCF) services (introduced in .NET 3.0), which have the extension `.svc` and offer much-improved security and scalability features.
`.master`	Master pages are like ASPX pages but are used as templates for other pages, having the look and feel and base functionality.

We can create two types of ASP.NET web applications in Visual Studio:

- ASP.NET web sites
- ASP.NET web applications

Web sites are preferable in certain scenarios, including the following:

- You want to include both C# and Visual Basic code in a single web project. (By default, a web application is compiled based on language settings in the project file. Exceptions can be made, but making an exception is relatively difficult.)

- You want to open the production site in Visual Studio and update it in real time by using FTP.

- You do not want to have to explicitly compile the project in order to deploy it.

- If you do precompile the site, you want the compiler to create multiple assemblies for the site, which can include one assembly per page or user control, or one or more assemblies per folder.

- You want to be able to update individual files in production by just copying new versions to the production server, or by editing the files directly on the production server.

- If you precompile the site, you want to be able to update individual ASP.NET web pages (ASPX files) without having to recompile the entire site.

- You like to keep your source code on the production server because it can serve as an additional backup copy.

Web applications, on the other hand, offer better functionality if

- You want to be able to use the Edit and Continue feature of the Visual Studio debugger.

- You want to run unit tests on code that is in the class files that are associated with ASP.NET pages.

- You want to refer to the classes that are associated with pages and user controls from stand-alone classes.

- You want to establish project dependencies between multiple web projects.

- You want the compiler to create a single assembly for the entire site.

- You want control over the assembly name and version number generated for the site.

- You want to use MSBuild or Team Foundation Build to compile the project. For example, you might want to add prebuild and postbuild steps.

- You want to avoid putting source code on a production server.

Another important choice to make is the type of controls we'll have in our application. We can choose HTML or web server controls, or both. In general, a Web Forms web page can contain basic controls such as `<input type="text"../>`, which are standard to HTML, and/or much more powerful web server controls such as `<asp:TextBox.../>`. The difference between the two types of controls is functionality. HTML controls have limited functionality because they work only on the client (browser), while web server controls work on both the client and the server. Web server controls are the only ones that are accessible in the code-behind file of the web page, and they generate the appropriate HTML markup when rendered to the client.

Consider using HTML controls when any of the following conditions exists:

- You are migrating existing, classic ASP pages over to ASP.NET.

- The control needs to have custom client-side JavaScript attached to the control's events.

- The web page has lots of client-side JavaScript that is referencing the control.

In nearly all other cases, you should consider using the more powerful web server controls, which follow a programming model and naming standard similar to Windows Forms. A web server control can generate extremely complex HTML markup. For example, `<asp:Calendar>` renders a `<table>` with multiple `<tr>` and `<td>` elements. These controls also have other benefits, such as multi browser rendering support, a powerful programming model, layout control, and theme support.

■ **Note** For more information about the differences between HTML server controls and web server controls, visit `http://bit.ly/ASPNETWebServerControls`.

ASP.NET Web Pages

ASP.NET Web Pages (now in version 2) is a framework for building web applications in which pages use the Razor syntax.

ASP.NET Razor uses a simple programming syntax that lets you embed server-based code into a web page. Razor pages use the extension `.cshtml` or `.vbhtml` depending on the language of choice (C# or VB.NET). Because the code is embedded in the web page, the idea of a code-behind file doesn't exist in Razor. The content in Razor pages is created with HTML, and there are no web server controls such as `<asp:Button />`.

You can use Visual Studio to create ASP.NET Web Pages, but the main tool to use is Microsoft WebMatrix 2. With WebMatrix 2, you have access to *web helpers*, which let your applications use common services such as Twitter, reCAPTCHA, Gravatars, Bing Maps, and more. Also, your applications can be extended using packages from the NuGet Gallery. You use NuGet's graphic interface or command line window to request the packages you want and then they will be downloaded, installed, and configured in your application automatically.

WebMatrix 2 also includes SQL Server Compact Edition (SQL CE), a lightweight, free, embedded database solution. You can create, edit, and delete database schema and data directly within WebMatrix. You can run web applications in WebMatrix using IIS Express, which is included when you install it; that way, you don't have to worry about configuring a full-blown IIS just to test your application.

Support for Windows Azure is also baked into WebMatrix 2. You can publish your application directly to Windows Azure, but what's really nice is that you can open your application directly from Windows Azure and make changes to it.

■ **Note** For more information about ASP.NET Web Pages, visit `http://bit.ly/ASPNETWebPages`.

ASP.NET MVC

ASP.NET MVC is a free and fully supported framework for building web applications that use the model-view-controller pattern. Like ASP.NET Web Forms, ASP.NET MVC is built on top of the ASP.NET Framework. This means you can use in ASP.NET MVC applications the same APIs for security, state management, membership, caching, and so on that you could use in traditional ASP.NET Web Forms applications.

In the ASP.NET MVC world, many improvements to ASP.NET have been included in the framework itself. The main purpose of this design pattern is to isolate business logic from the user interface in order to focus on better maintainability, improved testability, and a cleaner structure to the application.

Every ASP.NET MVC application has three core parts: a model, views, and controllers. In short, the model consists of all the classes that handle data and business logic. Data processing using model classes is initiated by the controllers that are in charge of user requests. Once the data processing is complete the controller creates a response to the user by sending the results to a View who then produces HTML to be rendered in the browser.

The MVC Pattern

Figure 1-2 illustrates a simple implementation of the MVC pattern. The straight arrows indicate direct associations while the curved arrows identify indirect associations.

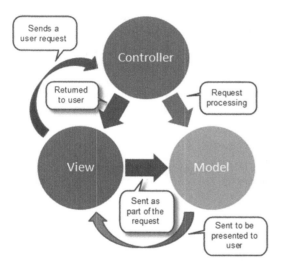

Figure 1-2. *Model-view-controller implementation*

The *model* in the MVC pattern represents the parts of the application that implement the data domain logic. The operation of the model might come from the generation of classes representing objects in a data store such as a database (for example, Entity Framework data classes).

Views are the visible elements in the application. They are the components that typically show users data from the model. A view page typically receives a view model object from the controller (the view doesn't care how this data was obtained—that's the controller's responsibility!). The view page contains HTML (and possibly some UI-related code) to determine how to render the model data back to the browser.

The *controllers* are classes that collect the user requests, work with the model, and ultimately select a view to render the appropriate UI.

When to Use ASP.NET MVC

ASP.NET MVC has certain capabilities that make it the best option to choose if you need one or more of the following:

- *A high level of control over the generated HTML*: Unlike Web Forms, Views in ASP.NET MVC render HTML exactly as you tell them to. Recently, Web Forms have been improved in this area but still don't have the level of control MVC has.

- *Easier unit testing*: With ASP.NET MVC, it is very easy to follow testing patterns such as test-driven development (TDD). Because of the complex event lifecycle in Web Forms, on top of a control-based framework, TDD is a lot easier with MVC.

- *Separation of concerns*: This refers to having all aspects of the system clearly separated from one another. Because of the pattern it implements, an MVC application is divided into discrete and loosely bound parts (model, views, and controllers), which makes it easy to maintain.

ASP.NET MVC Benefits

Compared to Web Forms, ASP.NET MVC applications benefit by including all ASP.NET core features but also by the features in the MVC pattern. Some of those benefits are:

- The MVC pattern itself makes it easier to manage complexity by clearly separating the functionality of the application into three core parts, the model, the view, and the controller.

- ASP.NET MVC web applications do not use view state or server-based forms. This makes the MVC framework ideal for developers who want full control over the behavior of an application. View state can become very large, which is a problem for devices like smartphones running over slow networks (transmitting all that information can be very slow). In a Web Forms page, you could only have one <form> per page. This is quite a major restriction. In MVC, there is no such restriction—that is, you can have as many<form> elements as you like.

- ASP.NET MVC provides better support for test-driven development (TDD).

- ASP.NET MVC works well for web applications that are supported by large teams of developers and for web designers who need a high degree of control over the HTML.

ASP.NET MVC Request Processing

One of the most important concepts to understand about MVC applications is that no relationship exists between a page request and a physical file inside the web server. In a traditional Web Forms and Web Pages application, every page request is translated into a call to a physical file in the webserver. For example, if your request is something like http://myapp/mypage.aspx, the web server interprets the request by looking at the root of the website for a file named mypage.aspx.It then processes the file and returns the generated HTML.

In the case of an MVC application, when you make a request (e.g.,http://myapp/product/list), a component called *routing engine* matches the request to a specific route. A *route* defines requests using a pattern string and establishes the controller and method in the controller class that should process the request. Once the route is identified, the routing engine creates a request handler that in turn will create the controller object that will process the request (in our example, the controller is "product"). The controller then invokes the method in the controller class that will process the request (in the example is named "list"). These methods in controller classes that process requests are called *action methods*. When the processing of the request ends, the action method produces a result to send back to the user. Normally the result is some HTML (rendered by a View) the user will see in the browser.

We will examine the routing engine in more detail in Chapter 10. Figure 1-3 illustrates the entire server-side processing life cycle in an ASP.NET MVC web application.

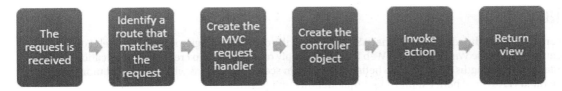

Figure 1-3. *ASP.NET MVC request process*

A LITTLE ASP.NET MVC HISTORY

The first version of ASP.NET MVC, released on March 13, 2009, was a full-featured implementation of the MVC pattern built on top of ASP.NET. This version included features such as a routing engine, helper methods to create HTML and AJAX elements in pages, data binding, the Web Forms view engine, and more.

ASP.NET MVC 2 debuted in March 2010 and added even more features, including a rich set of UI helpers for automatic scaffolding; customizable templates; strongly typed HTML helper methods; asynchronous controllers; the concept of areas, allowing the separation of large applications into different projects; attribute-based model validation in the client and the server; and better tools in Visual Studio.

Less than a year later (10 months to be precise), Microsoft released ASP.NET MVC 3, which introduced a whole bunch of new features, including .NET 4 data annotations and a new view engine (Razor). JavaScript got its own improvements with unobtrusive JavaScript, jQuery validation, and JSON binding.

Slowing down the pace a bit, ASP.NET MVC 4 shipped on August 15, 2012 (19 months after version 3) and was included in Visual Studio 2012 when it shipped in September of the same year.

ASP.NET MVC 4 Features

ASP.NET MVC 4 is built on top of the many features of its previous versions and include new features like:

- ASP.NET Web API, a new framework for building HTTP and RESTful services.

- A new HTML5-based default template in Visual Studio and a new Mobile Application project template.

- Automatic selection of rendered views with Display Modes. This is particularly useful when building applications that will run not only on desktop browsers but on mobile browsers as well. It will let the application determine the best view to render based on the browser making the request.

- jQuery Mobile and mobile features.

- Task support for asynchronous controllers.

- Microsoft Windows Azure SDK support for deploying ASP.NET MVC 4 applications to Windows Azure.

- Bundling and minification for CSS and JavaScript files to help reduce the amount of HTTP requests as well as the size of those requests.

- Facebook, OpenID, and OAuth authentication.

Summary

You have seen in this introductory chapter what ASP.NET is and the core technologies it contains: Web Forms, Web Pages, and MVC. While Web Forms and Web Pages are simply other options to create web applications, MVC has some advantages and strengths that make it a better fit for certain scenarios, such as where you need more control over the generated HTML and better support for implementing unit testing.

You have seen that the way in which MVC handles requests differs from how Web Forms and Web Pages handle requests. This is a very important concept, as it highlights the decoupling of the request from the physical page, using a powerful routing engine.

Among the features in ASP.NET MVC 4 is Web API, a powerful new framework for building HTTP and RESTful services. A mobile template is included in ASP.NET MVC 4 so that you can support mobile browsers out of the box. Asynchronous controllers can be implemented using tasks. Easy Facebook and OAuth implementations are also included to create a friendlier authentication scheme.

Integration with Windows Azure via the Windows Azure SDK is now available, as well as bundling and minification of CSS and JavaScript files to improve speed and bandwidth consumption.

Having read this chapter, you now have the information to know when to choose ASP.NET MVC as the technology for your project. ASP.NET MVC is a better fit if you want a clear separation of concerns by having a model, controllers and views thus reducing the complexity of the project. Also, ASP.NET MVC works well if you have a large team with people doing specific tasks.

CHAPTER 2

Installing ASP.NET MVC 4

Preparing your environment to develop applications using ASP.NET MVC 4 is a very straightforward process. You have a few options for the development tools, some of which already include ASP.NET MVC 4.

This chapter describes the system requirements for ASP.NET MVC 4, explains what to install and where to get it, and, most important, shows you how to prepare properly to start developing applications.

Software Requirements for ASP.NET MVC 4

ASP.NET MVC 4 runs on the following operating systems:

- Windows XP Service Pack 3, Windows Vista Service Pack 2, Windows 7, and Windows 8

- Windows Server 2003 Service Pack 2, Windows Server 2003 R2 (32-bit x86), Windows Server 2003 R2 x64 editions, Windows Server 2008, Windows Server 2008 R2, and Windows Server 2012

The minimum .NET version required is 4.0, and for development you need the following:

- Windows PowerShell 2.0. Windows PowerShell is a task-based, command-line shell and scripting language designed especially for system administration. The built-in Windows commands, known as *cmdlets*, help you to manage your Windows environment as well as other applications installed, such as the database SQL Server.

- Either Visual Studio 2010 Service Pack 1, Visual Web Developer Express 2010 Service Pack 1, Visual Studio 2012, or Visual Studio Express 2012 for Web. The Express editions are free downloads, and the only difference from the paid versions is that they are missing certain features, such as add-ins, an extended set of project templates, XML and UML features, performance and analysis features, and so on.

Note   You can download Visual Studio 2012 from `http://bit.ly/DownloadVS2012`.

Installing ASP.NET MVC 4 Development Components

One of the questions often asked by developers who are new to MVC is whether ASP.NET MVC 4 can run side by side with older versions of ASP.NET MVC. The answer is yes. After installing MVC 4, you can still create and work with applications using MVC 1, 2, and 3.

For your development environment, all versions of Visual Studio 2012 include ASP.NET MVC 4, so if you are using a version of Visual Studio 2012, you can skip ahead to the section "Visual Studio Application Templates." If you are using Visual Studio 2010, you need to install ASP.NET MVC 4 separately. For this task, you can use either the Microsoft Web Platform Installer (WebPI) or the stand-alone installer.

- WebPI is a free, tiny (2MB) tool that allows you to download and install the latest components of the Microsoft Web Platform. Those components may be server components such as Internet Information Services (IIS), frameworks such as ASP.NET MVC or PHP, databases like SQL Server or MySQL, tools like Visual Studio Express 2012 and Microsoft WebMatrix 2,or even Windows Azure components like SDKs and libraries.

- The stand-alone installer is a single executable file that you download from Microsoft. The advantage of the stand-alone installer is that it works offline, so it can be used for distribution in corporate environments.

Personally, I like to use Web PI simply because it does all the work of finding any required dependencies and includes them for installation if they are not already present (and it does so in the correct order). Therefore, I'll present that option first, and then present the option of using the stand-alone installer.

Using Web Platform Installer

As previously mentioned, all versions of Visual Studio 2012 already include ASP.NET MVC 4. If you instead have Visual Studio 2010 installed, either Express or another version, you need to follow the instructions in this section if you want to include support for developing ASP.NET MVC 4 applications.

You can download Web PI from `http://bit.ly/DownloadWebPI`. Once you have downloaded it, run the executable, which opens the interface shown in Figure 2-1. Note that WebPI's interface is divided in three areas, top, middle, and bottom. The top area includes the general categories of components and a search box. The middle area is divided into two sections. The section on the left is a submenu of the category selected in the top area. Whichever item you select in the submenu filters the components available in the section on the right. The Install column on the right identifies whether the particular component is already installed on your system; if it isn't, you can click the Add button to add the component to the list of components to install. Finally, the bottom area provides a summary count of the components to be installed, an Options link to further customize WebPI (such as the components feed and interface language), an Install button (which is enabled once there are components selected for installation), and an Exit button to quit the Web PI tool.

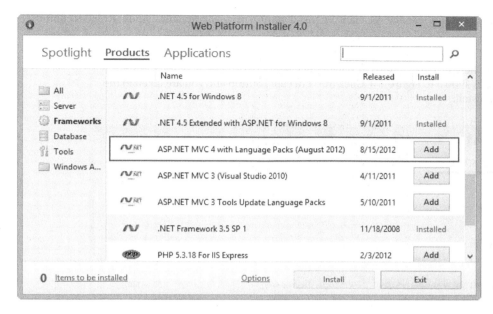

Figure 2-1. *Locating ASP.NET MVC 4 in Web PI for installation*

Figure 2-1 shows the Web Platform Installer window with the Products category selected. With the Products category selected, choose the Frameworks submenu, as shown, and scroll down the list on the right to find the component ASP.NET MVC 4 with Language Packs. The date of the installer release is indicated there too. Once you locate the component, click the "Add" button to its right to instruct WebPI that you want the component to be installed.

After you've added the component to the install list, you can click the link "Items to be installed" at the bottom of the window to see what exactly will be installed, including all the dependencies. The resulting window is shown in Figure 2-2. Click Close to return to the Web PI window.

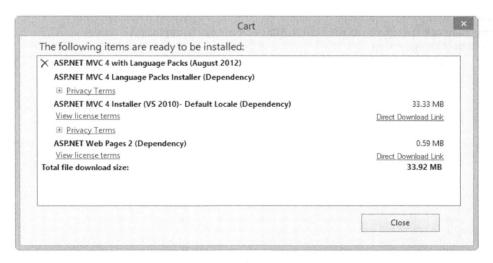

Figure 2-2. *Packages to be installed. The list of dependencies will vary based on what is already installed on the system*

Now that everything is ready for installation, click the Install button to kickoff the installation, which is composed of four steps:

- *Prerequisites*: This step shows you what will be installed, just as you saw in Figure 2-2. The difference here is that you need to accept the licenses associated with the selected components, as shown in Figure 2-3. Click the "I Accept" button and you are taken to the second step, Install.

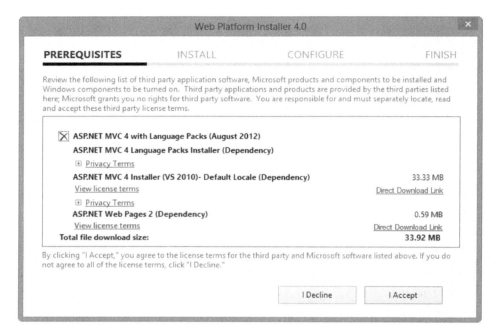

Figure 2-3. *WebPI Prerequisites step*

- *Install*: This step is simple and requires no interaction (see Figure 2-4). WebPI downloads the required components and proceeds to install them. After everything is complete, you move automatically to the Configure step.

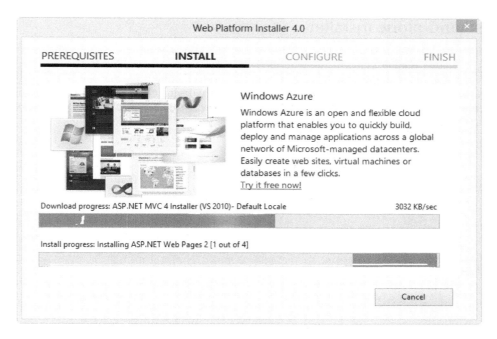

Figure 2-4. *WebPI Install step*

- *Configure*: Depending on the selected components, additional configuration is required, such as the definition of a port to host an application or any other type of configuration. All that is done during the Configure step. Once all the configuration options are set, you are taken to the Finish step.

- *Finish*: This step shows the summary of the installations and offers you only one option, "Finish," as shown in Figure 2-5. Click "Finish" and the installation wizard will take you back to WebPI, where you can select and install other components.

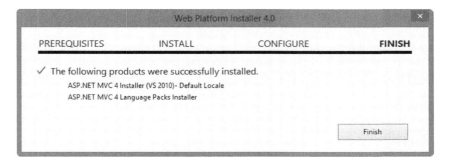

Figure 2-5. *WebPI Finish step*

Using the Stand-alone Installer

If you choose not to use the Web Platform Installer to install ASP.NET MVC 4, your other option with Visual Studio 2010 (either Express or another version) is to use the stand-alone installer.

As described earlier in the chapter, the stand-alone installer is an executable file that you download from http://bit.ly/DownloadMVC4, shown in Figure 2-6. The advantage of the installer file is that it runs offline, so after you download the file, you can disconnect from the Internet (if you need to) and share the file using any offline method, such as USB keys.

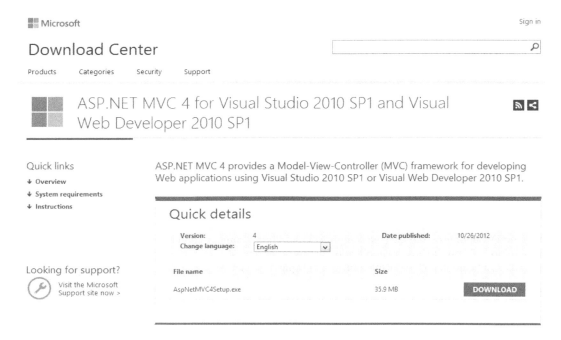

Figure 2-6. *Download page for the stand-alone installer*

After you download the file, just double-click it and it will run, as shown in Figure 2-7. The process is really simple. Select the "I agree to the license terms and conditions" check box to enable the Install button. Click the "Install" button, and the program handles all the installation tasks. When it finishes, it prompts you to exit.

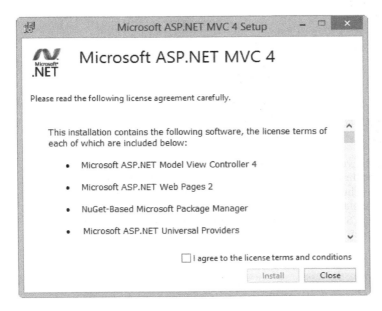

Figure 2-7. The license agreement page of the stand-alone installer

Installing ASP.NET MVC 4 Server Components

Let's look now at the server that will host the application once we finish the development. Just as we needed to install ASP.NET MVC 4 on the development machine in order to develop applications, we need to install it on the server so that it can host the applications. In the server you also use one of the two available methods to install ASP.NET MVC 4, the stand-alone installer or Web PI.

Installing ASP.NET MVC 4 on a server is different from installing it on your development machine in the sense that the stand-alone installer (or WebPI) will skip installation of the development tools, recognizing that you're installing it on a server and that the operating system is different (e.g., Windows Server 2012). By making this distinction and skipping unnecessary components, the server ends up having only the components that it needs to host and serve ASP.NET MVC 4 applications.

An additional advantage of installing ASP.NET MVC 4 on the server is that the required assemblies are registered in the Global Assembly Cache (GAC), which means that any web site that runs on ASP.NET MVC 4 in that server now has the required assemblies available because the GAC works as a repository of assemblies for the whole server, not just for individual applications

The limited component installation is also important for security and performance considerations, because administrators don't want any unnecessary software on the servers—and definitely don't want development tools on the server. The problem with installing development tools on the server is that they sometimes open network ports and/or enable services that otherwise will be closed or turned off, and that increases the risks of security breaches and performance problems.

Visual Studio Application Templates

After you have installed ASP.NET MVC 4 to work with Visual Studio 2010, or have installed Visual Studio 2012 (which already includes ASP.NET MVC 4), you can start creating new ASP.NET MVC 4 projects.

To start creating a new project, open Visual Studio (2010, 2012, or Express) and choose FILE ➤ New Project, as shown in Figure 2-8. Alternatively, you can use the keyboard shortcut Ctrl+Shift+N.

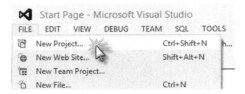

Figure 2-8. Creating a new project in Visual Studio 2012

This option opens the New Project dialog, shown in Figure 2-9, which is divided into four sections. The navigation pane on the left allows you to navigate through the available project templates, either online or installed in your computer. As shown in Figure 2-9, expand the navigation pane to Installed ➤ Templates ➤ Visual C#. That instructs Visual Studio to display from the set of installed project templates all those that are preconfigured to work with the Visual C# language. As you can see, Visual Studio can be used to build all kinds of different projects under the Visual C# node. We're going to be creating a web application, so select Web.

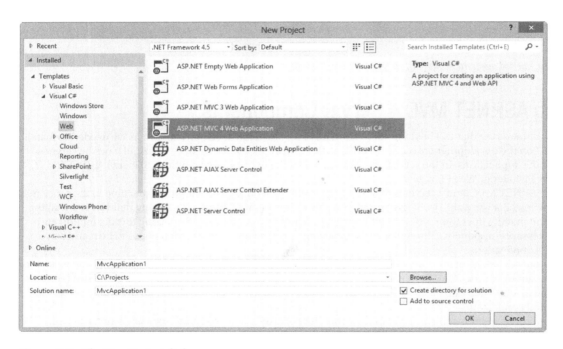

Figure 2-9. The New Project dialog

The middle section displays all the different types of Web project templates available for Visual C#. Select the ASP.NET MVC 4 Web Application template, as shown in Figure 2-9.

■ **Note** In Visual Studio, the term "solution" refers to the collection of individual projects that compose the application you are building. You will see in a moment how an ASP.NET MVC 4 application can have two projects, one for the web application and one for unit tests.

In the drop-down list boxes at the top of the middle section of the dialog, you can select the version of .NET Framework to work with and how the list of templates should be sorted. For the samples in the book, we will use .NET Framework 4.5.

The section on the right side of the dialog provides a brief description of the template selected in the middle section. Above that description is a search box, enabling you to search for a specific installed template.

At the bottom of the dialog, you type the name of your application and specify the directory where Visual Studio will save the solution files. To the right are two checkboxes:

- *Create directory for solution*: Selecting this instructs Visual Studio to create a separate directory for the solution files.

- *Add to source control*: Selecting this will add your application to a source-control system.

I strongly suggest keeping all solution files in a separate folder, so select the "Create directory for solution" checkbox (if it isn't already selected). As for the source control checkbox, if you already use a source-control system, you can use it (as long as it is compatible with Visual Studio).

■ **Note** Several commercial and free source-control systems are available. If you don't have a source-control system, you are missing a great technology that can save you from unwanted file/code deletions, team collaboration issues, and so forth. Microsoft has its own product, called Microsoft Team Foundation Server, which gives you not only source control but other features as well, such as continuous unit testing, code review, team collaboration, agile planning, and more. Microsoft also offers a cloud-based service, named Team Foundation Service (at `http://tfs.visualstudio.com`). You can sign up for free and get an account for up to five developers.

After you have filled in all the necessary information in the New Project dialog, click the "OK" button. The New ASP.NET MVC 4 Project dialog is displayed (see Figure 2-10), which gives you three important options: choose the ASP.NET MVC 4 project template for your new project, choose a view engine, and choose whether to create a unit test project or not. Each option is discussed in turn next.

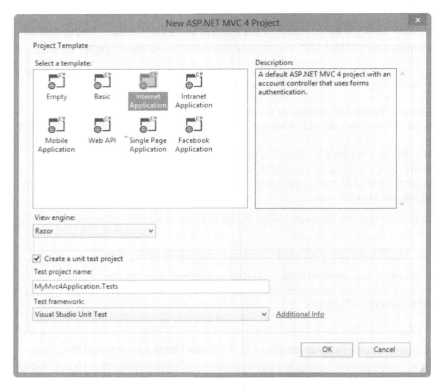

Figure 2-10. *New ASP.NET MVC 4 Project dialog*

Choose the Project Template

You can choose the ASP.NET MVC 4 project template from one of the following eight available options. Each of the templates serves a specific purpose depending on what kind of project you are building.

- *Empty*: This template creates a solution and project with only the references and minimum configuration to start building an ASP.NET MVC 4 application from scratch. Only the directory structure is added. It does not create any controllers, views, or functionality.

- *Basic*: Similar to the Empty template, the Basic template has a minimum configuration, but it adds some shared views for an initial (very) basic layout but still no controllers are added and no default functionality implemented.

- *Internet Application*: This template creates an entire working website that implements a nicely done HTML5-based layout with CSS files, jQuery, and some plug-ins already setup. It has Forms Authentication implemented in the Account controller for handling users with the ASP.NET Membership system. This template is intended for public-facing applications, enabling users to be authenticated using either username and password or OAuth with Facebook, Google, or Twitter.

- *Intranet Application*: This template is similar to the Internet Application template but, instead of implementing Forms Authentication, it uses Windows Authentication. Windows Authentication is used here because normally intranet users are authenticated against an Active Directory domain.

- *Mobile Application*: This template is a new kid on the block. It implements a new layout based on jQuery Mobile specifically designed for mobile browsers.

- *Web API*: Another new kid on the block, this template is similar to the Internet Application template but is specifically designed for creating HTTP services that can reach a broad range of clients, including browsers and mobile devices. With it, you can also build RESTful services, which are nothing more than HTTP services that implement the principals of REST (REpresentational State Transfer).

- *Single Page Application*. ASP.NET Single Page Application (SPA) helps you build applications that include significant client-side interactions using HTML 5, CSS 3 and JavaScrip. This template is available after installing the Web Tools 2012 update for Visual Studio 2012. It allows you to build single page applications using Knockout.js and ASP.NET Web API. Knockout (http://knockoutjs.com) is a Javascript library that helps you implement the Model-View-ViewModel (MVVM) pattern including templates. The template includes a "to do" list application that demonstrates common practices for building a JavaScript HTML5 application that uses a RESTful server API

- *Facebook Application*. The Web Tools 2012 update also includes this template. It helps you build Facebook applications. The template includes a new library that takes care of all the plumbing involved in building a Facebook application to let you focus in the logic of the application rather than in the integration with Facebook.

Choose a View Engine

ASP.NET MVC is highly configurable and allows you to select a *view engine* in the New Project dialog. A view engine is simply a templating language that will ultimately generate HTML in your application once the view has been processed.

You need to select one view engine, but you are not limited to the out-of-the-box options, which are ASPX (or the Web Forms view engine) and Razor (see Figure 2-11).

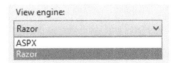

Figure 2-11. *View Engine drop-down list*

■ **Note**   Other view engines, such as Spark and NHaml, are available, but you have to download and install them separately from http://bit.ly/SparkViewEngine and http://bit.ly/NHamlViewEngine, respectively. The ASPX and Razor view engines are very easy to work with, and I suggest you give them a try before trying a new one.

Create a Unit Test Project for Your Application

The last portion of the New ASP.NET MVC 4 Project dialog, shown in Figure 2-12, is related to unit testing your application. This is an optional step, the purpose of which is to create an additional project that will be used to host unit tests for the application. Although this is optional, keep in mind that the capability to test more easily the functionality you are building is one of the core benefits of using ASP.NET MVC 4. Therefore, I recommend that you choose this option.

☑ Create a unit test project

Test project name:

MyMvc4Application.Tests

Test framework:

Visual Studio Unit Test ▾   Additional Info

Figure 2-12. *Create a unit test project option*

In this section of the dialog, you are given the option to enter the name of the project. By default, it is given the same name as your MVC application but with the suffix "Tests," which I personally think is a nice name selection. Then you can select the test framework. Visual Studio Unit Test, which uses the Microsoft Test Framework,is selected by default (and is the only option unless you have installed and configured a custom testing framework such as NUnit, MbUnit, or xUnit.net).

Anatomy of an ASP.NET MVC 4 Internet Application

After creating an ASP.NET MVC 4 Internet Application (and test project), you will see in the Solution Explorer window a solution with two projects, as shown in Figure 2-13. The default directory structure is simple but provides a well-structured convention to create elements in your application.

Figure 2-13. *Solution structure of an ASP.NET MVC 4 Internet Application*

The directory structure can handle almost any scenario you will encounter. If by chance it doesn't, you can modify the structure. I do not advise doing so unless you know how to properly do it. Modifying this structure is an advanced topic that is outside the scope of this book.

■ **Note**   Should you need to modify the directory structure you can use "Areas." More information on areas can be found at http://bit.ly/MVCAreas.

Table 2-1 describes the folders in the two projects shown in Figure 2-13.

Table 2-1. *ASP.NET MVC 4 Internet Application Directory Structure*

Directory	Description
App_Data	You can place in this folder the files for which you require read/write permissions, such as LocalDB database files.
App_Start	This folder contains the configuration files for the different technologies you use in the application, such as authentication, bundling, filtering, routing, and Web API.
Content	This folder is designed for CSS files and other assets in your website design.
Controllers	This folder is where you create controller classes. These classes are in charge of handling user requests. The methods in the classes are called *action methods* because they return some kind of action result. The action result can be HTML, a file, an object, or even an exception. Action methods and controllers are mapped to request URLs, which is how controllers know how to handle the requests.
Filters	*Action filters* are custom attributes that provide a declarative means to add a specific behavior to controller action methods. They are used to simplify the implementation of logic in action methods that otherwise would have to be added manually (and repetitively) in every action method. They facilitate the centralization of logic that will then be reused by any action method that needs it.
Images	This folder is a place to store the images you will be using in your website.
Models	This is the folder where you create the data and business logic classes.
Scripts	You add JavaScript files to this folder.
Views	This folder is for the files containing the UI logic. The files are normally just called *views* and use a syntax defined by the view engine you selected when you created the project. Views are used to render HTML to the client browser.
Properties	Double clicking on the Properties node will open the project's properties window where you can modify options such as the .NET version used by the project, build and publishing options and many more. Expanding the node gives you access to the AssemblyInfo.cs file that stores metadata associated with the project's assembly.
References	The References node contains all assemblies used in the application.
Configuration files	The Web.Config and App.Config files are files in XML format that define configuration options for ASP.NET applications.
Global.asax	Is a file where ASP.NET applications declare and handle application and session-level events.
Packages.Config	Is a file in XML format that stores the information of NuGet packages installed in the application.

Summary

This chapter introduced you to the different options for installing and using ASP.NET MVC 4.

As you discovered, ASP.NET MVC 4 is already included in Visual Studio 2012 and Visual Studio 2012 Express for Web. To build ASP.NET MVC 4 applications with Visual Studio 2010 or Visual Web Developer Express 2010, you have to install it separately, using either of two options: use the free, tiny Web Platform Installer tool, or use the stand-alone installer. The choice depends on whether you want to handle the dependencies automatically (WebPI) or by yourself (stand-alone installer). The difference between installing MVC 4 on client computers and installing it on servers is that the development tools aren't installed on servers.

When creating projects with Visual Studio, you can choose from among several ASP.NET MVC 4 templates for your project and select the view engine of your choice. Optionally, you can create an additional project for unit testing your application using either the default Microsoft Test Framework or any third-party testing framework you have downloaded and installed separately, such as NUnit or MbUnit.

Finally, you were introduced to the anatomy of an ASP.NET MVC 4 Internet Application and the default directory structure. This structure is just a starting point and can be modified to fit your needs.

■ ■ ■

The "Have You Seen Me?" ASP.NET MVC 4 Web Application

The purpose of this book is to teach you how to use ASP.NET MVC 4, and there's no better way to do that than to guide you through the development of an actual application. Whereas most ASP.NET MVC 4 tutorials and books base their examples and code on some kind of e-commerce application, I've decided to show you in this and the following chapters how to create something different. You will still learn how to use ASP.NET MVC 4 in the process, but the application will also be both fun and useful.

The application is simple yet features all the elements that you'll need to create applications that are useful to your everyday work. Although you will create this application from scratch, I'll provide all the code for the elements that are beyond the scope of this book.

In this chapter you will create the ASP.NET MVC 4 application using the Internet Application project template that is installed in Visual Studio 2012. Additionally, you will create the database with the tables that will store the information. In future chapters you will create the functionality described for the components in the application; for example, in chapter 4 you will create the main controller for the application and in chapter 9 you will create the controllers that will be accessible only to registered users.

Description of the Application

Our sample ASP.NET MVC 4 application is called "Have you seen me?" and is a web site that allows people to post information about missing pets so that they potentially can get information from the public on the whereabouts of their beloved animals.

The application has the following three sections, access to each of which will depend on the type of user. There are three types of users: application administrators, registered members, and anonymous users.

- *Administrative section*: This section is accessible only to application administrators.

- *Public section*: This section is accessible to everyone (anonymous users) and displays photos and additional information about the missing pets.

- *Members section*: This section is accessible to registered members and enables them to manage the details about their missing pets.

Administrative Section

The purpose of the administrative section is to provide a place for the owner of the web site (in this case, you) to configure the general web site settings and perform administrative actions, such as:

- Designate which types of pets can be registered.

- Enable/disable the e-mail messages feature. With this feature enabled, members of the public can send e-mail messages to pet owners who have registered their missing pets on the web site.

- Suspend or even cancel member accounts.

- See reports about membership, the number of found pets, and so forth.

Public Section

The public section of the web site is accessible to anyone with a web browser and is the place where members of the public can go to:

- View missing pets

- See photos and additional information

- Send an e-mail message to a pet owner to report a sighting of his or her pet, ask for more information, and so forth

- Register to gain access to the members section

Members Section

The members section is where pet owners can create profiles of their pets and report them as missing. To access the members section, pet owners are required to register an account to uniquely identify them. To facilitate the registration and authentication process, the members section supports not only the classic username and password mechanism but also the OAuth and OpenID protocols using the DotNetOpenAuth library included in the ASP.NET MVC 4 application Visual Studio template. Because this library is incorporated into the template, users can authenticate using a Twitter, Facebook, Microsoft or Google account, meaning they don't have to create a new profile. They simply authorize the application to use their information already stored in one of these services.

In the members section, pet owners can

- Update their password (for local accounts)

- Register missing pets

- Upload pet photos

- Manage additional information about missing pets

- Deactivate the record for a missing pet

  - Mark as a found pet

  - Mark as never found

- Read messages

- Reply to messages

- Cancel their account

Creating the ASP.NET MVC 4 Sample Application

For the development of our sample application, you need either Visual Studio 2012 (any of the paid versions or the free Visual Studio Express 2012 for Web), which you can download from `http://bit.ly/VS2012Download`, or Visual Studio 2010 with the ASP.NET MVC 4 with Language Packs installed, as described in Chapter 2.

To create the application, follow these steps:

1. Open Visual Studio.

2. Choose File ➤ New Project, as shown in Figure 3-1.

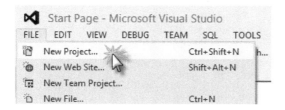

Figure 3-1. *Creating a new project in Visual Studio*

3. In the New Project dialog, navigate to Templates ➤ Visual C# ➤ Web and select ASP.NET MVC 4 Web Application, as shown in Figure 3-2.

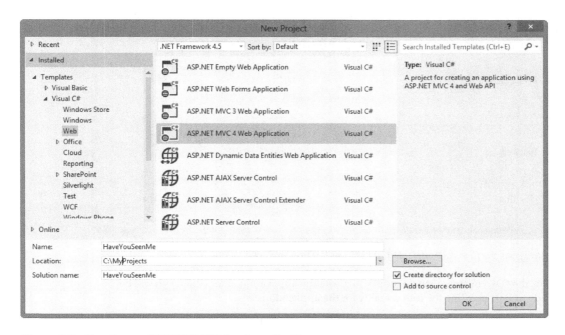

Figure 3-2. *Creating an ASP.NET MVC 4 web application*

4. Name the project **HaveYouSeenMe**, leave the other options at their default values, and then click the "OK" button.

5. In the New ASP.NET MVC 4 Project dialog, select the Internet Application template, select the Razor view engine from the drop-down menu, and check the "Create a unit test project" check box, as shown in Figure 3-3.

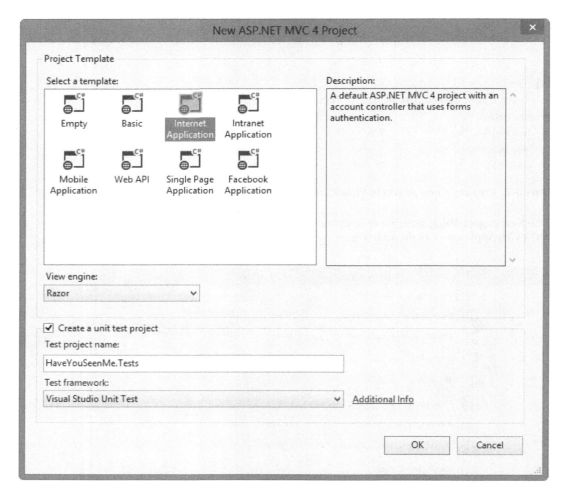

Figure 3-3. *Settings for the new ASP.NET MVC 4 web application project*

6. Click the "OK" button. Visual Studio will create the application, after which you will be ready to start building the functionality for the application.

Creating the Database

The application's database is built using Microsoft SQL Server 2012 LocalDB. We will use this small database while we are developing the application because it is easy to use, requires minimal configuration (none, actually), and can be modified using Visual Studio itself, thus avoiding use of different tools.

We will review the database again in Chapter 12, as we will need to examine options for deploying the web site in a production environment. In that scenario, we will need to find a replacement for LocalDB that can handle bigger loads of information and provide more features in regard to security, performance, and scalability.

The database consists of several tables that will be used to store the information. At a glance, the tables are as follows:

- Setting: Used to store information about the general settings governing the application
- PetType: Used to store information that identifies the different types of pets, such as Dogs, Cats, Reptiles, etc.
- Pet: Used to store specific information about each pet, such as name, age, gender, breed, and more
- PetPhoto: Used to store photos for each pet
- Status: Serves as a catalog of the different statuses that can be assigned to pets (for example, "missing" and "found")
- Message: Used to store messages sent to pet owners

In addition to the preceding application-specific tables, the database includes the following set of tables to manage user accounts. These tables are used to store account and authentication information about members who register with a username and password (local accounts) and members who register using third-party services such as Facebook or Twitter.

- UserProfile
- webpages_Membership
- webpages_OAuthMembership
- webpages_Roles
- webpages_UsersInRoles

The UserProfile table is used to store the registered members' information. The webpages_ tables are used to store specific information about the authentication method used for each user; for example, webpages_Membership stores the information about passwords on local accounts, while webpages_OAuthMembership stores information about users who authenticate via Facebook, Twitter, and so forth.

The tables webpages_Roles and webpages_UsersInRoles can be used to identify individual users as part of a group of users that has a specific set of permissions within the application. For example, one role may be called Moderators and another role may be called Administrators. A user in the Moderators role could review and approve/deny pet registrations and member registrations. Users in the Administrators role would be the only ones with permission to access the administrative section of the web site.

The technology behind the user account management system and these tables is called *ASP.NET SimpleMembership*. This technology is built into the ASP.NET framework, so it is not exclusive to MVC. The configuration of SimpleMembership happens automatically with the first request to the AccountController class (this class is automatically generated by Visual Studio when you create an ASP.NET MVC 4 Internet Application). Why is it configured with the first request to this class? Because the AccountController class handles the requests to log in and register user accounts. Listing 3-1 shows part of the AccountController class. Note that the class is decorated with the [InitializeSimpleMembership] attribute. For any user account operation to happen, the application must guarantee that the supporting tables are present so that the requested functionality works properly. If the database and tables are not present for some reason, the [InitializeSimpleMembership] attribute instructs ASP.NET to create a new LocalDB database complete with the tables introduced in this section.

Listing 3-1. Partial listing of the AccountController Class

```
namespace HaveYouSeenMe.Controllers
{
    [Authorize]
    [InitializeSimpleMembership]
    public class AccountController : Controller
    {
        ...
    }
}
```

Now we are going to create the database table's script. A script is recommended over the graphical interface to create tables as a way to document our work. After the script is ready we are going to create the database and then run the script to create the tables.

Defining Scripts to Create Database Tables

To create the application tables, we have two options: we can use Visual Studio to create one table at a time, or we can use a script that contains all the instructions to create all the tables in one go. Creating a script is the recommended best practice. That way, you have documented your work and if you discover an error or if you want to tweak the database, you can simply change the script and reapply it or better yet, create a new script with the modifications to document what has happened in the database.

Listing 3-2 includes all the necessary script commands to create the application tables (it is included in the book resources and is available to download so that you don't have to type it).

Listing 3-2. T-SQL Script to create the application-specific tables in our application

```
CREATE TABLE [dbo].[Setting]
(
    [Id] INT NOT NULL IDENTITY(1,1),
    [Key] VARCHAR(50) NOT NULL,
    [Value] VARCHAR(500) NULL,
    CONSTRAINT [PK_Setting] PRIMARY KEY ([Id])
);

CREATE TABLE [dbo].[PetType]
(
    [PetTypeID] INT NOT NULL IDENTITY(1,1),
    [PetTypeDescription] VARCHAR(50) NULL,
    CONSTRAINT [PK_PetType] PRIMARY KEY ([PetTypeID])
);

CREATE TABLE [dbo].[Status]
(
    [StatusID] INT NOT NULL IDENTITY(1,1),
    [Description] VARCHAR (50) NOT NULL,
    CONSTRAINT [PK_Status] PRIMARY KEY ([StatusID])
);

CREATE TABLE [dbo].[Pet]
(
    [PetID] INT NOT NULL IDENTITY(1,1),
```

```
    [PetName] VARCHAR(100) NOT NULL,
    [PetAgeYears] INT NULL,
    [PetAgeMonths] INT NULL,
    [StatusID] INT NOT NULL,
    [LastSeenOn] DATE NULL,
    [LastSeenWhere] VARCHAR(500) NULL,
    [Notes] VARCHAR(1500) NULL,
    [UserId] INT NOT NULL,
    CONSTRAINT [PK_Pet] PRIMARY KEY ([PetID]),
    CONSTRAINT [FK_Pet_Status] FOREIGN KEY ([StatusID])
        REFERENCES [Status] ([StatusID]),
    CONSTRAINT [FK_Pet_User] FOREIGN KEY ([UserId])
        REFERENCES [UserProfile] ([UserId])
);

CREATE TABLE [dbo].[PetPhoto]
(
    [PhotoID] INT NOT NULL IDENTITY(1,1),
    [PetID] INT NOT NULL,
    [Photo] VARCHAR(500) NOT NULL
        CONSTRAINT [DF_PhotoFile] DEFAULT '/content/pets/no-image.png',
    [Notes] VARCHAR(500) NULL,
    CONSTRAINT [PK_PetPhoto] PRIMARY KEY ([PhotoID]),
    CONSTRAINT [FK_PetPhoto_Pet] FOREIGN KEY ([PetID])
        REFERENCES [Pet] ([PetID])
);

CREATE TABLE [dbo].[Message]
(
    [MessageID] INT NOT NULL,
    [UserId] INT NOT NULL,
    [MessageDate] DATETIME NOT NULL,
    [From] VARCHAR(150) NOT NULL,
    [Email] VARCHAR(150) NOT NULL,
    [Subject] VARCHAR(150) NULL,
    [Message] VARCHAR(1500) NOT NULL,
    CONSTRAINT [PK_Message] PRIMARY KEY ([MessageID]),
    CONSTRAINT [FK_Message_User] FOREIGN KEY ([UserId])
        REFERENCES [UserProfile] ([UserId])
);
```

Listing 3-3 includes a modification to the ASP.NET SimpleMembership UserProfile table that enables the application to store more details about the registered user.

Listing 3-3. T-SQL script to modify the UserProfile table with new columns

```
ALTER TABLE [dbo].[UserProfile]
ADD
    [FirstName] VARCHAR(150) NOT NULL,
    [LastName] VARCHAR(150) NOT NULL,
    [Email] VARCHAR(150) NOT NULL;
```

The scripts in listings 3-2 and 3-3 will be executed once the database is created. You will create the database in the next section of this chapter.

The scripts in listings 3-2 and 3-3 are created using standard T-SQL commands. T-SQL is the language the database (Microsoft SQL Server) uses to execute commands. LocalDB is a reduced version of SQL Server, so it understands most T-SQL syntax. Also, the scripts can be used when deploying the application to a production environment, which will most likely use a different version of SQL Server. (Application deployment will be covered in Chapter 12.)

Running the Scripts

We'll execute the scripts in Listings 3-2 and 3-3 in our database using Visual Studio. The following steps walk you through the process.

1. Open Visual Studio (if it is not already open).

2. Open the ASP.NET MVC 4 application you just created (if it is not already open) by selecting the menu File ➤ Open Project and then browse for the folder where the application is. Figure 3-4 shows the open application.

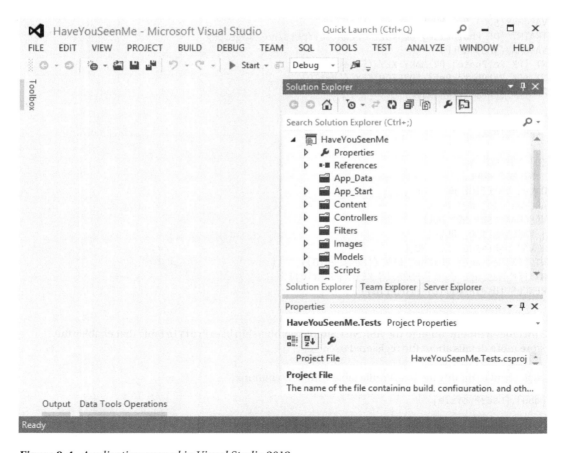

Figure 3-4. *Application opened in Visual Studio 2012*

3. Run the application by pressing F5 or by choosing Debug ➤ Start Debugging (see Figure 3-5).

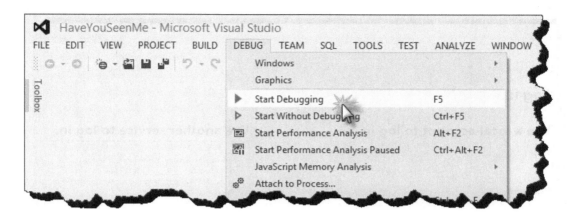

Figure 3-5. *Start Debugging option in the Debug menu*

4. On the application home page that opens, click the "Log in" link in the top-right corner of the page, as shown in Figure 3-6. As described earlier in the chapter, we are trying to execute a user account operation with the `AccountController` class. The operation will open the login page to authenticate users, but first the `AccountController` class must determine if the supporting database and tables are ready to handle such operations; if they are not, `ASP.NET` will create the database and tables, which will take a minute or less depending on your machine.

Figure 3-6. *"Log in" link on the application home page*

The login page appears, as shown in Figure 3-7.

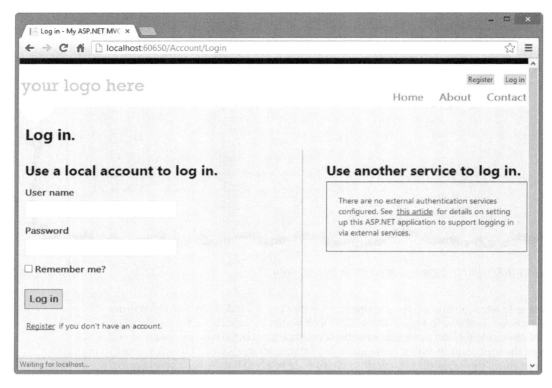

Figure 3-7. Login page

5.   Once you reach the login page, close the web browser and then click the "Stop Debugging" button in Visual Studio, as shown in Figure 3-8. This has effectively created a LocalDB database and populated the tables for the initial configuration of SimpleMembership.

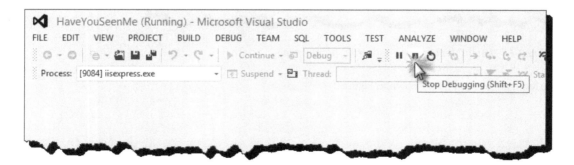

Figure 3-8. Stop Debugging button in the toolbar

6. To work with the database, in the Solution Explorer window, click the HaveYouSeenMe project (not the Tests project) to select it, and then click the "Show All Files" button, as shown in Figure 3-9. Clicking the Show All Files button displays all files in the project folders whether they are a part of the project or not (including those folders and files that are normally hidden in Solution Explorer). Then, expand the App_Data folder and you will see the LocalDB database file.

***Figure 3-9.** Finding the LocalDB database file in the Solution Explorer window*

7. Right-click the LocalDB database file and select the option "Include in Project." This step is not required, but it saves you time and effort in the future by making the file available for editing without having to use the Show All Files button every time.

8. Double-click the LocalDB database file. This opens the Server Explorer window (which allows you to open data connections and to log on to servers and explore their databases and system services) with the contents of the LocalDB database file displayed. Expand the DefaultConnection node and then the Tables node, as shown in Figure 3-10. The DefaultConnection node represents the connection to the LocalDB database file as defined in the Web.Config file in the root of the application. The connection configuration provides the application with the information to locate and connect to the database. Note that the tables have been created in the database file.

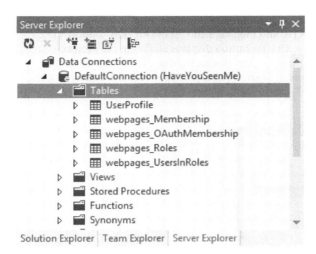

Figure 3-10. *Server Explorer window displaying the contents of the LocalDB database file*

9. To execute the database scripts in Listing 3-2 and Listing 3-3, right-click the Tables node and select "New Query," as shown in Figure 3-11.

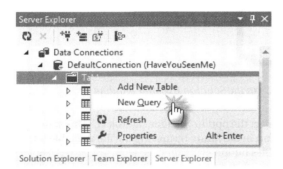

Figure 3-11. *Opening a new query window*

10. Copy the scripts from Listings 3-2 and 3-3 into the query window and click the "Execute" button, as shown in Figure 3-12.

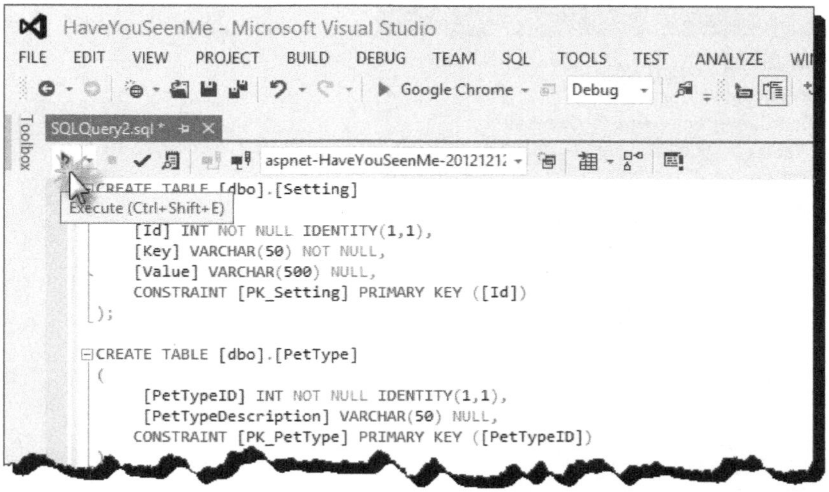
HaveYouSeenMe - Microsoft Visual Studio
FILE EDIT VIEW PROJECT BUILD DEBUG TEAM SQL TOOLS TEST ANALYZE
Google Chrome
Debug
SQLQuery2.sql*
Toolbox
Execute (Ctrl+Shift+E)
[dbo].[Setting]
[Id] INT NOT NULL IDENTITY(1,1),
[Key] VARCHAR(50) NOT NULL,
[Value] VARCHAR(500) NULL,
CONSTRAINT [PK_Setting] PRIMARY KEY ([Id])
);
CREATE TABLE [dbo].[PetType]
(
[PetTypeID] INT NOT NULL IDENTITY(1,1),
[PetTypeDescription] VARCHAR(50) NULL,
CONSTRAINT [PK_PetType] PRIMARY KEY ([PetTypeID])

Figure 3-12. *Executing the scripts in the query window*

The results window should display a message indicating successful execution, as shown in Figure 3-13.

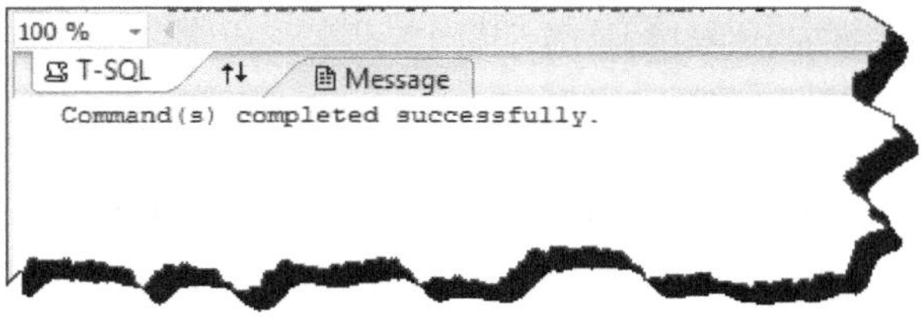
100 %
T-SQL
Message
Command(s) completed successfully.

Figure 3-13. *Query execution results window*

11. In the `Tables` node in the Server Explorer window, right-click the Tables node and select "Refresh." You will see that the new tables are now created in the database. Expand the `Pet` table, for example, and you will see all the columns of the table, as shown in Figure 3-14.

Figure 3-14. Server Explorer window displaying the new tables and the columns of the table Pet

Summary

This chapter described the application we are going to build and we used Visual Studio 2012 to create the ASP.NET MVC 4 web application that will be used to implement it. It is an application that publishes information about missing pets. By registering on the application's web site, a pet owner can gain access to the members section, where they can post information about their missing pet and upload photos of their pet. The information and photos are then displayed in the public section, which can be viewed by anyone and which allows anyone to send a message to an owner if they've seen the owner's missing pet. There is also an administrative section that administrators can use to manage the site features, user accounts, and data catalogs.

This chapter also introduced you to the database structure we are going to use and outlined the scripts used to create the new tables and modify the ASP.NET SimpleMembership UserProfile table.

At this point we have the bare bones of the HaveYouSeenMe ASP.NET MVC 4 web application with a Microsoft SQL Server 2012 LocalDB database. In the application, we will be using the C# programming language for the server-side code and the Razor view engine to build our views.

In the following chapters we will build our application's specific functionality, and in the process you will see how the concepts and technologies of ASP.NET MVC 4 provide the necessary building blocks to complete the application.

■ ■ ■

Controllers

In this chapter you will see that in the world of the MVC pattern, controllers process incoming HTTP requests from users. Each HTTP request is handled by a specific controller. ASP.NET MVC implements the concept of controllers with .NET classes that have methods to process such requests. The methods in a controller are called *action methods* because they return an object of type ActionResult.

The processing of a request starts with an element called the *routing engine*, which maps the request to a controller and a method (this chapter provides only a brief introduction to routing; Chapter 10 examines it in more detail). After that, the method is executed and produces an action result object that is returned to the user. The most common type of action result object is a View that renders HTML in the browser. Views are covered in more detail in Chapter 5.

We are going to create a controller named PetController with the main functionality for the HaveYouSeenMe web application. This controller, and the functionality implemented in it through the chapter, will be used to demonstrate how to work with controllers and action methods.

The Routing Engine

The ASP.NET MVC 4 Internet Application template in Visual Studio includes two default routes so that the project will run. Listing 4-1 shows the default routes. The first route instructs the routing engine to ignore requests for .axd resources such as ScriptResource.axd and WebResource.axd. These resources don't physically exist as files in the application; rather, they are HttpModules that load special content (such as images, scripts, CSS, etc.) that are embedded in DLL files so that they can be sent to the browser as part of the response. The second route is used to map requests to controllers and action methods.

Listing 4-1. Default Routes Created in the Internet Application Template in Visual Studio

```
routes.IgnoreRoute("{resource}.axd/{*pathInfo}");

routes.MapRoute(
    name: "Default",
    url: "{controller}/{action}/{id}",
    defaults: new { controller = "Home",
                    action = "Index",
                    id = UrlParameter.Optional }
);
```

To work correctly, routes need to be created when the application first starts. There is a handler called Application_Start in the Global.asax.cs file for this purpose. In ASP.NET MVC 4, the Application_Start event handler calls the static method RegisterRoutes() in the RouteConfig class located in the App_Start folder. The method accepts the existing routes table as a parameter so routes can be added to it.

The route definition is done by the MapRoute extension method in the RouteCollection class. The route definition contains the route name as the first parameter, the route pattern as the second parameter, and the default values for the elements in the route pattern as the third parameter. The route pattern in the default route is composed of three placeholders. Each placeholders is defined using curly braces,{ }.

The routing system actually doesn't know about controllers and their methods; it just matches the request to a pattern in a defined route (if one exists) and passes the information to the request pipeline, which in turn executes the method in a controller.

The route pattern identifies the controller name with the controller placeholder property, the action placeholder property defines the action method in the controller class that will be executed, and an additional third parameter indicates some kind of information that will be used by the method. Note that the HTTP request doesn't include the word "Controller" even though the controller class (per the naming convention) does use it. For example, with an HTTP request of http://myapp/Home/About, the route maps to the HomeController class and the action method About.

■ **Note**   When the routing engine was first launched, it was a part of ASP.NET MVC, but due to its success, it was later moved out of the ASP.NET MVC framework and baked into the core ASP.NET framework, thus making it available also to Web Forms and Web Pages.

The action methods in the controller class can have parameters. These parameters are matched to values in the request. For example, a request such as http://myapp/Product/Details?id=1 is mapped to the ProductController class to execute the Details action method, and the action method accepts a parameter named id that will be filled with the value from the request.

The defaults parameter supplies default values for the placeholders in the URL pattern—this allows the user a lot of flexibility in how they specify URLs in the browser. Table 4-1 lists some examples of URLs that the user might type in the browser, and how they would be matched by the routing engine using the default route.

Table 4-1. *Examples of How the Default Route Maps URL Requests to Controller Action Methods*

Request	Parameter Values	Execution
http://domain/	controller = Home action = Index	The Index method in the HomeController class
http://domain/Pet	controller = Pet action = Index	The Index method in the PetController class
http://domain/Pet/Details	controller = Pet action = Details	The Details method in the PetController class
http://domain/Pet/Details/1	controller = Pet action = Details id = 1	The Details action method in the PetController class passes the value 1 as the Id parameter of the action method

While it is very common to define default values for the placeholder properties in a route, they are not required. If you don't add default values to a route, the HTTP request must supply the values for all of the placeholders so that the route can be matched to the request.

Let's imagine for example that our route from Listing 4-1 doesn't have any default values. It would look like the one shown in Listing 4-2. If we now try to use the same example requests from Table 4-1, we will see the responses from Table 4-2.

Listing 4-2. Route Definition Without Default Values for Placeholders

```
routes.IgnoreRoute("{resource}.axd/{*pathInfo}");

routes.MapRoute(
    name: "Default",
    url: "{controller}/{action}/{id}"
);
```

Table 4-2. *Sample Requests with Default Route But No Default Values*

Request	Parameter Values	Execution
http://domain/		Error. The URL doesn't include values for controller, action, or id.
http://domain/Pet		Error. The URL doesn't include values for action or id.
http://domain/Pet/Details		Error. The URL doesn't include values for id.
http://domain/Pet/Details/1	controller = Pet action = Details id = 1	The Details method in the PetController class passing the value 1 as the Id parameter of the action method.

Creating Controllers

When creating controllers in ASP.NET MVC, the name of the controller classes has the form <*ControllerName*>Controller. For example, Listing 4-3 shows the skeleton of the PetController class in the PetController.cs file. The controller name is actually Pet, but the default behavior of the routing engine is to use classes that will have a name ending with the word Controller. This behavior can be modified, but that topic is outside the scope of this book. The class inherits from the Controller base class (in the System.Web.Mvc namespace).

Listing 4-3. Definition of the Pet Controller Class

```
using System;
using System.Collections.Generic;
using System.Linq;
using System.Web;
using System.Web.Mvc;

namespace HaveYouSeenMe.Controllers
{
    public class PetController : Controller
    {

    }
}
```

The Controller base class gives your classes the functionality to handle requests and the ability to create *action methods*, which, as described at the beginning of the chapter, are simply regular methods that return an ActionResult object. There are different types of ActionResult objects such as views, files, a redirection to another route, and so forth. Technically, an ActionResult object represents a command that the framework will perform on behalf of the action requested by the user. The ActionResult class is the base class for all the specific implementations of action results. The following classes derive from the ActionResult class and can be used as an action method's return type:

- ViewResult: Used to return a view to render HTML in the browser. This is the most common ActionResult.

- PartialViewResult: Similar to ViewResult, it returns a partial view.

- ContentResult: Used to return any type of content. By default, it is used to return plain text, but the actual content type can be explicitly defined (e.g. text/xml).

- EmptyResult: This is the equivalent of a void method—it is by definition an action result object, but it does nothing.

- FileResult: Used to return binary content (e.g., if you want to download a file).

- HttpUnauthorizedResult: You can return an HttpUnauthorizedResult object when the request tries to access restricted content that, for example, is not available to anonymous users. The browser is then redirected to the login page.

- JavaScriptResult: Used to return JavaScript code.

- JsonResult: Used to return an object in JavaScript Object Notation (JSON) format.

- RedirectResult: Used to perform an HTTP redirect to another URL. You can define it as a temporary (code 302) or permanent (code 301) HTTP redirect.

- RedirectToRouteResult: used to perform an HTTP redirect, but to a specific route rather than a URL.

Working with Action Methods

The example in Listing 4-4 shows an action method in our Pet controller. Although the stated return type of the method is ActionResult, we are actually returning a ViewResult object that represents a view. The ViewResult class inherits from ActionResult, so the framework will accept it.

Listing 4-4. The Display Action Method in the PetController Class

```
public ActionResult Display()
{
    var name = (string)RouteData.Values["id"];
    var model = PetManagement.GetByName(name);

    if (model == null)
        return RedirectToAction("NotFound");

    return View(model);
}

public ActionResult NotFound()
{
    return View();
}
```

When a request from a user such as http://domain/Pet/Display/Fido is made to the application, the routing engine matches it to the Display action method in the PetController class. Next, the action method examines the RouteData dictionary in search of the value in the {id} placeholder, which is Fido. Once the pet name has been identified, the action method uses a business model class named PetManagement to retrieve a record from the database (if any exists) and place it in the model variable. (The business model is examined in Chapter 6.)

The method PetManagement.GetByName() will return an object if the pet's record exists; otherwise it will return null. If the value returned is null, then the action method redirects to another action method called NotFound. This action method will return a view with specific functionality to inform the user that there is no pet with the name Fido in the system.

If a record is found for Fido, then a view will be returned along with the newly found record so that the view can render the pet's details.

Using FileResult

Let's now add functionality to allow users to download pictures of the pets. In Listing 4-5, the action method DownloadPetPicture returns a FileResult object. The content of the FileResult object is the pet picture file, which is in the Content/Uploads folder.

Listing 4-5. Downloading Files Using FileResult

```
public FileResult DownloadPetPicture()
{
    var name = (string)RouteData.Values["id"];
    var picture = "/Content/Uploads/" + name + ".jpg";
    var contentType = "image/jpg";
    var fileName = name + ".jpg";
    return File(picture, contentType, fileName);
}
```

The FileResult object expects three parameters: the path where the file is located, a content type of image/jpg (because we are using pictures and assuming it's a JPG file), and the name of the file, because we want it to display to the user when they are prompted to download. Figure 4-1 shows the result in the browser.

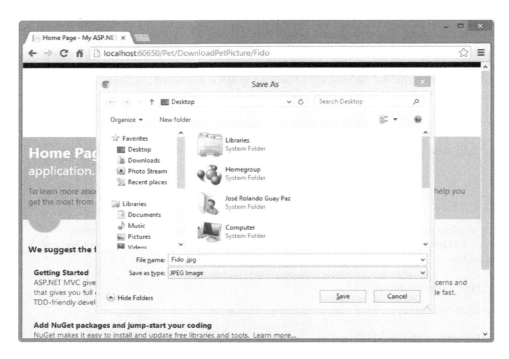

Figure 4-1. *Downloading a file with a FileResult action method*

Additionally, if you modify the code to remove the third parameter of the File method, then the action method will, instead of downloading the picture, display the picture in the browser, as shown in Figure 4-2. The modified code is shown in Listing 4-6.

Figure 4-2. *Displaying a picture using FileResult*

Listing 4-6. Displaying Pictures Using FileResult

```
public FileResult DownloadPetPicture()
{
    var name = (string)RouteData.Values["id"];
    var picture = "/Content/Uploads/" + name + ".jpg";
    var contentType = "image/jpg";
    return File(picture, contentType);
}
```

Using HttpStatusCodeResult

The action result HttpStatusCodeResult is useful when recognizing that a specific area of the application is accessible only to authorized users. With a system such as Forms Authentication, you can implement a certain level of access control. For example, imagine you have a banking application that allows employees to see reports. You want certain reports to be accessible to managers but not the people in the customer service team. Your action method can check for this access level and then, if it finds that the user is a member of the customer service team, issue an error that results in a redirection to the login page, as shown in Figure 4-3.

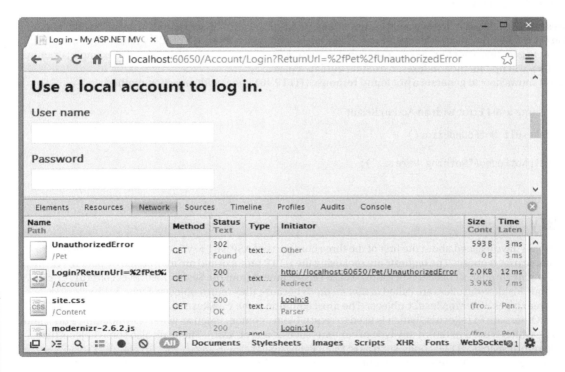

Figure 4-3. Identifying unauthorized access and then redirecting to the login page

Listing 4-7. Issuing a 401 Error

```
public HttpStatusCodeResult UnauthorizedError()
{
    return new HttpUnauthorizedResult("Custom Unauthorized Error");
}
```

■ **Tip**   Modern browsers such as Chrome, Firefox, and Internet Explorer include tools (also known as developer tools) that enable you to see different aspects of the pages being rendered, including the network traffic generated by requests. In Chrome, for example, if you press F12, the developer tools window opens.

In Figure 4-3 you can see in the Network tab of the developer tools that a request was made to /Pet/UnauthorizedError. Then this was correctly identified as a request to a restricted (secured) page. Finally, the application issued an HttpUnauthorizedResult response, which resulted in a redirection to the login page.

Using HttpNotFoundResult

In some cases it is a good idea to intentionally return a "not found" HTTP error. For example, consider search engine optimization (SEO). When dealing with dynamic content, such as an online store, if a product is no longer available, you might want to generate a not found response so that when search engines' crawlers (Google's, for example) examine the web site, they will update their indexes to exclude outdated pages.

Listing 4-8 shows how to generate a not found response (HTTP 404 code) with an action method.

Listing 4-8. Issuing a 404 Error with an Action Result

```
public ActionResult NotFoundError()
{
    return HttpNotFound("Nothing here...");
}
```

Summary

In this chapter you have learned about the first of the three core parts of ASP.NET MVC, controllers. Controllers are classes that handle user requests. The requests are sent using the HTTP protocol and are interpreted by patterns defined in the routing engine through a collection of routes. These classes inherit from the System.Web.Mvc.Controller class.

The methods inside controllers are called *action methods* because they return objects of type ActionResult. There are different types of ActionResult objects. The most common is the ViewResult object used to return HTML to the browser. Others are FileResult, which is used to return binary content (such as when downloading a file), and ContentResult, which is used to return any type of content (such as text or XML). There are also some objects that can be used to return specific HTTP codes, such as HttpNotFoundResult.

In the next chapter we will study views in more detail, including how we can use some features in which controllers send information to views so that they render HTML properly.

Views

In Chapter 4 you saw how action methods return an ActionResult. One of the most commonly used types of action results in an ASP.NET MVC application is the ViewResult. When you return a ViewResult from an action method, it indicates that ASP.NET MVC should invoke a view page to render HTML back to the client browser.

You store view pages in the Views directory inside the application. Views often include server-side code to produce the final HTML. When you create a view, you need to specify the view engine that will be used to process server-side code. Out of the box, ASP.NET MVC includes two view engines:

- *ASPX view engine*: The original view engine included in ASP.NET MVC 1. It uses a syntax similar to Web Forms.

- *Razor view engine*: A new view engine that uses a new, simple and fluid syntax.

An important addition in ASP.NET MVC 4 is the Display Modes feature, which lets the application choose which view to render based on which client browser is making the request. This is relevant now that mobile browsers are widely used.

In this chapter we are going to describe some of the features that will be implemented in the "Have You Seen Me?" application in relation to view pages. Particularly important is the concept of *layouts* that will help keep a consistent look-and-feel across the entire application.

Understanding View Engines

The ultimate goal of a view is to render HTML to the browser in response to a user request. A view can be as simple as the one presented in Listing 5-1.

Listing 5-1. A Simple View

```
<!DOCTYPE html>
<html>
<head>
    <meta name="viewport" content="width=device-width" />
    <title>View1</title>
</head>
<body>
    <h1>View1</h1>
</body>
</html>
```

Note that the view content is basically only HTML. This is perfectly OK, but it doesn't do much for an application except to display static content.

To make views really useful, they should render HTML based on information produced in the server. To work with this information, views must be able to access and manipulate the information, and that's where *view engines* come into play.

View engines provide a specific syntax to work with server-side elements and process the view to render the HTML in the browser. As indicated in the introduction to the chapter, ASP.NET MVC 4 includes two view engines: the original ASPX view engine, which works similarly to the syntax in Web Forms applications, and the new Razor view engine, which uses a simpler and compact syntax that is very easy to use.

A few examples of the syntax in both view engines are provided in Listings 5-2, 5-3, and 5-4. Note that Razor uses fewer characters and that the syntax is far easier to read than the ASPX syntax.

Listing 5-2. Print the Current Date

```
<%--ASPX--%>

<%=DateTime.Now %>

@*Razor*@

@DateTime.Now
```

Listing 5-3. if Statement

```
<%--ASPX--%>

<% if (DateTime.Today.Year == 2013) { %>
<span> Current year </span>
<% }
  else { %>
<span> Past year </span>
<% } %>

@*Razor*@

@if (DateTime.Today.Year == 2013) {
<span> Current year </span>
}
else {
<span> Past year </span>
}
```

Listing 5-4. foreach Loop

```
<%--ASPX--%>

<ul>
<% foreach (var t in tweets) { %>
<li><%= t.content %></li>
<% } %>
</ul>

@*Razor*@
```

```
<ul>
@foreach (var t in tweets) {
<li>@t.content</li>
}
</ul>
```

You can also have code blocks. A *code block* is a section of the view that contains strictly code rather than a combination of markup and code. An example is shown in Listing 5-5.

Listing 5-5. Code Blocks

```
<%--ASPX--%>

<%
var name = "Jose";
var message = "Welcome " + name;
%>

<p>Hello! <%= message %> </p>

@*Razor*@

@{
var name = "Jose";
var message = "Welcome " + name;
}

<p>Hello! @message </p>
```

Working with Views

Creating views is a very straightforward process. Let's take, for example, our Pet controller class created in Chapter 4. It has an action method called NotFound that is called if we have a request to display information about a pet that is not in the system. The view basically just needs to say that the pet has not been found. The action method is shown in Listing 5-6.

Listing 5-6. NotFound Action Method in the PetController Class

```
public ActionResult NotFound()
{
    return View();
}
```

One of the easiest ways to create a view for an action method is to right-click anywhere inside the action method and select the option "Add View," as shown in Figure 5-1.

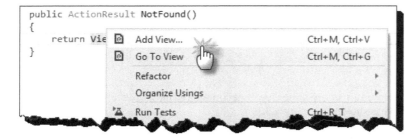

```
public ActionResult NotFound()
{
    return Vie
}
```

Figure 5-1. *Right-click anywhere inside the action method to create a view*

Doing this opens the Add View dialog, shown in Figure 5-2. In the dialog, you can set the properties of the view, which I'll describe in a moment.

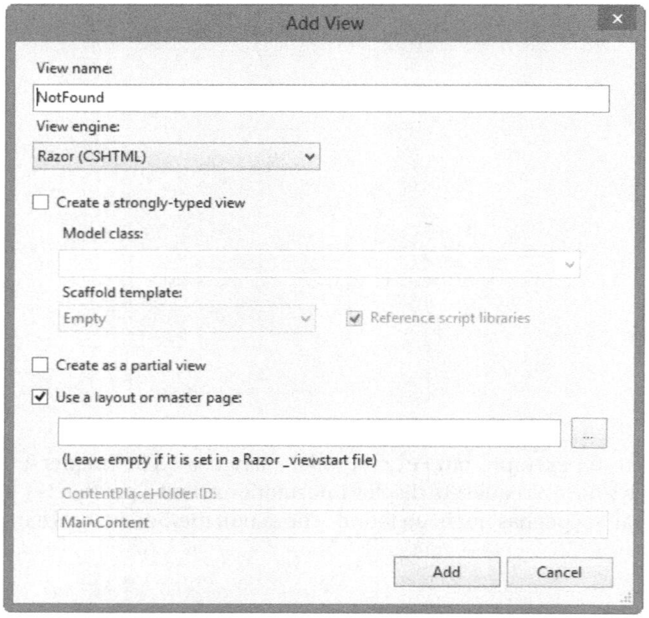

Figure 5-2. *Add View dialog*

In the "View name" text box, enter the name of the view. Generally, you'll want to give the view the same name as the action method that triggered it. Sometimes, though, you'll want the view to have a different name from that of the action method. In this case, the action method must specify the name of the view as follows:

```
return View(name-of-view);
```

The "View engine" drop-down list of the Add View dialog enables you to choose which view engine your view will use to process server-side code. As described earlier in the chapter, you can choose between the ASPX view engine and the more modern Razor view engine.

The following check boxes in the Add View dialog offer three additional view characteristics that you can specify:

- *Create a strongly-typed view*: Check this box if you want to make your view a *strongly typed view*, which is a view that receives a known type of "model" object as a parameter from the controller action method. Using strongly typed views has several advantages, such as:

  - *IntelliSense*: Visual Studio will be capable of displaying IntelliSense using the Model property based on the view model class. This allows the view page to access properties on the model object, call methods, and so forth.

  - *Automatic scaffolding*: Selecting this option instructs Visual Studio to create a view with a <form> tag that includes all the fields and validation options based on the properties defined in the view model class.

  - *Compile-time type checking*: The compiler is able to detect problems with data type handling in the view because it knows the view model class and its properties. For example, if the view page tries to access a property that doesn't exist on the model object, you'll get a compiler error rather than a runtime error. This is a good thing, because it helps you fix problems in your code more easily.

- *Create as a partial view*: Check this box to define the view as a *partial view*, which is a chunk of HTML that can be reused in other views. For example, a partial view can contain the logic to display a chart based on a set of data. This chart then can be placed in different views, but the logic remains centralized in a single partial view. This means that if you modify the chart type, for example, from a bar chart to a pie chart, all views having the same chart will be displayed as a pie chart.

- *Use a layout or master page*: Checking this box allows you to define a view that serves as a general layout with elements such as a logo, a top menu, and a footer that will be the same across all views that use it. This is a good way to give your web site a consistent look and feel. Also, changes that you make in this shared view apply to all views that use it, which is much easier than having to make the changes in each individual view. In Razor, there is a default layout view called _ViewStart.cshtml (or _ViewStart.vbhtml if your server-side language is VB.NET). The _ViewStart.cshtml view is used if you selected the check box "Use a layout or master page" and left the layout input box empty (as shown in Figure 5-2).

The last field in the Add View dialog is the ContentPlaceHolder ID, which you use when you choose ASPX as the view engine. It is the ID of the ContentPlaceHolder element in the master page that defines where the view content will be rendered to create a whole HTML document to be sent to the client browser. If you are using the Razor view engine, then this field is not available (as shown in Figure 5-2). Using the ASPX view engine is the old way, and I strongly suggest you use Razor instead. The best way to see how the ContentPlaceHolder ID setting works is with an example. Listing 5-7 includes a master page that defines a general layout for other views. Note that the HTML code includes two server-side elements, one in the <head> section and another in the <body> section. These elements are defined by <asp:ContentPlaceHolder>.

Listing 5-7. Sample Master Page That Uses the ASPX View Engine

```
<%@ Master Language="C#" Inherits="System.Web.Mvc.ViewMasterPage" %>

<!DOCTYPE html>
<html>
<head runat="server">
    <meta name="viewport" content="width=device-width" />
    <title><asp:ContentPlaceHolder ID="TitleContent" runat="server" /></title>
</head>
```

```
<body>
    <div>
        <asp:ContentPlaceHolder ID="MainContent" runat="server">
        </asp:ContentPlaceHolder>
    </div>
</body>
</html>
```

The ContentPlaceHolder elements are meant to be replaced at runtime by HTML generated from the specific views that use the master page. For example, the view in Listing 5-8 has two <asp:Content> elements, each of which has a ContentPlaceHolderID property that refers to the ID of the ContentPlaceHolder elements in the master page.

Listing 5-8. View Implementing the Master Page from Listing 5-7

```
<%@ Page Title="" Language="C#"
    MasterPageFile="~/Views/Shared/ViewMasterPage1.Master"
    Inherits="System.Web.Mvc.ViewPage<dynamic>" %>

<asp:Content ID="Content1" ContentPlaceHolderID="TitleContent" runat="server">
    Index
</asp:Content>

<asp:Content ID="Content2" ContentPlaceHolderID="MainContent" runat="server">

<h2>Index</h2>

</asp:Content>
```

At runtime, a call to the view will cause the HTML in the master page to be rendered as part of the HTML in the view, as shown in Listing 5-9; the areas where the view HTML was inserted in the master page appears in bold.

Listing 5-9. Resulting HTML Sent to the Browser Based on the Master Page and the View

```
<!DOCTYPE html>

<html>
<head><meta name="viewport" content="width=device-width" />
<title>Index</title>
</head>
<body>
    <div>
        <h2>Index</h2>
    </div>
</body>
</html>
```

The Rendering Process

Once you have created the view for the action method in Listing 5-6, all you need to do is compile the application so it can start accepting requests to render the view. Let's see what happens when you create a view and name it, for example, not-found.cshtml instead of NotFound.cshtml, which is the expected view name for the NotFound() action method.

If you run the application and make a request to Pet/NotFound, the request will be handled by the NotFound action method in the PetController class. The NotFound() action method returns a ViewResult by calling return View(). Because a specific view was not requested, the framework will try to render a view named NotFound.cshtml and you will get a response like the one shown in Figure 5-3.

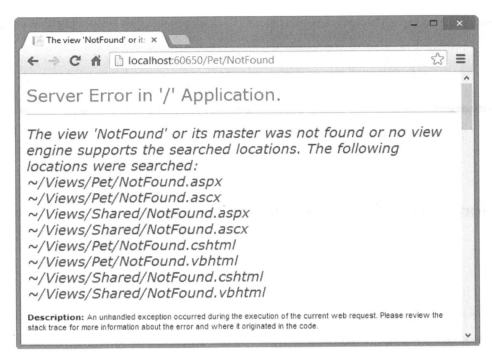

Figure 5-3. Error displayed when rendering a view that doesn't exist or has a different name than the action method

Figure 5-3 displays a lot of information that is important to examine. First, notice that the framework looked for a view with the name NotFound in two different directories: Views/Pet and Views/Shared. The Pet directory inside the Views directory represents a place for all views created based on the PetController class; it is another convention of ASP.NET MVC, by default it will look for a folder with the name of the controller class for views that are to be rendered by action methods defined in the controller. The second directory, Views/Shared, is a directory for views that don't have a direct relationship with an action method in a controller class but can be used by many action methods in different controllers (layout pages and partial views are good examples of shared views).

Second, notice in Figure 5-3 that the framework looks for files with different extensions, because each view engine uses different file extensions. The extensions .aspx and .ascx are used by the ASPX view engine, while the .cshtml and .vbhtml file extensions are used by the Razor view engine. In the world of the ASPX view engine, .aspx files are for views and .ascx files are for partial views. When you use the Razor view engine, you have only one file extension for your views: .cshtml is defined for views (and partial views) when your project uses the C# language, and .vbhtml is defined for views when your project uses VB.NET.

Third, the message states that one probable cause for the error is that it could not find the master page the view is using. This can happen if you renamed the master page or moved it to a different location.

If the view was created following the conventions and has the content in Listing 5-10, you will see the result shown in Figure 5-4.

Listing 5-10. Content of the Views/Pet/NotFound.cshtml View

```
@{
    ViewBag.Title = "NotFound";
}

<h1>The information you are looking could not be found</h1>
```

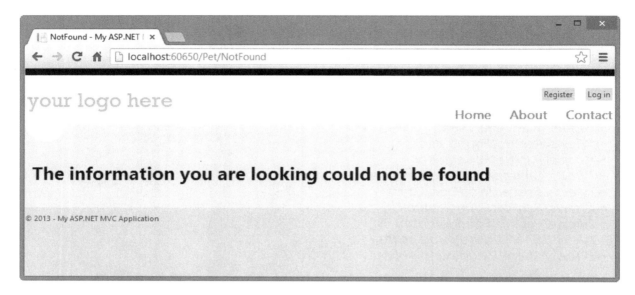

Figure 5-4. *Result of the NotFound view rendered in the browser*

Understanding the Razor View Engine

We are now going to work with Razor and explore the functionality it provides. The ASP.NET MVC 4 project template created a default _ViewStart.cshtml view (shown in Listing 5-11). The view actually uses another view to render content. This is a Razor feature called *layouts* in which the Layout property of the view defines a shared view that will be used as a template for the content in the view that implements it (similar to what a master page is in the ASPX view engine).

Using layouts helps you to keep look-and-feel consistency across your entire web site. You also get the benefit of having a centralized place from which to make changes.

Listing 5-11. Content of _ViewStart.cshtml

```
@{
    Layout = "~/Views/Shared/_Layout.cshtml";
}
```

The view named _Layout.cshtml (located in the Views/Shared directory) contains the HTML content for the "layout" (or "master"). When creating views with the Add View dialog (shown earlier, in Figure 5-2), you can refer directly to _Layout.cshtml by specifying it in the layout input box. The content of _Layout.cshtml is presented in Listing 5-12.

Listing 5-12. Content of _Layout.cshtml

```
<!DOCTYPE html>
<html lang="en">
    <head>
        <meta charset="utf-8" />
        <title>@ViewBag.Title - My ASP.NET MVC Application</title>
        <link href="~/favicon.ico" rel="shortcut icon" type="image/x-icon" />
        <meta name="viewport" content="width=device-width" />
        @Styles.Render("~/Content/css")
        @Scripts.Render("~/bundles/modernizr")
    </head>
    <body>
        <header>
            <div class="content-wrapper">
                <div class="float-left">
                    <p class="site-title">
                        @Html.ActionLink("your logo here", "Index", "Home")
                    </p>
                </div>
                <div class="float-right">
                    <section id="login">
                        @Html.Partial("_LoginPartial")
                    </section>
                    <nav>
                        <ul id="menu">
                            <li>@Html.ActionLink("Home", "Index", "Home")</li>
                            <li>@Html.ActionLink("About", "About", "Home")</li>
                            <li>@Html.ActionLink("Contact Us", "Contact", "Home")</li>
                        </ul>
                    </nav>
                </div>
            </div>
        </header>
        <div id="body">
            @RenderSection("featured", required: false)
            <section class="content-wrapper main-content clear-fix">
                @RenderBody()
            </section>
        </div>
        <footer>
            <div class="content-wrapper">
                <div class="float-left">
                    <p>&copy; @DateTime.Now.Year - My ASP.NET MVC Application</p>
                </div>
            </div>
        </footer>

        @Scripts.Render("~/bundles/jquery")
        @RenderSection("scripts", required: false)
    </body>
</html>
```

Listing 5-12 has two commands in the <head> portion of the page: @Scripts.Render() and @Styles.Render(). They are used to create script and style references to external files, respectively. The code in the page will produce the following HTML:

```
<link href="/Content/site.css" rel="stylesheet"/>
<script src="/Scripts/modernizr-2.6.2.js"></script>
```

As with the ASPX view engine, you can include HTML sections where content from views will be "slotted in" to the layout page—in the case of Razor they are called *sections*, as opposed to *ContentPlaceHolders* in the ASPX view engine.

The syntax to create a section is @RenderSection("name of section"). Note in Listing 5-12 the section named "featured" that will be rendered just above the body content. Pages are obliged to provide content for a section unless the section is defined as not required with an additional parameter. To define a section as not required, use @RenderSection("name of section", required : false).

Sections in Razor views created with @RenderSection() are a totally different concept from the HTML5 semantic tag <section>. When you use @RenderSection(), don't expect to get a <section> tag in the rendered HTML.

@RenderBody() renders the main content for a view page—that is, any content that isn't part of a named section. The view presented in Listing 5-13 has one named section (featured), denoted by @section featured {...}. The featured section is followed by HTML that is not enclosed in a @section{...} block. Razor automatically treats this as the "body" section and merges it into the layout page where indicated by @RenderBody().

Listing 5-13. View with a Named Section (Featured) and an Unnamed Section (Body)

```
@{
    ViewBag.Title = "Home Page";
}
@section featured {
    <div class="featured">
        <div class="content-wrapper">
            <hgroup class="title">
                <h1>@ViewBag.Title.</h1>
                <h2>@ViewBag.Message</h2>
            </hgroup>
            <p>
                To learn more about ASP.NET MVC visit
                <a href="http://asp.net/mvc" title="ASP.NET MVC Website">http://asp.net/mvc</a>.
                The page features <mark>videos, tutorials, and samples</mark> to help you get the
most from ASP.NET MVC.
                If you have any questions about ASP.NET MVC visit
                <a href="http://forums.asp.net/1146.aspx/1?MVC" title="ASP.NET MVC Forum">our
forums</a>.
            </p>
        </div>
    </div>
}
<h3>We suggest the following:</h3>
<ol class="round">
    <li class="one">
        <h5>Getting Started</h5>
        ASP.NET MVC gives you a powerful, patterns-based way to build dynamic websites that
        enables a clean separation of concerns and that gives you full control over markup
        for enjoyable, agile development. ASP.NET MVC includes many features that enable
        fast, TDD-friendly development for creating sophisticated applications that use
        the latest web standards.
```

```
    <a href="http://go.microsoft.com/fwlink/?LinkId=245151">Learn more...</a>
</li>

<li class="two">
    <h5>Add NuGet packages and jump-start your coding</h5>
    NuGet makes it easy to install and update free libraries and tools.
    <a href="http://go.microsoft.com/fwlink/?LinkId=245153">Learn more...</a>
</li>

<li class="three">
    <h5>Find Web Hosting</h5>
    You can easily find a web hosting company that offers the right mix of features
    and price for your applications.
    <a href="http://go.microsoft.com/fwlink/?LinkId=245157">Learn more...</a>
</li>
</ol>
```

Working with HTML Helper Methods

In the previous section, you may have noticed a few lines in Listing 5-12 that are not familiar to you, such as the following line:

```
<li>@Html.ActionLink("Contact Us", "Contact", "Home")</li>
```

This is called an *HTML helper method*. The idea behind HTML helper methods is that you can encapsulate functionality into libraries to generate HTML markup that can then be reused across the web application. ASP.NET MVC 4 already includes a rich set of HTML helper methods, but you can also create your own.

Html is a property of type HtmlHelper in the ViewWebPage class. ViewWebPage encapsulates the properties and methods that are needed to render a view that uses ASP.NET Razor syntax. The Html property has a lot of methods that render different types of HTML snippets.

In the example shown in listing 5-12, the @Html.ActionLink() helper method is used to create three HTML hyperlinks. The helper method takes the following three arguments (but it has nine overloads with different options):

- The text that will appear in the hyperlink

- The action method

- The controller where the action method is declared

At runtime, the example HTML helper method will render the following:

```
<a href="/Home/Contact">Contact Us</a>.
```

Another important helper method is @Html.Partial(). This helper method is used to render a partial view inside the main view. For example, in Listing 5-11 you may have noticed the following lines:

```
<section id="login">
    @Html.Partial("_LoginPartial")
</section>
```

This code tells the view to render the HTML contained in the partial view named _LoginPartial.cshtml, shown in Listing 5-14. To use this helper method, you don't need to specify the extension of the partial view.

Listing 5-14. Content of the Partial View _LoginPartial.cshtml

```
@if (Request.IsAuthenticated) {
    <text>
        Hello, @Html.ActionLink(User.Identity.Name, "Manage", "Account", routeValues: null,
htmlAttributes: new { @class = "username", title = "Manage" })!
        @using (Html.BeginForm("LogOff", "Account", FormMethod.Post, new { id = "logoutForm" })) {
            @Html.AntiForgeryToken()
            <a href="javascript:document.getElementById('logoutForm').submit()">Log off</a>
        }
    </text>
} else {
    <ul>
        <li>@Html.ActionLink("Register", "Register", "Account", routeValues: null, htmlAttributes:
new { id = "registerLink" })</li>
        <li>@Html.ActionLink("Log in", "Login", "Account", routeValues: null, htmlAttributes: new {
id = "loginLink" })</li>
    </ul>
}
```

Listing 5-14 includes some other helper methods, such as @Html.BeginForm(), which renders a <form> element, and @Html.AntiForgeryToken(), which generates a hidden form field (antiforgery token) that is validated when the form is submitted. The latter helper method is a security mechanism that we will examine in more detail in Chapter 9.

Working with ViewData and ViewBag

When passing information from an action method to a view, you basically have three options:

- Use the ViewData dictionary
- Use ViewBag (starting in MVC 3)
- Use a strongly typed view with a view model object

ViewData and ViewBag allow you to add information (primitive types such as integers or even complex objects) that will later be accessible to the view for generating HTML. Using strongly typed views is discussed in the next section.

ViewData is simply a dictionary that uses the key/value pattern. An example of how to use ViewData is provided in Listing 5-15. Note that the information in the ViewData dictionary is simply added by giving it a name and setting its value.

Listing 5-15. Using ViewData to Pass Information from the Action Method to the View

```
// Action Method
public ActionResult ShowError()
{
    ViewData["ErrorCode"] = 12345;
    ViewData["ErrorDescription"] = "Something bad happened";
    ViewData["ErrorDate"] = DateTime.Now;
    ViewData["Exception"] = new Exception();

    return View();
}
```

```
@* View *@
<h1>An error was found</h1>
<h2>Error Code: @ViewData["ErrorCode"]</h2>
<h2>Error Date: @ViewData["ErrorDate"]</h2>
<h2>@ViewData["ErrorDescription"]</h2>
```

ViewBag is different from ViewData in the sense that it implements the dynamic features introduced in C# 4. Basically, the difference is that properties can be added to ViewBag dynamically. Listing 5-16 shows the code in Listing 5-15 modified to use ViewBag.

Listing 5-16. Using ViewBag to Pass Information from the Action Method to the View

```
//Action Method
public ActionResult ShowError()
{
    ViewBag.ErrorCode = 12345;
    ViewBag.ErrorDescription = "Something bad happened";
    ViewBag.Exception = new Exception();

    return View();
}

@* View *@
<h1>An error was found</h1>
<h2>Error Code: @ViewBag.ErrorCode</h2>
<h2>@ViewBag.ErrorDescription</h2>
```

After viewing the code in Listings 5-15 and 5-16, you will notice that they are very similar—and there is a good reason for that. ViewBag is simply a dynamic implementation of ViewData. Under the hood, ViewBag uses ViewData as a storage mechanism, so either way you end up using a dictionary; the difference is the syntax used to set and get the information.

You might be thinking now, "If they are using the same dictionary, I can use them interchangeably." Well, yes and no. Technically, there is no reason not to do so (nor any associated problems); for example, you can use ViewBag.ErrorCode = 12345; in the action method and then use <h2>@ViewData["ErrorCode"]</h2> in the view. However, I recommend using ViewBag simply because it is a bit easier than ViewData due to its dynamic nature.

One last thing to consider when using ViewData and ViewBag is that the information in the dictionary is lost after the view is rendered. This is important because you could, for example, use RedirectToAction in your action method to call a different action method (as you saw in Listing 4-4 in Chapter 4). If a RedirectToAction happens after you add values to ViewData (or ViewBag), it will cause the browser to issue a 302 HTTP redirect (a temporary redirect). At this point, a completely new request is sent to the server and the new action method won't have access to the information previously added to ViewData. In this scenario, you will have to use a different object that is designed to have a short life but is capable of surviving redirects. The object is TempData, which, as opposed to ViewData, is stored in the current session instead of a dictionary. Use TempData with caution, as the information is promptly discarded once the redirect is complete. If you refresh the page, the information in TempData won't be available.

■ **Note** Two great articles on TempData are "ASP.NET MVC: Do You Know Where Your TempData Is?" by Gregg Shackles (http://bit.ly/GregShackles-TempData) and "When to Use ViewBag, ViewData, or TempData in ASP.NET MVC 3 Applications" by Rachel Appel (http://bit.ly/RachelAppel-ViewBag-ViewData-TempData).

Working with Strongly Typed Views

While ViewData and ViewBag (and TempData) are easy to use, they are not suitable for more complex scenarios that include any of the following:

- Master-detail data

- Larger sets of data

- Complex relational data

- Reporting and aggregate data

- Dashboards

- Data from disparate sources

- Data sent from the view to the controller

For such scenarios, it is better to use a view model object. When you associate a view model to a view, the view become a strongly typed view. I will cover models (including view models) in Chapter 6; for now, simply understand that a view model is a class with properties that represent information that you want to pass from the controller action method to the view, so that the view can render it.

An example of a view model class is presented in Listing 5-17. Note that it is just a class with properties, and each property is decorated with some attributes.

Listing 5-17. A View Model Class

```
public class LoginModel
    {
        [Required(ErrorMessage = "The UserName is required")]
        [Display(Name = "User name")]
        public string UserName { get; set; }

        [Required(ErrorMessage = "The Password is required")]
        [StringLength(20, MinimumLength = 6, ErrorMessage = "The Password is invalid")]
        [DataType(DataType.Password)]
        [Display(Name = "Password")]
        public string Password { get; set; }

        [Display(Name = "Remember me?")]
        public bool RememberMe { get; set; }
    }
```

In this case, we need to tell the view that it has an associated view model. We do so with the @model directive, as shown in Listing 5-18, which is generated automatically when you specify the model class in the Add View dialog (refer to Figure 5-2).

Listing 5-18. Strongly Typed View Using the LoginModel View Model Class

```
@model HaveYouSeenMe.Models.LoginModel

@{
    ViewBag.Title = "Log in";
}
```

```
<hgroup class="title">
    <h1>@ViewBag.Title.</h1>
</hgroup>

<section id="loginForm">
<h2>Use a local account to log in.</h2>
@using (Html.BeginForm(new { ReturnUrl = ViewBag.ReturnUrl })) {
    @Html.AntiForgeryToken()
    @Html.ValidationSummary(true)

    <fieldset>
        <legend>Log in Form</legend>
        <ol>
            <li>
                @Html.LabelFor(m => m.UserName)
                @Html.TextBoxFor(m => m.UserName)

            </li>
            <li>
                @Html.LabelFor(m => m.Password)
                @Html.PasswordFor(m => m.Password)

            </li>
            <li>
                @Html.CheckBoxFor(m => m.RememberMe)
                @Html.LabelFor(m => m.RememberMe, new { @class = "checkbox" })
            </li>
        </ol>
        <input type="submit" value="Log in" />
    </fieldset>
    <p>
        @Html.ActionLink("Register", "Register") if you don't have an account.
    </p>
}
</section>

<section class="social" id="socialLoginForm">
    <h2>Use another service to log in.</h2>
    @Html.Action("ExternalLoginsList", new { ReturnUrl = ViewBag.ReturnUrl })
</section>

@section Scripts {
    @Scripts.Render("~/bundles/jqueryval")
}
```

What's important about a strongly typed view is that it not only enables you to pass information back and forth to a controller but also enables you to use the view model properties simply by calling the implicit Model object. Note that the Model object is written with capital M as opposed to the model declaration with the @model statement. Visual Studio also makes the list of properties available in IntelliSense, as shown in Figure 5-5.

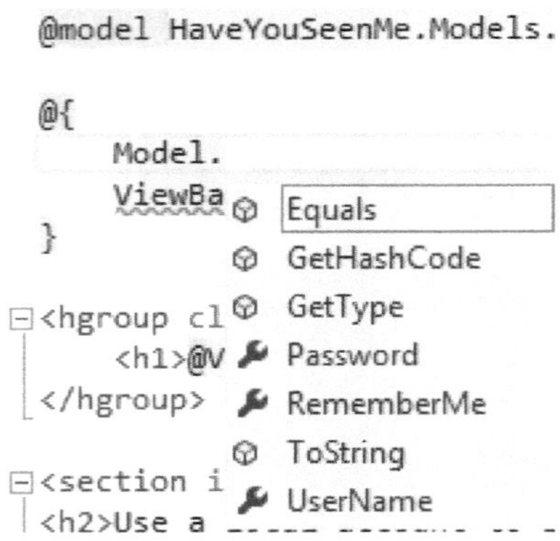

```
@model HaveYouSeenMe.Models.

@{
    Model.
    ViewBa ⊕  Equals
}          ⊕  GetHashCode
□<hgroup cl ⊕  GetType
    <h1>@v  🔑 Password
  </hgroup>  🔑 RememberMe
            ⊕  ToString
□<section i 🔑 UserName
  <h2>Use a
```

Figure 5-5. *Properties of the view model object displayed in Visual Studio IntelliSense*

Additionally, you can use the view model object's properties in HTML helper methods, and you don't even need to reference the Model object. For example:

```
@Html.LabelFor(m => m.UserName)
@Html.TextBoxFor(m => m.UserName)
```

These two helper methods will create a label and a text box, respectively, based on the attributes set for the property UserName in the view model class. The following is the rendered HTML for the two lines:

```
<label for="UserName">User name</label>
<input data-val="true" data-val-required="The UserName is required"
       id="UserName" name="UserName" type="text" value="" />
```

Introducing ASP.NET MVC 4 Mobile Features

The world in which we live is changing rapidly. Almost everyone now seems to own a smartphone, a tablet, or both, and we spend a lot of our time (too much?) viewing web sites on these devices. This trend has created a challenge for developers because mobile browsers and desktop browsers behave differently. Adding to that challenge is the fact that there is a plethora of devices with different form factors. Building web applications that look good and are fully functional on these devices can quickly become a titanic task.

ASP.NET MVC 4 introduces a new set of features that is intended to help developers create web applications that work seamlessly both in desktop browsers and in mobile browsers. Views can now be created to target specific browsers. Also, with the help of CSS3, we can apply styles based on the form factor of the device.

Let me start by saying that, to provide the best user experience across desktop and mobile browsers, you should work with HTML5 for the markup and CSS3 for the styling of elements. In Listing 5-12, presented earlier in the chapter, the _Layout.cshtml view is built with HTML5. You can quickly identify in the listing the enhanced HTML5 markup, known as *semantic markup*, with tags such as <header>, <footer>, <nav>, <section>, and a simplified <!DOCTYPE html>.

Another important aspect of mobile browsers is the *viewport*, a virtual browser window that is defined in most mobile browsers. This virtual window is normally defined with dimensions that are larger than the actual device screen, which allows users to zoom in on page content that is of interest. If the viewport, on the other hand, is defined by the developer with the actual device screen dimensions, then zooming is not available as the content in the page is supposed to fit correctly.

We can control the viewport using a `<meta>` tag in the `<head>` section of a web page. Note in Listing 5-12 the following tag:

```
<meta name="viewport" content="width=device-width">
```

This tag instructs the mobile browser to set the width of the viewport to the actual width of the device's screen. This is achieved with the constant `device-width`, whose value is defined in every device with the screen's width. This is important because we want to provide to mobile users a version of the web application that is suitable for their devices, not just the full desktop version with zoom capabilities.

To provide styles for specific form factors, we need to implement CSS3 media queries. A *media query* is nothing more than a definition of a type of media and a set of characteristics for the media. A type of media identifies the means by which a page is viewed (for example, onscreen or printed). The characteristics of the media may be, for example, the screen dimensions and whether or not the media supports colors.

The default ASP.NET MVC 4 Internet Application project template that we are using for our sample application includes in the `Content` directory a CSS style sheet called `Site.css`. If you open the file, you will find the following media query:

```
@media only screen and (max-width: 850px){
...
// set of styles when the media query is applied
...
}
```

The media query specifies that it will apply the set of styles only when the application is viewed onscreen. This means that if the page is printed, for example, then the styles won't be printed. Also, the media characteristics state that the maximum width is 850 pixels. The browser interprets this as, "If the page is viewed in a screen with a width of 850 pixels or less, then apply the following set of styles."

Listing 5-19 shows a few modifications I added to the `Site.css` file to clearly show the difference between rendering a view in a desktop browser (see Figure 5-6) and rendering a view in a mobile browser (see Figure 5-7).

Listing 5-19. Modifications to the Media Query in Site.css File

```
.main-content,
.featured + .main-content {
    background-position: 10px 0;
    background-image: none;
}

.featured .content-wrapper {
    padding: 10px;
    background-color: #e80c4d;
    background-image: -ms-linear-gradient(left, #e80c4d 0%, #e6507d 100%);
    background-image: -o-linear-gradient(left, #e80c4d 0%, #e6507d 100%);
    background-image: -webkit-gradient(linear, left top, right top, color-stop(0, #e80c4d),
    color-stop(1, #e6507d));
    background-image: -webkit-linear-gradient(left, #e80c4d 0%, #e6507d 100%);
    background-image: linear-gradient(left, #e80c4d 0%, #e6507d 100%);
    color: #fff;
}
```

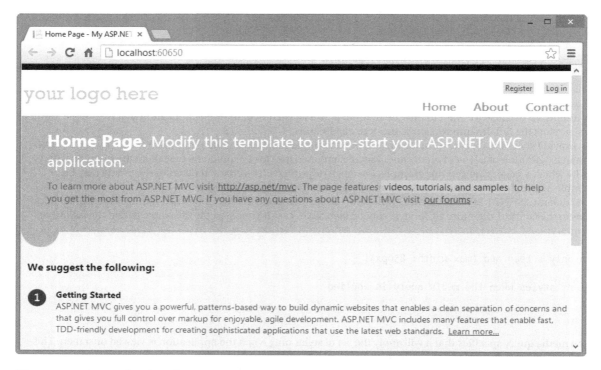

***Figure 5-6.** View rendered in Chrome desktop browser on a Windows computer*

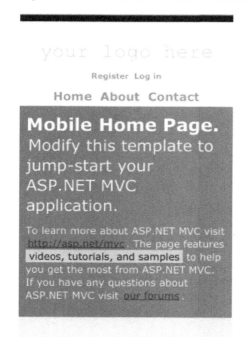

***Figure 5-7.** View rendered in Mobile Chrome running in iOS*

You can immediately see the differences between the browsers and how the media query affected the way styles were applied. The desktop version has a light blue background for the main, featured-content area, and the header is split in left and right sections (the left section for the site title and the right section for the menu options). In the mobile version, the light blue background is changed to fuchsia and the header is simplified and placed in a single stacked column for all the menu options.

There is another difference that probably didn't catch your eye at first glance. In Figure 5-6, the featured section reads "Home Page," but in Figure 5-7, the mobile browser says "Mobile Home Page." How did that happen? CSS media queries cannot do that. That is a feature in ASP.NET MVC 4 called *view override*, a simple mechanism in which ASP.NET MVC identifies that the request is made by a mobile browser. It does only that—recognizes that a mobile browser made the request.

To override a view, you need to create a view that ends with `.Mobile.cshtml`, as opposed to the normal desktop browser views, which just use `.cshtml`. The examples shown in Figures 5-6 and 5-7 use the views shown in Figure 5-8.

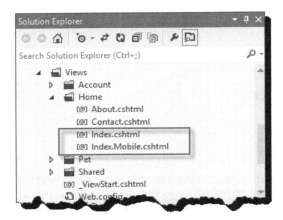

Figure 5-8. *Views used to implement view override*

With this simple mechanism, you can provide a much better experience to users who are using mobile browsers. You don't need to mix code, HTML markup, and CSS styles in a single view to handle different browsers. The mobile version of the view can be completely different from the desktop version, both from the style perspective and in the content it presents. In an extreme case, you could even use the mobile browser view simply to tell the user to use a desktop browser because the content cannot be correctly viewed in a mobile browser.

One thing that view override cannot do is identify a specific browser or a specific platform. For that, we need to create a custom display mode. Let's say, for example, that we want to target specifically browsers in iPhones. To do so, we need to do two things: first, add the new display mode in the `Application_Start` event in the `Global.asax.cs` file, and then create a new view that targets the specific display mode.

Listing 5-20 adds a new display mode object identified as `iPhone` to the `DisplayModeProvider`. The new display mode object defines which properties it wants to recognize in the browser in order to render the view with the `ContextCondition` property. The condition states that if the information in the `UserAgent` piece passed by the browser in the request has the word "iPhone" (ignoring all casing rules), then the requested view should be rendered with the iPhone version.

Listing 5-20. Creating a Custom Display Mode to Target iPhone Mobile Browsers

```
using System;
using System.Web.Http;
using System.Web.Mvc;
using System.Web.Optimization;
```

```
using System.Web.Routing;
using System.Web.WebPages;

namespace HaveYouSeenMe {
    public class MvcApplication : System.Web.HttpApplication {
        protected void Application_Start(){
            DisplayModeProvider.Instance.Modes
                .Insert(0, new DefaultDisplayMode("iPhone")
                {
                    ContextCondition = (context =>
                        context.GetOverriddenUserAgent().IndexOf
                        ("iPhone", StringComparison.OrdinalIgnoreCase) >= 0)
                });

            AreaRegistration.RegisterAllAreas();

            WebApiConfig.Register(GlobalConfiguration.Configuration);
            FilterConfig.RegisterGlobalFilters(GlobalFilters.Filters);
            RouteConfig.RegisterRoutes(RouteTable.Routes);
            BundleConfig.RegisterBundles(BundleTable.Bundles);
            AuthConfig.RegisterAuth();
        }
    }
}
```

In Listing 5-20, we are creating a new DefaultDisplayMode with the name iPhone. This tells the ASP.NET MVC 4 framework to look for views in files whose names end with .iPhone.cshtml. If we want a view with file name Index.cshtml to render differently in iPhone devices, then we need to create a version of the view named Index.iPhone.cshtml, as shown in Figure 5-9.

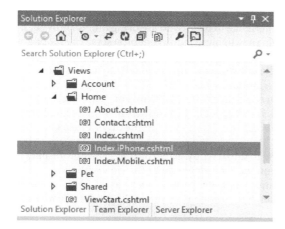

Figure 5-9. *New view to be rendered when a request is made from iPhone devices*

For our example, I made a simple change in the view content to indicate that it is the view to be rendered in iPhone devices. The result is shown in Figure 5-10.

Figure 5-10. *View rendered in an iPhone*

Summary

In this chapter we examined what views are and how they are built and processed. The goal of views is to send HTML to browsers in response to a user request. The type of action result an action method needs to implement to return a view is ViewResult.

To process server-side code views, you implement a view engine. View engines provide a specific syntax to work with server-side elements and process the view to render the HTML in the browser. Two view engines are included out of the box in ASP.NET MVC 4: the original ASPX view engine, and the newer Razor view engine.

Creating views is a simple process, but you have to make some important decisions to do it properly. By convention, a view should be named the same as the action method that renders it. If you don't follow the convention, then you need to specify the name of the view to be returned using return View(name of view). Each view can use a different view engine, but as a best practice, the entire application should use a single view engine (I strongly suggest Razor). You can choose to create a strongly typed view by selecting a view model class that will be used by the view. Additionally, Visual Studio can create a scaffold view to perform insert or update operations based on the view model class. Finally, you can choose to have your view use a general layout or master page.

We examined the Razor view engine in more detail than the ASPX view engine because it is simpler and easier to use than ASPX. You can create in Razor the same elements from ASPX—that is, master pages (known as *layouts* in Razor) to share parts of the content and keep a consistent look across all views in the application.

You also learned that you have at your disposal a rich set of HTML helper methods, such as @Html.ActionLink(...), that you can use to produce HTML based on server-side information such as hyperlinks and forms.

Passing data from a controller to a view can be achieved by using a series of available mechanisms such as ViewData, ViewBag, TempData, and a view model class. ViewData is a dictionary. ViewBag is a wrapper around ViewData that implements dynamic properties. TempData is similar to ViewData but is used for redirections only. View model classes provide the best solution for transporting data to and from views for more complex scenarios, and in general they should be your preferred option. A view that uses a view model object becomes strongly typed.

ASP.NET MVC 4 includes various features to support mobile browsers. These features allow you to create a rich experience for users with smartphones and tablets. As a rule, if the application supports mobile browsers, it should use HTML5 for the HTML markup in views and CSS3 for styles. CSS media queries provide a mechanism to identify the type of media used by the user and certain properties around that media to conditionally apply specific styles to the markup.

You can override views to target mobile browsers in general simply by creating views with the same name but ending with Mobile.cshtml. Also, you can target specific mobile platforms and browsers by creating new display modes that can render specific views created for those platforms or browsers.

CHAPTER 6

Models

This chapter describes the last of the three core parts of an ASP.NET MVC application: models.

Several different types of models exist, but this chapter narrows the scope to the three MVC pattern model types that are most relevant when developing MVC applications: the data model, the business model, and the view model.

The data model is particularly important because it allows you to interact with the database. The business model is used to perform general processing and in most cases it interacts with the data model to obtain data from the database and save data back to the database. View models are classes in charge of passing information from controllers to views.

The chapter covers what model binding is and why is important. It is a mechanism to convert the data from incoming HTTP requests to objects that can be easily manipulated in the server.

What Are Models?

The term *model* refers to a set of objects that implements a piece of functionality. A model in the MVC pattern can be classified further as either a data model, a business model, or a view model. Each of the different model types has a specific purpose, as described in Table 6-1. As a whole, the data and business models are known as the *domain model*. View models are not part of the domain model, as their purpose is only to pass in data from the controller to the views and vice versa.

Table 6-1. *Types of Models*

Type	Description
Data model	The objects in the data model represent classes that interact with a database. Normally, you can think of the data model as the set of classes created by tools such as Entity Framework (EF). These classes can either start as existing tables in the database which are then read to generate classes (database-first approach) or start as classes which will be used to generate tables in the database (code-first approach). Also, you can manually create such classes using ADO.NET to implement the particular database interaction that your application needs.
Business model	The classes in the business model normally implement functionality that represents business rules or processing (for example, the calculation of a particular shipping cost for a shopping cart item based on the weight of the item being purchased). As part of the processing, the business model classes can interact with the data model classes to read or save data in the database.
View model	The view model classes provide information passed in from controllers to views, so that the views know what to render in the user's browser. For example, a view model class can contain product information that is used by a view to display the product name, price, and images. The function of a view model class is not to process anything; rather, its only function is to contain data and optional metadata for the view to render properly. A view model is also used when a user makes a request from a previously rendered view (for example, when submitting a contact form).

Creating the Data Model

As described before, the data model is a set of classes that interact with the database in order to provide a means to store and retrieve data in the database. In an ASP.NET application (whether it's MVC or Web Forms), working with classes is far easier than working with database tables because object-oriented languages such as C# or VB.NET are not designed to interact directly with databases. Instead, an abstraction layer is used to send commands to the database. The level of abstraction may be as simple as working with ADO.NET connections and commands or as elaborate as working with a tool such as Entity Framework.

What Are ORMs?

ORM stands for *object-relational mapping*. The idea behind ORM is to create a translation (mapping) mechanism that will allow developers to work with familiar object-oriented (OO) languages such as C# or VB.NET to manipulate tables, views, stored procedures, and more in a relational database (e.g., SQL Server).

The result of an ORM is a set of classes that, for example, implements the functionality necessary to read, create, and delete rows of data in a database table. Other functionality that might result from an ORM is a class that interact with stored procedures and allow you to execute them from your C# code. Tools that implement ORMs include both commercial tools (e.g., LLBLGen Pro from Solutions Design and eXpress Persistent Objects [XPO] from DevExpress) and free tools (e.g., OpenAccess ORM from Telerik and Entity Framework from Microsoft), but you can easily create classes that provide such functionality. The major benefit of using a tool is that you save the time it takes to create classes. Also, most modern ORM tools enable you to modify the behavior of the class-generation engine and provide utility programs that, for example, help you to analyze and profile the generated code to ensure it is optimal for your project.

For the purpose of our sample application, we will use Microsoft Entity Framework (EF). EF is included in Visual Studio, but newer versions (released after Visual Studio shipped) are available as the EntityFramework NuGet package. Although working with the latest version of EF is recommended, because it provides richer functionality and improvements, you are not required to upgrade.

ABOUT NUGET

NuGet is an open source project licensed under the Apache version 2 license. NuGet was originally developed by Microsoft, which then transferred it to the Outercurve Foundation (www.outercurve.org).

Microsoft recognized that it needed to provide .NET developers with an easy method to incorporate third-party components so that the developers could improve their productivity when using development tools such as Visual Studio or WebMatrix. The result was a repository for components packaged in a way that could be understood by clients (e.g., Visual Studio) by using a command-line or graphical interface. Each package includes not just the required files to run the component but also metadata with information for the client to configure the component in the development project (e.g., an ASP.NET MVC 4 application), thus minimizing the time to implement such components. Another benefit of NuGet packages is that they are very easy to upgrade, and updates are applied only at the request of the developer.

The NuGet Package Manager tool is already installed in Visual Studio 2012; it needs to be installed separately for Visual Studio 2010 editions. If you are not familiar with the NuGet Package Manager, you can find more information at www.nuget.org. NuGet is not limited to working only with Visual Studio, and clients can be developed to provide the ability to include packages from the NuGet Gallery.

Anyone can develop their own package and share it via the NuGet Gallery, and many of the existing packages are also open source projects that you can get involved with to improve them.

Adding the Entity Framework Model

Chapter 3 explained how to create the database for the "Have You Seen Me" application and add a set of tables to support the application's functionality. It is now time to use EF to create the classes in the data model that will interact with the database. The following steps guide you through the process of adding the data model using EF in Visual Studio 2012.

1. Open the ASP.NET MVC 4 application created in Chapter 3.

2. Create an ADO.NET Entity Data Model using either of the following procedures:

   Right-click the Models folder and select Add ➤ ADO.DB Entity Data Model, as shown in Figure 6-1, and type the name of the data model in the Specify Name for Item dialog. For example, enter **DataModel**, as shown in Figure 6-2. Click the "OK" button to start the Entity Data Model Wizard, which will guide you through the steps to create the EF-based data model.

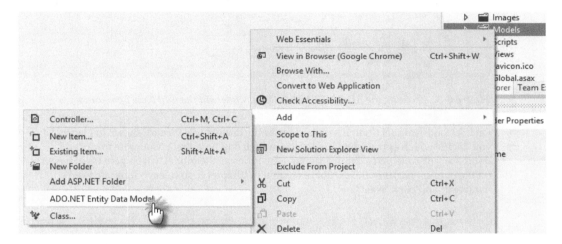

Figure 6-1. *Creating the ADO.NET Entity Data Model from the context menu*

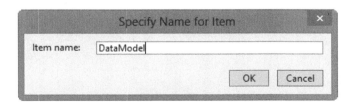

Figure 6-2. *Naming the ADO.NET Entity Data Model*

Alternatively, select Add ➤ New Item. In the Add New Item dialog (see Figure 6-3), click "Data" in the left pane, click "ADO.NET Entity Data Model" in the middle pane, and enter a name such as **DataModel** in the Name text box. Then click the "Add" button to launch the Entity Data Model Wizard.

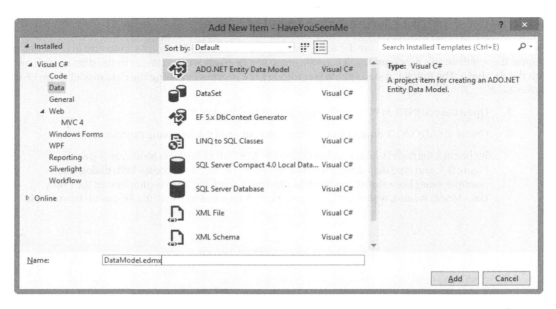

Figure 6-3. Creating the ADO.NET Entity Data Model via the Add New Item dialog

3. On the Choose Model Contents page of the Entity Data Model Wizard, shown in Figure 6-4, you decide which approach to use for the model: database first ("Generate from database") or code first ("Empty model"). In our case, the model will be generated based on the existing tables in the database created in Chapter 3, so select "Generate from database" and click "Next."

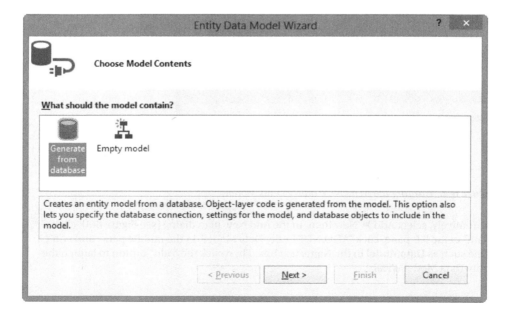

Figure 6-4. Selecting the database-first approach to generate the data model

4. The next step in the wizard is Choose Your Data Connection, as shown in Figure 6-5. The connection includes the name of the server (or IP address) where the database resides, the database name, and the connection credentials. Complete this wizard step as follows:

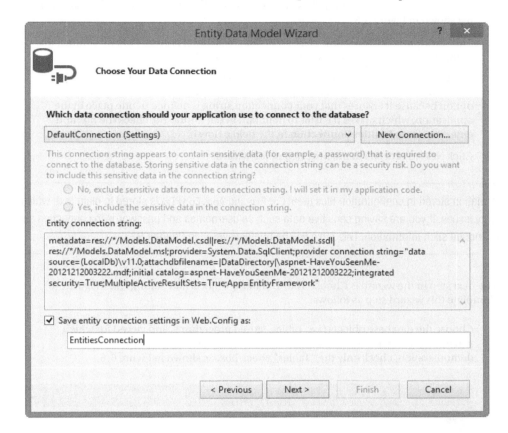

Figure 6-5. *Creating and saving the EF connection string*

a. The wizard first asks which data connection your application should use to connect to the destination database. The only option available in the drop-down list is DefaultConnection, so you don't need to make a change. This connection was created by the ASP.NET MVC 4 application template and is used to connect to the LocalDB database where our tables reside.

Alternatively, if the database is not already listed, you can click the "New Connection" button to create a new connection string. This opens the Choose Data Source dialog, in which you identify the type of database you are connecting to (e.g., SQL Server or Oracle). The available data sources depend on the EF providers installed. By default, you have Microsoft SQL Server, Microsoft SQL Server Compact 4.0, and Microsoft SQL Server Database File. If, for example, you are connecting to a LocalDB database, select Microsoft SQL Server Database File and click "Continue." The Add Connection dialog appears. You can either browse for the database file or, if you know the exact location, type the location in the box. Then select how you are connecting, either with Windows Authentication or with SQL Server Authentication. Leave the default setting, Windows Authentication. Click the "Test Connection" button at the bottom of the dialog to test the connection. You should get the message "Test connection succeeded." Click "OK." If you don't get that message, then something is wrong with the configuration and you should review the entered values. Now click "OK" to finish and save the new connection. This new connection will be available in the drop-down list shown in Figure 6-5.

b.   The "Entity connection string" section in this wizard step previews the EF connection string that is generated based on the database selection.

c.   The check box at the bottom of this step gives you the choice of saving the EF connection string in the Web.Config file. It's generally a good idea to select this option because it ensures that your connection string is defined in one place in the application, which makes it easier to maintain in the future. So, check the box and enter the name **EntitiesConnection** in the field below it.

d.   Click Next to proceed to the next step of the wizard.

■ **Note**   Information stored in configuration files (Web.Config and App.Config) is stored in plain text, which could have potential security issues. If you are saving sensitive data such as usernames and passwords in connection strings, there is an option to encrypt such information. This topic will be briefly covered in Chapter 9.

---

5.   The next step in the wizard is Choose Your Database Objects and Settings (see Figure 6-6). Complete this wizard step as follows:

a.   Choose the database objects (i.e., tables, stored procedures, and views) for which you want the wizard to create classes in the data model. For the purpose of this demonstration, check only the "Tables" check box, as shown in Figure 6-6.

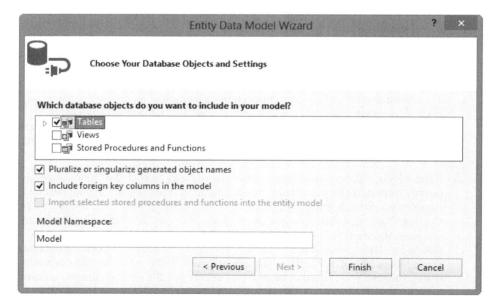

Figure 6-6. *Selecting the database objects and other options to generate the data model*

b. Because the tables (and other objects) in the database may have been created by different people, following different standards (or none at all), their names might not have been set with specific conventions or rules. To help establish consistent naming conventions, the wizard offers the "Pluralize or singularize generated object names" check box. When checked, this option will normalize the names of the classes and properties so that they are easier to work with in the application. By default, this check box is selected. For our project, leave it selected. The rules enforced by this selection are as follows:

    i. Use singular names for all the entity classes (e.g., if your database table is `Pets`, the EF wizard will generate a class named `Pet`).

    ii. Use plural names to represent collections of entities. As you'll see shortly, the EF wizard generates a "context" class that contains a bunch of properties (one property per table). Each property contains a collection of entity objects for a particular table—thus, there will be properties named `Pets`, `Owners`, `Messages`, etc. These properties will be named as plural nouns, which makes sense.

c. Leave the "Include foreign key columns in the model" check box selected. By doing so, for example, if the table `Pet` is referenced in the table `PetPhoto` with a foreign key, the `Pet` class will have a navigation property that is a collection of `PetPhoto` objects, and the `PetPhoto` class will have a navigation property that is a `Pet` object.

d. Leave the default name of "Model" in the Model Namespace field.

6. Click "Finish" to complete the Entity Data Model Wizard.

After you click the Finish button, you may encounter a security warning similar to the one shown in Figure 6-7. The reason for the warning is simple: In order to create the classes in the data model, Visual Studio needs to execute the commands in the T4 template files generated by the wizard. (T4 template files, which have the extension .tt, are instructions or commands that Visual Studio executes in order to generate code classes.) Theoretically, these template files could originate from anywhere, which is a potential security threat (hence the warning message). However, the T4 templates for the EF wizard originate from Microsoft, so they're perfectly safe to use. Thus, you can click the "OK" button to dismiss this warning. If you don't want to see such messages in the future, select the "Do not show this message again" check box before you click OK. (Alternatively, you can choose Tools ➤ Options ➤ Text Templating and set the Show Security Message option to `False`.)

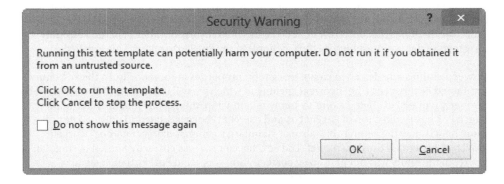

Figure 6-7. *Warning dialog that is displayed when executing T4 templates*

When you accept to run the T4 template files by clicking the OK button in the Security Warning dialog, the wizard creates `DataModel.edmx`, which is the data model designer file. It is used by Visual Studio to create a graphical representation of the classes in the data model, as shown in Figure 6-8.

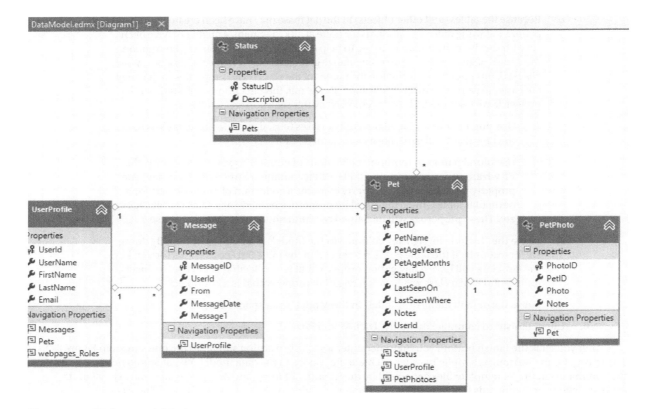

Figure 6-8. *EF data model designer*

The boxes in the data model designer shown in Figure 6-8 are the classes generated for the data model. The name of the class is in the dark gray section at the top of each box. Each box is known as an *entity* and represents a table or view in the database. For example, the entity named Pet has properties that match the fields in the Pet database table.

Each foreign key relationship between database tables is defined in the data model designer by a line between the two entities that are related. For example, the line between the Pet and PetPhoto entities represents a foreign key relationship. Also note that this line identifies that each row of data (represented by the number 1) in the Pet entity is related to zero, one, or many rows of data (represented by the * symbol) in the PetPhoto entity. This is called a *one-to-many relationship.*

Having relationships between entities enables EF to create navigation properties automatically. In the Pet entity there is a navigation property named PetPhotoes (the incorrect spelling of which we will fix next), and in the PetPhoto entity there is a navigation property named Pet. Being a one-to-many relationship, this means that the navigation properties are set such that each Pet has a collection of PetPhotos and each PetPhoto is related to only one Pet.

An important thing to note here is how the setting "Pluralize or singularize generated object names" worked when the Entity Data Model Wizard generated the data model. The PetPhoto entity was correctly named in singular, but the Entity Set Name property of the entity was not pluralized correctly and was set to PetPhotoes instead of PetPhotos. Having an incorrect entity set name in the PetPhoto entity also caused the navigation property in the Pet entity to be created incorrectly (see Figure 6-8).

Fortunately, this kind of error is very easy to fix. Just right-click the PetPhoto entity and select "Properties". In the Properties window, change the Entity Set Name property to **PetPhotos** to set the correct name in plural. Next, click in the navigation property from the Pet entity and, in the Properties window, change the Entity Set Name property to **PetPhotos** (see Figure 6-9). Now you have the correct names, plus you know how to use the Properties window to change any other property that you may need to change.

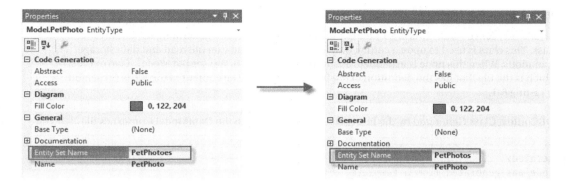

***Figure 6-9.** Entity Properties window*

■ **Tip** You don't have to use the same names for your database tables and your entities; for example, you could change the name of the Pet entity to Mascot. The definition of the entity states that, regardless of the name, such entity maps to the database table named Pet. Thus, your application can work with the entity Mascot and the database will know that it is Pet.

In the Solution Explorer window, expand the DataModel.edmx node in the Models folder to see additional files that were generated by the Entity Data Model Wizard, as shown in Figure 6-10.

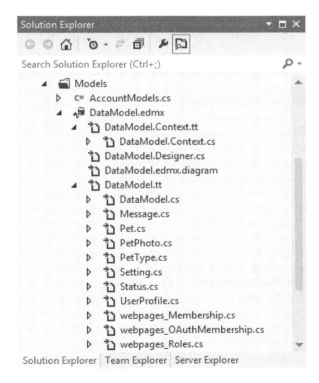

***Figure 6-10.** Additional files generated by the Entity Data Model Wizard*

The additional files are as follows:

- DataModel.Context.tt: This is a T4 template file that is in charge of generating the DbContext class. This class is used to open a connection to the database and execute read and data storage operations. When this node is expanded, as shown in Figure 6-10, you see DataModel.Context.cs, which is the file that has the definition of the DbContext class. The content of the file is presented in Listing 6-1.

Listing 6-1. DBContext Class Generated by the Entity Data Model wizard in the DataModel.Context.cs file

```
//------------------------------------------------------------------------------
// <auto-generated>
//     This code was generated from a template.
//
//     Manual changes to this file may cause unexpected behavior in your application.
//     Manual changes to this file will be overwritten if the code is regenerated.
// </auto-generated>
//------------------------------------------------------------------------------

namespace HaveYouSeenMe.Models
{
    using System;
    using System.Data.Entity;
    using System.Data.Entity.Infrastructure;

    public partial class EntitiesConnection : DbContext
    {
        public EntitiesConnection()
            : base("name=EntitiesConnection")
        {
        }

        protected override void OnModelCreating(DbModelBuilder modelBuilder)
        {
            throw new UnintentionalCodeFirstException();
        }

        public DbSet<Message> Messages { get; set; }
        public DbSet<Pet> Pets { get; set; }
        public DbSet<PetPhoto> PetPhotos { get; set; }
        public DbSet<PetType> PetTypes { get; set; }
        public DbSet<Setting> Settings { get; set; }
        public DbSet<Status> Status { get; set; }
        public DbSet<UserProfile> UserProfiles { get; set; }
        public DbSet<webpages_Membership> webpages_Membership { get; set; }
        public DbSet<webpages_OAuthMembership> webpages_OAuthMembership { get; set; }
        public DbSet<webpages_Roles> webpages_Roles { get; set; }
    }
}
```

- DataModel.Designer.cs: Visual Studio provides two ADO.NET templates that generate the Entity Framework object layer code: the ADO.NET EntityObject Generator and the ADO.NET Self-Tracking Entity Generator. By default, the Entity Data Model Wizard uses the ADO.NET EntityObject Generator, which in turn uses a T4 template file to generate the entity class's files. Because the DataModel.Designer.cs file is used for the ADO.NET Self-Tracking Entity Generator, in this particular case the file is empty and is not used (but don't delete it, please).

- DataModel.edmx.diagram: This file contains the information (in XML format) that is to be used by Visual Studio to draw the boxes and lines in the data model designer window. The content of the file is shown in Listing 6-2.

Listing 6-2. Content of the DataModel.edmx.diagram File

```xml
<?xml version="1.0" encoding="utf-8"?>
<edmx:Edmx Version="3.0" xmlns:edmx="http://schemas.microsoft.com/ado/2009/11/edmx">
 <!-- EF Designer content (DO NOT EDIT MANUALLY BELOW HERE) -->
  <edmx:Designer xmlns="http://schemas.microsoft.com/ado/2009/11/edmx">
    <!-- Diagram content (shape and connector positions) -->
    <edmx:Diagrams>
      <Diagram DiagramId="cada75ba5c654c2cbfdcd24b3475c346" Name="Diagram1">
        <EntityTypeShape EntityType="Model.Message" Width="1.5" PointX="5.25"
        PointY="3.5" IsExpanded="true" />
        <EntityTypeShape EntityType="Model.Pet" Width="1.5" PointX="8.25"
        PointY="2.875" IsExpanded="true" />
        <EntityTypeShape EntityType="Model.PetPhoto" Width="1.5" PointX="10.875"
        PointY="3.625" IsExpanded="true" />
        <EntityTypeShape EntityType="Model.PetType" Width="1.5" PointX="0.75"
        PointY="1" IsExpanded="true" />
        <EntityTypeShape EntityType="Model.Setting" Width="1.5" PointX="0.75"
        PointY="7" IsExpanded="true" />
        <EntityTypeShape EntityType="Model.Status" Width="1.5" PointX="6"
        PointY="0.75" IsExpanded="true" />
        <EntityTypeShape EntityType="Model.UserProfile" Width="1.5" PointX="3"
        PointY="3.25" IsExpanded="true" />
        <EntityTypeShape EntityType="Model.webpages_Membership" Width="1.5"
        PointX="2.75" PointY="7" IsExpanded="true" />
        <EntityTypeShape EntityType="Model.webpages_OAuthMembership" Width="1.5"
        PointX="4.75" PointY="7" IsExpanded="true" />
        <EntityTypeShape EntityType="Model.webpages_Roles" Width="1.5" PointX="0.75"
        PointY="3.75" IsExpanded="true" />
        <AssociationConnector Association="Model.FK_Message_User" ManuallyRouted="false" />
        <AssociationConnector Association="Model.FK_Pet_Status" ManuallyRouted="false" />
        <AssociationConnector Association="Model.FK_Pet_User" ManuallyRouted="false" />
        <AssociationConnector Association="Model.FK_PetPhoto_Pet" ManuallyRouted="false" />
        <AssociationConnector Association="Model.webpages_UsersInRoles" ManuallyRouted="false" />
      </Diagram>
    </edmx:Diagrams>
  </edmx:Designer>
</edmx:Edmx>
```

- DataModel.tt: This T4 template file generates the classes for the entities in the data model designer. Each entity has its own class file; for example, the entity Pet has a corresponding file named Pet.cs that contains the definition of the class Pet, as shown in Listing 6-3.

Listing 6-3. Generated Data Model Class for the Pet Database Table

```
//------------------------------------------------------------------------------
// <auto-generated>
//     This code was generated from a template.
//
//     Manual changes to this file may cause unexpected behavior in your application.
//     Manual changes to this file will be overwritten if the code is regenerated.
// </auto-generated>
//------------------------------------------------------------------------------

namespace HaveYouSeenMe.Models
{
    using System;
    using System.Collections.Generic;

    public partial class Pet
    {
        public Pet()
        {
            this.PetPhotoes = new HashSet<PetPhoto>();
        }

        public int PetID { get; set; }
        public string PetName { get; set; }
        public Nullable<int> PetAgeYears { get; set; }
        public Nullable<int> PetAgeMonths { get; set; }
        public int StatusID { get; set; }
        public Nullable<System.DateTime> LastSeenOn { get; set; }
        public string LastSeenWhere { get; set; }
        public string Notes { get; set; }
        public int UserId { get; set; }

        public virtual Status Status { get; set; }
        public virtual UserProfile UserProfile { get; set; }
        public virtual ICollection<PetPhoto> PetPhotos { get; set; }
    }
}
```

■ **Note** If you try to run the application at this point, you will get an error because the class UserProfile is defined twice. This happened after adding the EF data model. The data model created a new UserProfile class in the HaveYouSeenMe.Models namespace. The conflict happens with the UserProfile class in the Models/AccountModels.cs file, which is in the same namespace. Now that we have the EF data model, it is safe to remove the UserProfile class in the AccountModels.cs file because both classes refer to the same database table (only the one in the AccountModels.cs file was used to generate the database table). That will remove the conflict and will allow the application to run without issues.

And that's it. You have created the data model of the application and are ready to move on to add some specific functionality to it (business model).

Adding a Business Model

The business model is composed of classes that perform processing. The objects in the business model do not work directly in response to user requests; instead, they work per requests from action methods in the controller that received the user request.

For example, in our application, a class in the business model is in charge of sending out e-mail messages to pet owners when someone reports a pet sighting. Another class implements the creation of image thumbnails for pet photos. In short, any type of processing on the server is handled by business model classes.

Let's take a look at an example. We are going to build a class that handles images and creates thumbnails. This functionality is useful in the "Have You Seen Me?" application to create thumbnails of pet photos that can be used later to create a gallery for each pet. The way this will work is that, whenever the owner uploads a picture, the action method will process the upload and create the thumbnail at the same time.

The first task—and this is just to keep our classes in a structure that can be easily understood by anyone—is to create a new folder under the Models folder. Right-click the Models folder and choose Add ➤ New Folder, as shown in Figure 6-11. Name the new folder **Business**. In this new folder, we are going to create all the classes in our business model.

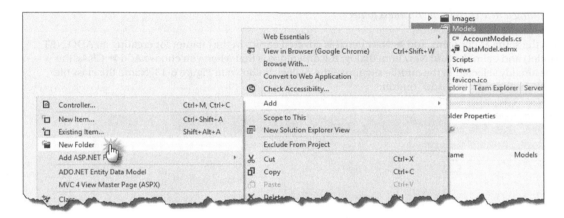

Figure 6-11. *Adding a new folder for the business model classes*

The next step is to create a new class. To do that, right-click the newly created Business folder and choose Add ➤ Class, as shown in Figure 6-12.

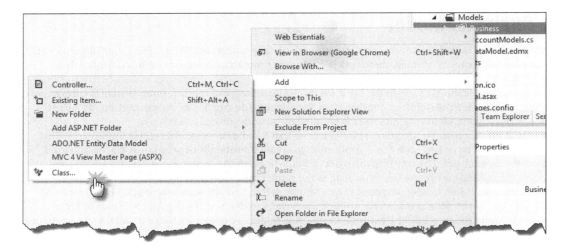

Figure 6-12. *Adding a new class in the Business folder*

This works the same as choosing Add ➤ New Item (as covered earlier in the chapter for creating an ADO.NET Entity Data Model) and open the Add New Item dialog; the difference is that when you choose Add ➤ Class, the Class file type is already selected in the middle section of the dialog, as shown in Figure 6-13. Name the class file **PetManagement.cs** and click the "Add" button.

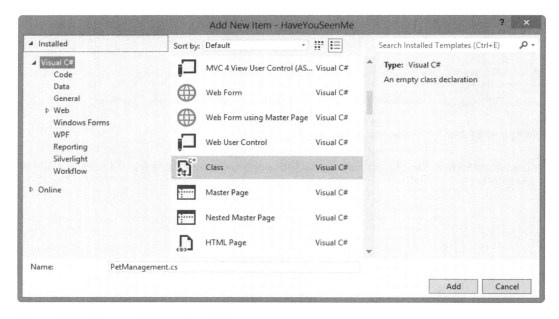

Figure 6-13. *Using the Add New Item dialog to create a new class*

You are now ready to start adding some functionality to your business class. Listing 6-4 shows the CreateThumbnail() method.

Listing 6-4. Content of the PetManagement.cs file in the Models/Business folder

```
using System;
using System.Collections.Generic;
using System.Drawing;
using System.Drawing.Drawing2D;
using System.IO;
using System.Linq;
using System.Web;

namespace HaveYouSeenMe.Models.Business
{
    public class PetManagement
    {
        public static void CreateThumbnail(string fileName, string filePath,
                                    int thumbWi, int thumbHi,
                                    bool maintainAspect)
        {
            // do nothing if the original is smaller than the designated
            // thumbnail dimensions
            var originalFile = Path.Combine(filePath, fileName);
            var source = Image.FromFile(originalFile);
            if (source.Width <= thumbWi && source.Height <= thumbHi) return;

            Bitmap thumbnail;
            try
            {
                int wi = thumbWi;
                int hi = thumbHi;

                if (maintainAspect)
                {
                    // maintain the aspect ratio despite the thumbnail size parameters
                    if (source.Width > source.Height)
                    {
                        wi = thumbWi;
                        hi = (int)(source.Height * ((decimal)thumbWi / source.Width));
                    }
                    else
                    {
                        hi = thumbHi;
                        wi = (int)(source.Width * ((decimal)thumbHi / source.Height));
                    }
                }
```

```
                thumbnail = new Bitmap(wi, hi);
                using (Graphics g = Graphics.FromImage(thumbnail))
                {
                    g.InterpolationMode = InterpolationMode.HighQualityBicubic;
                    g.FillRectangle(Brushes.Transparent, 0, 0, wi, hi);
                    g.DrawImage(source, 0, 0, wi, hi);
                }

                var thumbnailName = Path.Combine(filePath, "thumbnail_" + fileName);
                thumbnail.Save(thumbnailName);
            }
            catch
            {

            }

        }

    }
}
```

The method accepts five parameters. The first two parameters are the name of the image file that was just uploaded (fileName) and the folder where the file was saved (filePath). Next are two parameters that indicate the desired width (thumbWi) and height (thumbHi) for the thumbnail. Finally, a Boolean parameter (maintainAspect) indicates whether or not the thumbnail should maintain the aspect ratio of the source image.

The functionality is simple. First, the CreateThumbnail method verifies whether or not the size of the image is already small enough to be considered a thumbnail. It does so by comparing the image width and height with the desired width and height for the thumbnail, as shown next. If the image dimensions are smaller than or equal to those of the desired thumbnail size, then the method does nothing and exits.

```
var originalFile = Path.Combine(filePath, fileName);
var source = Image.FromFile(originalFile);
if (source.Width <= thumbWi && source.Height <= thumbHi) return;
```

If the image is sufficiently large for a thumbnail to be created from it, then the method needs to check the maintainAspect parameter to determine if it should maintain the image's aspect ratio for the thumbnail. The *aspect ratio* describes the proportional relationship of the image's width and height, which is relevant if the image is a rectangle. The image may be either a square or a rectangle. The image is considered a rectangle if either its width is larger than its height or its height is larger than its width. Maintaining the aspect ratio means that the thumbnail should have the same relationship between its width and height as does the source image. If the maintainAspect parameter indicates the aspect ratio does not need to be kept, then the method will just assign the width and height for the desired thumbnail size.

```
int wi = thumbWi;
int hi = thumbHi;

if (maintainAspect)
{
    // maintain the aspect ratio despite the thumbnail size parameters
    if (source.Width > source.Height)
    {
        wi = thumbWi;
        hi = (int)(source.Height * ((decimal)thumbWi / source.Width));
    }
```

```
    else
    {
        hi = thumbHi;
        wi = (int)(source.Width * ((decimal)thumbHi / source.Height));
    }
}
```

The last step, shown in the following code block, is to actually create the new thumbnail image using the calculated dimensions. First, we need to create a new `Bitmap` object with the calculated dimensions. Then, using a `Graphics` object based on the newly created `Bitmap`, the process creates a transparent rectangle, also with the calculated dimensions that will be the surface for the thumbnail. Once that is ready, the `Graphics` object draws the image on top of the rectangle. Because the drawing of the image will take place using new image dimensions, we need to tell the `Graphics` object how it should handle the size reduction. For this purpose, we need to set the `InterpolationMode` property. This property determines how intermediate values between two end points are calculated, which is important to make sure the quality of the image doesn't degrade with the reduction. There are different values that can be set for this property, and they are all included in the enumeration called `InterpolationMode`. For our method, we are going to use the mode that creates the highest quality of thumbnails, which is `HighQualityBicubic`.

Finally, the method saves the thumbnail in the same folder as the original image, using the same file name as the original but with the added prefix `thumbnail_`.

```
thumbnail = new Bitmap(wi, hi);
using (Graphics g = Graphics.FromImage(thumbnail))
{
    g.InterpolationMode = InterpolationMode.HighQualityBicubic;
    g.FillRectangle(Brushes.Transparent, 0, 0, wi, hi);
    g.DrawImage(source, 0, 0, wi, hi);
}

var thumbnailName = Path.Combine(filePath, "thumbnail_" + fileName);
thumbnail.Save(thumbnailName);
```

Let's now handle the thumbnail creation when the image is uploaded. For that we need an action method that handles the request to upload an image file. In the `PetController` class we created in Chapter 4, add an action method called `PictureUpload()`, as shown in Listing 6-5.

Listing 6-5. Action Method PictureUpload()

```
public ActionResult PictureUpload()
{
    return View();
}
```

This action method will render the view in Listing 6-6.

Listing 6-6. PictureUpload View

```
@model HaveYouSeenMe.Models.PictureModel

@{
    ViewBag.Title = "Picture Upload";
}

<h2>Picture Upload</h2>
```

85

```
@using (Html.BeginForm(null, null, FormMethod.Post, new { enctype = "multipart/form-data" }))
{
    @Html.AntiForgeryToken()
    @Html.ValidationSummary(true)

    <fieldset>
        <legend>PictureModel</legend>
        <div class="editor-label">
            @Html.LabelFor(model => model.PictureFile)
        </div>
        <div class="editor-field">
            @Html.TextBoxFor(model => model.PictureFile, new { type = "file" })
            @Html.ValidationMessageFor(model => model.PictureFile)
        </div>

        <p>
            <input type="submit" value="Save" />
        </p>
    </fieldset>
}
@section Scripts {
    @Scripts.Render("~/bundles/jqueryval")
}
```

Note in the view code that it is a strongly typed view with the view model of type PictureModel as defined with the @model line at the beginning of the listing. It then has an HTML helper method to create a form element. The form must submitted using the "multipart/formdata" encoding in order to be able to handle file uploads. Also, the helper method has the value null for the first two parameters, which represent the controller and action method to post the form. This will cause the helper method to use the current controller and action method to render the <form> tag.

In order to have a file upload field, we need to create a text box using the HTML helper method @Html.TextBoxFor() and specify that it should use the property PictureFile from the model object. This statement would normally create a simple text box, but the helper method includes an additional optional parameter to add properties to the rendered text box, and because we said type = "file", when the view is rendered, it will in fact create an <input> tag of type file.

When rendered in the browser, the view produces the HTML in Listing 6-7, the result of which is shown in Figure 6-14.

Listing 6-7. HTML Produced by the View Shown in Figure 6-14

```
<h2>PictureUpload</h2>

<form action="/Pet/PictureUpload" enctype="multipart/form-data" method="post">
<input name="__RequestVerificationToken" type="hidden"
value="xK79CryunxPFezkUWw7WYqSQsFHxHRLJ5YnNr88mh1mTVNG2GKm_tD4v4cWycFFg7FPsH1-fJu7Az3Dmf8thIwpyzS5S
cmbDZ5UdvTOwbRo1" />
<fieldset>
        <legend>PictureModel</legend>

        <div class="editor-label">
            <label for="PictureFile">PictureFile</label>
        </div>
        <div class="editor-field">
            <input data-val="true"
                    data-val-required="The PictureFile field is required."
                    id="PictureFile" name="PictureFile"
```

```
                    type="file"
                    value="" />
            <span class="field-validation-valid"
                data-valmsg-for="PictureFile"
                data-valmsg-replace="true"></span>
        </div>

        <p>
            <input type="submit" value="Save" />
        </p>
    </fieldset>
</form>

<script src="/Scripts/jquery-1.9.0.js"></script>
<script src="/Scripts/jquery.unobtrusive-ajax.js"></script>
<script src="/Scripts/jquery.validate.js"></script>
<script src="/Scripts/jquery.validate.unobtrusive.js"></script>
```

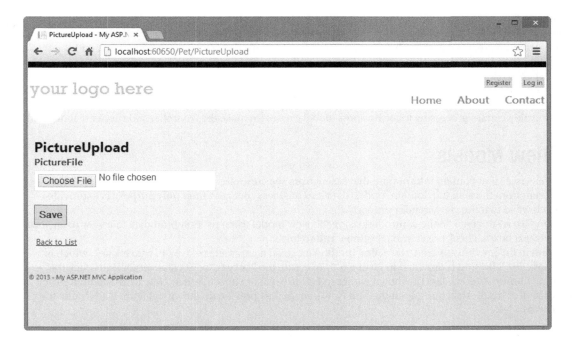

Figure 6-14. *Rendered view from Listing 6-6*

Now we need a way to receive the file. Listing 6-8 presents a second action method, also called PictureUpload, but this one is an overload method for the one in Listing 6-5. If you noticed in Listing 6-8 the action method has been decorated with the [HttpPost] and [ValidateAntiForgeryToken] attributes and has a parameter for the object that contains the information coming in the request. The [HttpPost] attribute instructs the controller to use the action method when the request is using the HTTP POST method. This is necessary because in order to upload a file using a page, an HTTP POST needs to be executed. The [ValidateAntiForgeryToken] attribute is a security mechanism to validate that the POST execution is coming from a valid source and the information has not been tampered with.

Listing 6-8. PictureUpload Action Method

```
[HttpPost]
[ValidateAntiForgeryToken]
public ActionResult PictureUpload(PictureModel model)
{
    if (model.PictureFile.ContentLength > 0)
    {
        var fileName = Path.GetFileName(model.PictureFile.FileName);
        var filePath = Server.MapPath("/Content/Uploads");
        string savedFileName = Path.Combine(filePath, fileName);
        model.PictureFile.SaveAs(savedFileName);
        PetManagement.CreateThumbnail(fileName, filePath, 100, 100, true);
    }

    return View(model);
}
```

The action method in Listing 6-8 does two things. First, it checks the information in the PictureModel object to see if there is actually a file to be processed. It does so by verifying that the size of the file is more than 0 bytes. If that is the case, then it creates a path to save the file based on a specific directory and the file name, and then it saves the file. The second thing the action method does is call the method CreateThumbnail in the PetManagement class that we just created.

Note here that although the action method does contain code to process the file upload, it relays the thumbnail generation processing to the PetManagement class. This is particularly important because it helps structure the application, delegating certain processing to the business model classes (to make the controller code easier to maintain).

Adding View Models

View models are classes that contain information that is sent from the controller to the view to be rendered. These classes are different from those in the domain model (data and business) because their only purpose is to provide information to views so that the views render properly.

Information also is sent back to the controllers using the view model when users submit data in a view using form elements such as text boxes, check boxes, radio buttons, and so forth.

In Listing 6-8 in the previous section, the action method received a parameter of type PictureModel, which is a view model class. Its definition is provided in Listing 6-9. To create the PictureModel class, either right-click the Models folder and choose Add ➤ Class (as shown earlier in Figure 6-12) or choose Add ➤ New Item and then select Class from the list of items. Both actions open the Add New Item dialog, previously shown in Figure 6-13. Name the new class **PictureModel**.

Listing 6-9. PictureModel Class

```
using System;
using System.Collections.Generic;
using System.ComponentModel.DataAnnotations;
using System.Linq;
using System.Text;
using System.Web;

namespace HaveYouSeenMe.Models
{
    public class PictureModel
```

```
{
    [Required]
    public HttpPostedFileBase PictureFile { get; set; }
}
}
```

The class has a single property, PictureFile, of type HttpPostedFileBase. This property is automatically populated with the file from the file upload control in the view shown earlier in Listing 6-7. The <form> in Listing 6-7 sends the information to the controller, but because it uses HTTP POST to do so, the action method that handles the request is the one in Listing 6-8 as opposed to the one in Listing 6-5.

An important question to address now is: how does the mapping between the PictureFile property and the PictureFile <input> field in the <form> happen automatically? The answer is: thanks to model binding.

Understanding Model Binding

As you just saw, a view can display a form that has fields such as text boxes, check boxes, radio buttons, and so forth, and a submit button. When the user submits the form, the information in the fields is sent to the controller.

Generally speaking, ASP.NET uses an HttpRequest object to handle requests. Information coming in the request is stored in different collection objects depending on how the request was sent and the type of information. For example, if the request was sent via HTTP GET, such as http://mydomain.com/page?t=1&s=true, then the values for the parameters t and s are stored in the HttpRequest.QueryString collection. If the request is sent using HTTP POST, then the values are stored in the HttpRequest.Form collection. Uploaded files are stored in the HttpRequest.Files collection. If the request is based on a route, then the values are stored in the RouteData.Values dictionary.

When a user submits a form in a strongly typed view, ASP.NET MVC automatically examines the HttpRequest object and maps the information sent to fields in the model object. That way you only have to examine the model object for the information being sent. This process of mapping the information in the HttpRequest object to the model object is called *model binding*.

The benefits of model binding are huge; for example:

- No manual code is needed to extract the data from the HttpRequest object, which avoids coding errors.

- Data type conversions happen automatically.

- Data can be easily validated (data validation will be covered in chapter 7).

Model binding is possible thanks to the built-in binder class DefaultModelBinder. This class is used by ASP.NET MVC when no custom binder classes are defined.

An important aspect of the DefaultModelBinder class is that it relies on values' names in the HttpRequest object, which must be the same as the names of the properties in the model object (including casing) or it won't be able to do the mapping.

Another consideration is that the DefaultModelBinder class will try to do a data type conversion to the model's property data type, and if it fails it will throw an exception.

Let's look at another example of using a view model. The ASP.NET MVC 4 Internet project template used for our sample application created an AccountController class, an AccountModel.cs file with several models for handling user accounts, and some views in the Views/Account directory. If you open the Login.cshtml file in the Views/Account folder you will see the code shown in Listing 6-10.

Listing 6-10. Login View

```
@model HaveYouSeenMe.Models.LoginModel

@{
    ViewBag.Title = "Log in";
}

<hgroup class="title">
    <h1>@ViewBag.Title.</h1>
</hgroup>

<section id="loginForm">
<h2>Use a local account to log in.</h2>
@using (Html.BeginForm(new { ReturnUrl = ViewBag.ReturnUrl })) {
    @Html.AntiForgeryToken()
    @Html.ValidationSummary(true)

    <fieldset>
        <legend>Log in Form</legend>
        <ol>
            <li>
                @Html.LabelFor(m => m.UserName)
                @Html.TextBoxFor(m => m.UserName)
                @Html.ValidationMessageFor(m => m.UserName)
            </li>
            <li>
                @Html.LabelFor(m => m.Password)
                @Html.PasswordFor(m => m.Password)
                @Html.ValidationMessageFor(m => m.Password)
            </li>
            <li>
                @Html.CheckBoxFor(m => m.RememberMe)
                @Html.LabelFor(m => m.RememberMe, new { @class = "checkbox" })
            </li>
        </ol>
        <input type="submit" value="Log in" />
    </fieldset>
    <p>
        @Html.ActionLink("Register", "Register") if you don't have an account.
    </p>
}
</section>

<section class="social" id="socialLoginForm">
    <h2>Use another service to log in.</h2>
    @Html.Action("ExternalLoginsList", new { ReturnUrl = ViewBag.ReturnUrl })
</section>

@section Scripts {
    @Scripts.Render("~/bundles/jqueryval")
}
```

This view is a strongly typed view based on the LoginModel class (located in Models/AccountModels.cs), which is shown in Listing 6-11. This class contains the properties UserName, Password, and RememberMe.

Listing 6-11. LoginModel Class

```
public class LoginModel
{
    [Required]
    [Display(Name = "User name")]
    public string UserName { get; set; }

    [Required]
    [DataType(DataType.Password)]
    [Display(Name = "Password")]
    public string Password { get; set; }

    [Display(Name = "Remember me?")]
    public bool RememberMe { get; set; }
}
```

To see how the view presented in Listing 6-10 works, run the application from Visual Studio either by pressing the F5 key or choosing Debug ➤ Start Debugging. On the application home page, click the login link in the top-right corner of the page. On the web page that opens, right-click and select "Source" or "View Page Source," depending on which browser you're using, and you will see the HTML produced by the view. A part of the HTML is shown in Listing 6-12.

Listing 6-12. Rendered Login View

```
<form action="/Account/Login" method="post">
<input name="__RequestVerificationToken" type="hidden"
value="d57MEurvCLFzLI8mAWIK6qimA_66Cb1MeRfL_
zvYAqyKreGuOra7Il3BQETad6BnuyGX7C4hvaOhmtQ1ewZ3DUjLmFx22fMeZVy9FmtrkQo1" />
<fieldset>
        <legend>Log in Form</legend>
        <ol>
            <li>
                <label for="UserName">User name</label>
                <input data-val="true"
                        data-val-required="The User name field is required."
                        id="UserName"
                        name="UserName"
                        type="text"
                        value="" />
                <span class="field-validation-valid"
                        data-valmsg-for="UserName"
                        data-valmsg-replace="true">
                  </span>
            </li>
            <li>
                <label for="Password">Password</label>
                <input data-val="true"
                        data-val-required="The Password field is required."
                        id="Password"
```

```
                            name="Password"
                            type="password" />
                <span class="field-validation-valid"
                        data-valmsg-for="Password"
                        data-valmsg-replace="true">
                    </span>
            </li>
            <li>
                <input data-val="true"
                        data-val-required="The Remember me? field is required."
                        id="RememberMe"
                        name="RememberMe"
                        type="checkbox" value="true" />
                <input name="RememberMe" type="hidden" value="false" />
                <label class="checkbox" for="RememberMe">Remember me?</label>
            </li>
        </ol>
        <input type="submit" value="Log in" />
    </fieldset>
    <p>
        <a href="/Account/Register">Register</a> if you don't have an account.
    </p>
</form>
```

When the user submits the form, the information is sent to the server using HTTP. At the server, the MVC routing mechanism deduces that it needs to invoke the Login() action method in the AccountController class. This action method expects a LoginModel object, so the MVC model binder creates a LoginModel object automatically—it initializes the LoginModel object's properties from the correspondingly named fields in the HTTP form. The LoginModel object is then passed into the Login() action method.

Now take a look at Listing 6-13, which shows the action method is actually expecting a LoginModel object as a parameter, instead of a low-level HttpRequest object. At the server, the data is automatically scraped from the HttpRequest object and put into a nice object (LoginModel), so you don't have to write the manual code to examine the request yourself.

Listing 6-13. Login() Action Method in the AccountController Class

```
[HttpPost]
[AllowAnonymous]
[ValidateAntiForgeryToken]
public ActionResult Login(LoginModel model, string returnUrl)
{
    if (ModelState.IsValid && WebSecurity.Login(model.UserName, model.Password, persistCookie:
    model.RememberMe))
    {
        return RedirectToLocal(returnUrl);
    }

    // If we got this far, something failed, redisplay form
    ModelState.AddModelError("", "The user name or password provided is incorrect.");
    return View(model);
}
```

The WebSecurity.Login() method is then used to validate the username and password passed in the LoginModel object. If the validation is successful, the user is taken to the destination URL; otherwise, an error is generated and returned to the view to inform the user about it.

Additionally, there is another kind of model binding that doesn't involve complex objects such as the LoginModel object. You can also take advantage of model binding in cases where you are using a view that is not strongly typed or are sending information via parameters in the URL; for example: http://my app/GetPet?id=5. The values for id is stored in the QueryString collection. An action method such as the one presented in Listing 6-14 would be able to handle the request because the name of the parameter is id and that matches the name of the value in the URL.

Listing 6-14. ActionResult Method with an Integer Parameter

```
[AllowAnonymous]
public ActionResult GetPet(int id)
{
    // code here
}
```

The default binder class also provides the automatic conversion, so the values in the URL (which are always interpreted as text) can be cast to the destination data type, in this case an integer. This ensures that your method will always get an integer value and will return an error if a value of another type is passed. What's more, you could even declare the parameter as nullable (just by changing it to int?), in which case the method will automatically accept URLs with or without the parameter, or, more usefully, you could give the parameter a default value such as int id = 0.

■ **Note** There is actually no limit to how many parameters you can create on your action methods, but with a view model class, your code will be cleaner and a lot easier to maintain.

Summary

You have seen in this chapter how important the domain model is. It is formed by the data and business models. The data model is composed of the classes that interact with the database. The business model is in charge of all the server-related processing, including data processing, application-specific functionality, business rules, and more. The view models are in charge of sending information from controllers to views so that the views can properly render HTML to the client browser.

The data model can be created either automatically by using an ORM tool or manually by implementing ADO. NET for the specific database functionality. One advantage of using an ORM tool is the time you can potentially save when implementing the data model for an existing large database. Another advantage of using an ORM tool is all the functionality you get that is automatically added for working with the data model classes. The data model classes normally only perform operations to store and retrieve information to and from the database, and any other functionality is delegated to the business model.

Model binding provides an automatic mechanism for converting data in the low-level HttpRequest object to an easier object. ASP.NET MVC includes the DefaultModelBinder class, which provides the functionality of mapping the HttpRequest object to a view model object. It does so by matching the names of the values in the HttpRequest object to the names of the properties in the view model object. It also attempts to do a data type conversion to the destination data type, and throws an exception if such conversion is not possible.

Data Validation

As you know from the previous chapters, users can make requests using URLs and send data to the application by submitting a form in a view that is then handled by a controller. However, an important question that hasn't been addressed yet is how to ensure that the data submitted by users is valid. One of the most important tasks when developing software is to include validation logic that ensures that the data received from users is valid, so that the application can work with it. This very important task is also quite challenging for developers because they not only must ensure the data is analyzed for validity but also provide timely feedback to the users so that they can fix any invalid data and resubmit it.

Validation logic should be implemented not only in the client browser, to provide immediate feedback to the user, but also in the server, because the server can examine the data using more complex business rules. Another reason to implement validation logic in the server is that, in general, you can never be completely sure that incoming data (from the network) is perfectly safe.

As will be described in this chapter, ASP.NET MVC has several built-in mechanisms to help implement client and server validation logic and to help provide feedback to the user. This will be used in the "Have You Seen Me?" application to validate input from users, for example, when sending messages to pet owners or creating new pet profiles.

Note Because data normally is sent to the server bound to an object (a view model), thanks to the process of data binding (described in Chapter 6), the process of data validation is often referred as *model validation*.

The Validation Workflow

It is important to understand how validation works in order to provide users with the best experience possible while ensuring the integrity of the application.

As mentioned in the introduction, validation happens in two places: first in the client browser, and second in the server. The steps in the validation workflow are as follows (see also Figure 7-1):

1. In the client browser, when the user submits data:

   - Verify that all required information is present.

   - Verify that the data format is correct. For example, to verify that the data sent in an e-mail address field is well constructed, you must check that it has the form of an e-mail address (a name, followed by the symbol @, followed by another name, and ending with a dot and two or three characters).

   - When possible, verify data types (for example, that a date field has an actual date).

   - If something is wrong at this point, the user is given immediate feedback about how to correct the problem, and the information is not sent to the server. The user can then resubmit the request with the corrections.

2. Once all client-side validation tests succeed, the data is sent to the server.

3. In the server, a second round of validation is performed to enforce business rules and to ensure that the request is not an attack.

   - If there is an error, then the request is not processed and information about the error is sent back to the browser so the user can make the necessary corrections.

4. Once all server-side validation tests succeed, the request is processed and a result is produced (a view is rendered, or a file is downloaded, etc.).

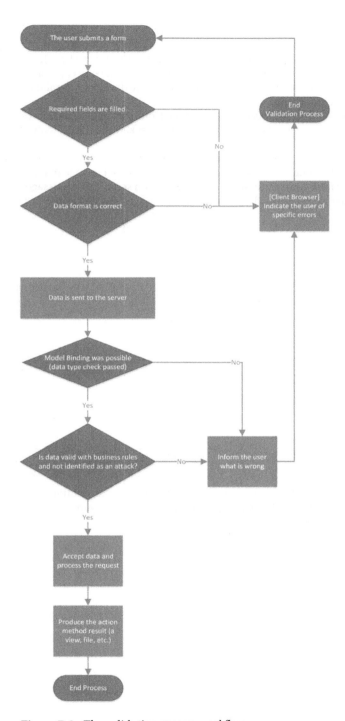

Figure 7-1. *The validation process workflow*

Manual Validation

The first approach to validation is to validate the data manually in each property in the view model object when the user submits a form. In this process, the data in the form fields is simply used to create the view model object (data binding), and then the object is sent to the controller for processing. It is the responsibility of the developer to validate each property by writing validation logic in the action method.

Because data binding has already occurred and the view model object has been created, one step in the validation process, the data type check, has been completed. This is important because the data type check, while not difficult, is a tedious and repetitive task that takes a lot of the developer's time.

To see how manua validation works let's take, for example, in the "Have You Seen Me?" application the feature in which a user can send a message to a pet owner. The view model shown in Listing 7-1 represents the message that is to be sent to the pet owner using a form in a view. It has four properties: the name of the person sending the message (From), the e-mail address of the person sending the message (Email), the subject of the message, and the content of the message.

Listing 7-1. View Model Class for Sending Messages

```
using System;
using System.Collections.Generic;
using System.Linq;
using System.Web;

namespace HaveYouSeenMe.Models
{
    public class MessageModel
    {
        public string From { get; set; }
        public string Email { get; set; }
        public string Subject { get; set; }
        public string Message { get; set; }
    }
}
```

Next, we need a controller for working with messages. Right-click the Controllers directory in the Solution Explorer window and select Add ➤ Controller. Name the controller **MessageController**, as shown in Figure 7-2, and select "Empty MVC controller" in the Template drop-down list. Then click Add.

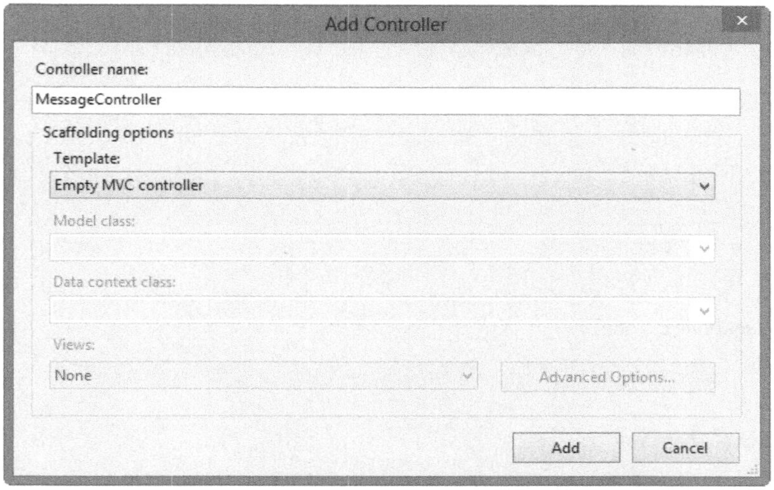

Figure 7-2. Adding the Message controller

Now we need to add some functionality to the controller to validate and send messages. The following steps will add the initial functionality to perform the manual validation:

1. The new controller class has a default action method called Index. Rename the action method to **Send()**.

2. Add a new action method, also called **Send()**, and add a parameter named **model** of type MessageModel.

3. Decorate the new Send() action method with the [HttpPost] attribute. This will instruct the controller to use this particular overload of the Send() action method when the request is made using HTTP POST.

4. The first validation is to ensure that the view model object is valid. We do this by checking the IsValid property of the ModelState object. ModelState.IsValid tells us if any model errors have been added to ModelState. The default model binder will add some errors for basic type-conversion issues (for example, passing a non-number for something that is an integer).

5. If the view model object is valid, we will just redirect to another action method to render a ThankYou view to tell the user the message has been sent.

6. If the model state is not valid, we are going to create an error message to be rendered in the view to inform the user something went wrong with the data submitted. To add the error, use the method AddModelError of the ModelState object.

All these steps produce the code shown in Listing 7-2.

Listing 7-2. Message Controller

```
using HaveYouSeenMe.Models;
using System;
using System.Collections.Generic;
using System.Linq;
using System.Web;
using System.Web.Mvc;
```

```
namespace HaveYouSeenMe.Controllers
{
    public class MessageController : Controller
    {
        public ActionResult Send()
        {
            return View();
        }

        [HttpPost]
        public ActionResult Send(MessageModel model)
        {
            if (ModelState.IsValid)
            {
                return RedirectToAction("ThankYou");
            }

            ModelState.AddModelError("", "One or more errors were found");
            return View(model);
        }

        public ActionResult ThankYou()
        {
            return View();
        }
    }
}
```

■ **Note**   As a best practice, always verify ModelState.IsValid is true when working with view model objects. Doing so will ensure that your action method can work with the view model, as no errors were generated by the model-binding operation. Further validation might be needed, but as a first step, this ensures that data type conversions were performed and all required information is present.

The ModelState.AddModelError() method expects two parameters. The first one is the specific property from the view model for which the error is generated. If the error is not specific to a property in the view model, but rather a general error, you can pass an empty string (as shown in Listing 7-2). The second parameter is the error description you want to show to the user.

Next, let's examine the code in the views. To create the Send view, right-click somewhere in the first Send() action method and choose "Add View." The Add View dialog will open, as shown in Figure 7-3. The name of the view should be Send.

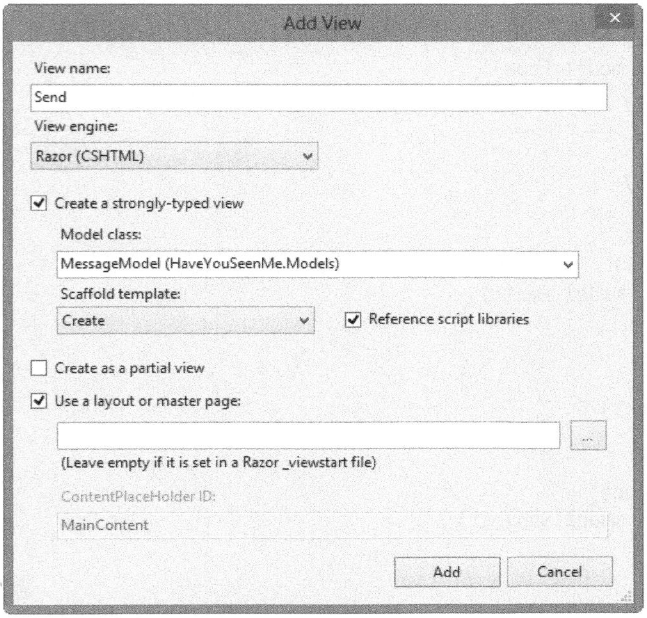

Figure 7-3. *Add View dialog*

Check the "Create strongly-typed view" check box to create a strongly typed view, and choose the `MessageModel` class from the "Model class" drop-down list. If the `MessageModel` class is not in the list, you will need to build the application first with the option Build Solution in the BUILD menu or the shortcut keys Ctrl+Shift+B. In the "Scaffold template" drop-down list, select "Create." Leave the rest of the properties at their default values. Selecting the scaffold template instructs the dialog to create an HTML form with fields corresponding to each property in the view model class in the view. The code for the view is shown in Listing 7-3.

Listing 7-3. The Newly Created Send View

```
@model HaveYouSeenMe.Models.MessageModel

@{
    ViewBag.Title = "Send";
}

<h2>Send</h2>

@using (Html.BeginForm()) {
    @Html.AntiForgeryToken()
    @Html.ValidationSummary(true)

    <fieldset>
        <legend>MessageModel</legend>

        <div class="editor-label">
            @Html.LabelFor(model => model.From)
        </div>
```

```
        <div class="editor-field">
            @Html.EditorFor(model => model.From)
            @Html.ValidationMessageFor(model => model.From)
        </div>

        <div class="editor-label">
            @Html.LabelFor(model => model.Email)
        </div>
        <div class="editor-field">
            @Html.EditorFor(model => model.Email)
            @Html.ValidationMessageFor(model => model.Email)
        </div>

        <div class="editor-label">
            @Html.LabelFor(model => model.Subject)
        </div>
        <div class="editor-field">
            @Html.EditorFor(model => model.Subject)
            @Html.ValidationMessageFor(model => model.Subject)
        </div>

        <div class="editor-label">
            @Html.LabelFor(model => model.Message)
        </div>
        <div class="editor-field">
            @Html.EditorFor(model => model.Message)
            @Html.ValidationMessageFor(model => model.Message)
        </div>

        <p>
            <input type="submit" value="Create" />
        </p>
    </fieldset>
}

<div>
    @Html.ActionLink("Back to List", "Index")
</div>

@section Scripts {
    @Scripts.Render("~/bundles/jqueryval")
}
```

The HTML helper method @Html.ValidationSummary(true) returns an unordered list (<ul>) with all the errors in the model state. If the Boolean parameter is set to true, the list of errors will include only model-level errors. If it's set to false, then all errors will be added to the list. Model-level errors are those that are not specific to a particular property in the view model—for example, the error we added with the method ModelState.AddModelError() in Listing 7-2 when the IsValid property was false.

There are several @Html.ValidationMessageFor() HTML helper methods in the view, one for each field in the form. Each of these helper methods is bound to a particular field from the view model. When an error is detected in the form fields, these methods will render a <span> element with the specific error for the field to which they are bound. These error messages are displayed automatically in the browser before the form is posted to the server, courtesy of some neat JavaScript code that MVC inserted into the web page when it rendered the view initially.

Let's now make a small change before testing the view. Change the <h2> tag at the top of the view to

```
<h2>Send Message</h2>
```

and change the value of the submit button at the bottom of the view to

```
<input type="submit" value="Send Message" />
```

Now create the ThankYou view that will be rendered when the validation tests succeed and everything is fine. Create a view that doesn't have a view model, and name it **ThankYou**. In the <h2> tag, modify the text to say **Thank You**, and add a sentence in the <p> tag to indicate the message has been sent, as shown in Listing 7-4.

Listing 7-4. ThankYou View

```
@{
    ViewBag.Title = "ThankYou";
}

<h2>Thank You</h2>
<p>Your message has been sent</p>
```

When you run the application and make the request /Message/Send, the browser will render the view just created, as shown in Figure 7-4.

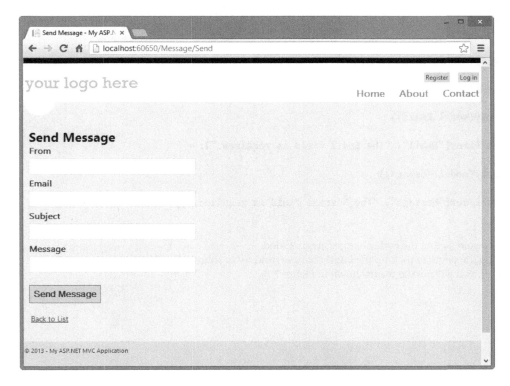

Figure 7-4. *Rendered view for the /Message/Send request*

If you click the Send Message button at this point, even with the fields empty, the model will still be valid because we haven't added any validation logic other than to verify that the model-binding operation was successful. You will see the ThankYou view shown in Figure 7-5.

Figure 7-5. *ThankYou view, shown after the model was successfully validated*

Let's now add the logic to validate some of the fields. Let's make the From, Email, and Message fields required fields. In the Send(MessageModel model) action method, before the if (ModelState.IsValid) statement, add the following:

```
if (string.IsNullOrEmpty(model.From))
{
    ModelState.AddModelError("From", "The From field is required.");
}
if (string.IsNullOrEmpty(model.Email))
{
    ModelState.AddModelError("Email", "The Email field is required.");
}
if (string.IsNullOrEmpty(model.Message))
{
    ModelState.AddModelError("Message", "The Message field is required.");
}
```

Build the application again so that the code changes are included.

Now when you re-load the page (to pick-up the latest changes) and try to submit the form without entering values (the same as before), you will get the result shown in Figure 7-6.

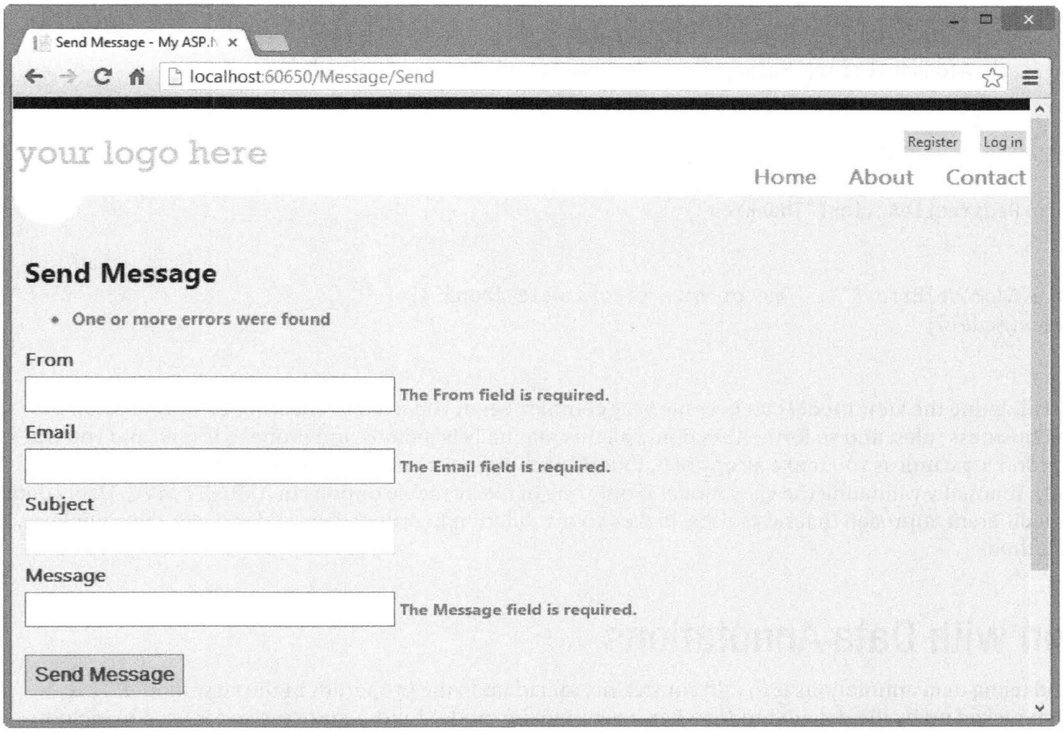

Figure 7-6. *Errors generated after the form is submitted*

Note that the specific error for each field is shown next to the corresponding field. This occurs because we specified to which field we were referring when we generated the errors in the action method code. The error messages are thus associated with the relevant @Html.ValidationMessageFor() in the view. At the top of the form, the validation summary shows the model-level error we added to indicate the view model is not valid. Also note that the ASP.NET MVC project template by default added eye-catching styles for displaying errors; the error messages are displayed in red, and the associated fields have a red border.

The modified action method is shown in Listing 7-5.

Listing 7-5. Modified Action Method with Manual Validation Checks

```
[HttpPost]
public ActionResult Send(MessageModel model)
{
    if (string.IsNullOrEmpty(model.From))
    {
        ModelState.AddModelError("From", "The From field is required.");
    }
    if (string.IsNullOrEmpty(model.Email))
    {
        ModelState.AddModelError("Email", "The Email field is required.");
    }
```

105

```
    if (string.IsNullOrEmpty(model.Message))
    {
        ModelState.AddModelError("Message", "The Message field is required.");
    }

    if (ModelState.IsValid)
    {
        return RedirectToAction("ThankYou");
    }

    ModelState.AddModelError("", "One or more errors were found");
    return View(model);
}
```

Manually validating the view model can become very complex when you need to check for errors based on the domain model, business rules, and so forth. Also, doing all this manually is tedious and prone to errors, and you can't reuse the validation logic unless you make a copy of it, thus duplicating your code and making it harder to maintain.

Fortunately, manually validating the view model is only one of the available options in ASP.NET MVC. Using data annotations is a different approach that saves time, makes your validation logic reusable, and reduces the complexity in the action methods.

Validation with Data Annotations

The idea behind using data annotations is to add constraints metadata to the properties in the view model. This metadata is then picked up by the default binder when executing the model-binding process and is used to include additional validations to the data in the form fields.

By adding the constraints metadata to the view model and allowing the default binder to do this validation as part of the model-binding process, we gain certain benefits, such as:

- The validation rules are enforced across the whole application, not just a single action method.

- We don't have to call a method, instantiate a class, or do anything else for the validation rules to be enforced; the default binder will do it automatically.

- The amount of code required to implement the validation rules with annotations is considerably less than when doing it manually.

Let's modify the code now to see data annotations in action. First, remove the manually added validations shown in Listing 7-5 and make the action method look as it was in Listing 7-2. Then, we will accomplish the following tasks:

- Make the From, Email, and Message fields required.

- Set the maximum length for the From field to 150 characters, because that is the length defined in the database field. The same constraint will be applied to the Email and Subject fields.

- Set the maximum length for the Message field to 1500 characters.

- Ensure that the e-mail address is correctly formatted.

- Specify custom error messages for all the annotations to further help the user fix any errors.

The result is the view model as shown in Listing 7-6. Note that all of the data annotations allow you to specify custom error messages with the ErrorMessage property.

Listing 7-6. Adding Data Annotations to the View Model

```
using System;
using System.Collections.Generic;
using System.ComponentModel.DataAnnotations;
using System.Linq;
using System.Web;

namespace HaveYouSeenMe.Models
{
    public class MessageModel
    {
        [Required(ErrorMessage="Please type your name")]
        [StringLength(150, ErrorMessage="You can only add up to 150 characters")]
        public string From { get; set; }

        [Required(ErrorMessage="Please type your email address ")]
        [StringLength(150, ErrorMessage = "You can only add up to 150 characters")]
        [EmailAddress(ErrorMessage="We don't recognize this as a valid email address")]
        public string Email { get; set; }

        [StringLength(150, ErrorMessage = "You can only add up to 150 characters")]
        public string Subject { get; set; }

        [Required(ErrorMessage="Please type your message")]
        [StringLength(1500, ErrorMessage = "You can only add up to 1500 characters")]
        public string Message { get; set; }
    }
}
```

There are other annotations that you can use to enforce validation rules in the view model. Some will work in the client browser, giving the user immediate feedback and the opportunity to fix the entries before sending them to the server. The data annotations are listed and described in Table 7-1.

Table 7-1. *Data Annotations List*

Annotation	Description
[CreditCard]	Defines the value as a credit card number (15 or 16 digits without spaces or dashes).
[EmailAddress]	Indicates that the value must be a well-formatted e-mail address.
[EnumDataType(typeof(name of enum))]	Enables a .NET Framework enumeration to be mapped to a data column. The value must be one of those defined in the enumeration.
[FileExtension(Extensions="")]	Validates that the file extension of the uploaded file is in the acceptable extensions defined; for example, [FileExtensions(Extensions=".jpg,.png,.gif")].
[Range(min, max)]	Indicates that the value must be between the specified minimum and maximum values.
[RegularExpression(pattern)]	Indicates that the value must match the specified regular expression pattern.
[Required]	Indicates that the property must contain a value. A validation exception is raised if the property is null, contains an empty string (""), or contains only whitespace characters. If you want to treat whitepace characters as valid characters, use [Required(AllowEmptyStrings=true)].
[StringLength(max)]	Indicates the maximum character length the value can have and, optionally, the minimum character length. This attribute is for properties of type string.
[Url]	Indicates that the value is a well-formatted URL.

Now when we execute the application, we can see different types of errors identified in the browser (client-side code), as shown in Figure 7-7.

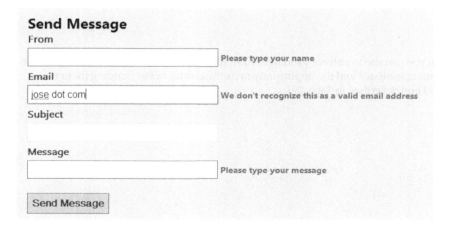

Figure 7-7. *Validation errors identified in the form fields based on the view model annotations*

Creating Custom Data Annotations

One of the major benefits of using data annotations is that you can create your own custom annotations. This allows you to reuse the validation logic in different view models. It also allows you to keep the validation logic in a centralized place, making it easier to maintain.

To create a custom annotation, you need to create a class that inherits from ValidationAttribute, and the name of that class must end with the suffix Attribute. As an example, suppose you want to validate that the name entered in the From field is a full name (contains a first name and last name). The following steps will guide you through the process of creating this custom data annotation:

1. Create a new class in the Models directory and name it **FullNameAttribute**.

2. Include the System.ComponentModel.DataAnnotations namespace at the top of the file with the rest of the default namespaces.

3. Make the FullNameAttribute class inherit from the class ValidationAttribute.

4. Override the method IsValid.

5. Add validation logic to identify if the value passed contains two words. This is done by splitting the string using spaces as separator. The Split() method of the String class will return an array of strings, so basically all we need to do is verify if the array has a length of 2; if it does, then return true, and otherwise return false.

The code in Listing 7-7 shows the result of implementing the previous steps to create a custom data annotation.

Listing 7-7. Custom Data Annotation to Validate a Full Name Has First and Last Names

```
using System;
using System.Collections.Generic;
using System.Linq;
using System.Web;
using System.ComponentModel.DataAnnotations;

namespace HaveYouSeenMe.Models
{
    public class FullNameAttribute : ValidationAttribute
    {
        public override bool IsValid(object value)
        {
            var nameComponents = value.ToString().Split(' ');
            return nameComponents.Length == 2;
        }
    }
}
```

We can now use this custom data annotation in our view model. Add it to the From property with an error message so that the user knows what the problem is, as follows:

```
[Required(ErrorMessage="Please type your name")]
[StringLength(150, ErrorMessage="You can only add up to 150 characters")]
[FullName(ErrorMessage="Please type your full name")]
public string From { get; set; }
```

When we run the application, we now see different types of messages depending on the error found, an example of which is shown in Figure 7-8.

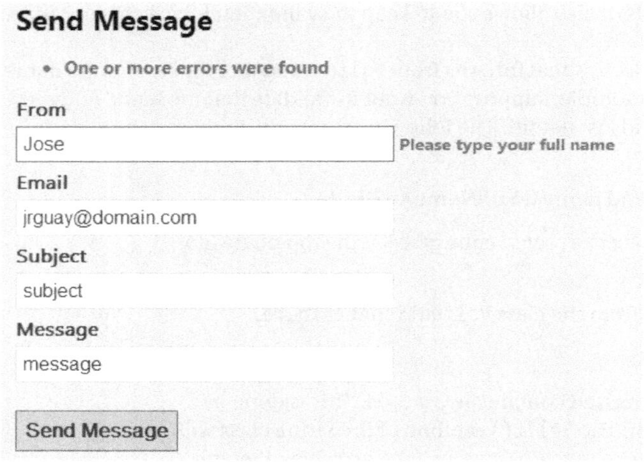

Figure 7-8. Validation error from the custom data annotation

Summary

The data validation process is an integral part of any application. As developers, we need to make sure the data sent by users is valid so that the application works properly. The validation process in ASP.NET MVC can be implemented in different ways, but the most common approach is to use data annotations.

When you implement the manual approach, you are responsible for implementing the logic under which the data should be analyzed and approved. This can be a huge task and normally involves creating a lot of code in the action method to verify that the data in the view model is valid. This approach not only is prone to errors but, most importantly, is very hard to maintain, and the validation logic cannot be reused.

Using data annotations is a much better approach because the constraints are implemented using metadata directly in the view model. This validation logic can be reused by many action methods. Also, by moving the validation logic to the view model instead of the action method, the validation happens wherever the view model is used across the entire application.

ASP.NET MVC supplies a considerable number of validation attributes that you can use in your view model, but if none of them fits your needs, you can always create your own custom data annotations by creating classes that inherit from the class `ValidationAttribute` and implement a suitable `IsValid` method.

CHAPTER 8

■ ■ ■

Ajax and jQuery

In this chapter we are going to cover a key technique in producing rich web applications: enhancing the user experience with Ajax and jQuery. Ajax stands for *Asynchronous JavaScript and XML*. It is a model that allows you to make requests to the server in the background from client-side code (JavaScript). This enables you to update the page without having to reload it completely, which greatly improves the performance of your web site and the user experience. To facilitate these requests, in addition to controllers, there is now a new technology called WebAPI that is designed to ease the transport of information over HTTP.

What's important about Ajax is that it is asynchronous. You can make a request to the server and then process the response whenever it is ready by handling an event that is raised when the request is completed.

In the early days of web applications and JavaScript, it was common to introduce client-side event handlers and even JavaScript code inside HTML tags. It was a model that allowed developers to implement processing logic in the browser, but the main problem was that it was too messy. The HTML code sometimes became unreadable, and the JavaScript code was hard to reuse and maintain.

ASP.NET MVC implements the concept of *unobtrusive JavaScript*, which means that, by following the principle of separation of concerns, it will keep JavaScript code separate from HTML code. The implementation of event handlers and other functionality is written in a separate file(s) that is (are) referenced in the page.

Unobtrusive JavaScript is based on the jQuery JavaScript library. Free and open source, jQuery provides a simple mechanism to find HTML elements (such as <div>, <button>, and form fields). Additionally, jQuery includes a fluent API to manipulate and animate such elements, and also implements wrappers to simplify Ajax calls.

jQuery's functionality is implemented by a layer that abstracts how each browser works with the Document Object Model (DOM). This allows developers to have a unified model of work that eliminates cross-browser differences. Developers only need to know one way to work with JavaScript and HTML elements, and jQuery will do the mapping to each browser implementation.

Introducing jQuery

jQuery is one of the most popular JavaScript libraries available and is included in Visual Studio in all the project templates for web applications. ASP.NET MVC uses jQuery for the implementation of its unobtrusive JavaScript features. You can find the jQuery library files in the Scripts directory of the web application template, as shown in Figure 8-1. The library is located in the jquery-[version].js file. The other three files listed in the box in Figure 8-1 are as follows:

- jquery-[version].intellisense.js: Helps Visual Studio display IntelliSense information.

- jquery-[version].min.js: A minified version of JQuery that doesn't include comments or whitespace characters and adds some other optimizations to reduce the size of the file so that it is transmitted faster to the browser.

- jquery-[version].min.map: The source map file that is used to translate the minified version of the library to the nonminified version so that you can debug jQuery's code from the browser. (At the time of this writing, only Google Chrome supports source maps.)

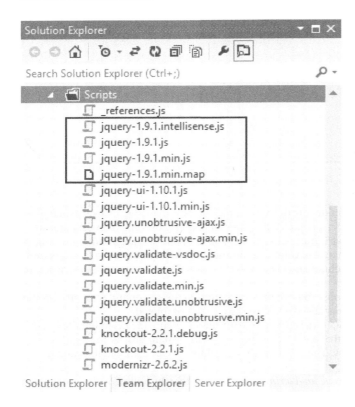

***Figure 8-1.** jQuery is included in the Scripts directory of the web application*

■ **Tip** The actual version of jQuery included in the ASP.NET MVC 4 project template is 1.8.2, but you can update it to the latest version with NuGet. To use NuGet with its graphical interface, go to Tools ➤ Library Package Manager ➤ Manage NuGet Packages for Solution. Or, using the Package Manager Console, issue the command `update-package jquery`.

Working with jQuery

To access the jQuery library and start working with it, you need to include the `jquery-[version].js` file in the pages that will use it. There are two mechanisms to do this. The first one is to just add a reference to the jQuery file in the page with a `<script>` tag. The other way is to include it in what is called a *bundle*.

Adding a reference with a script tag is a fairly simple process. You just need to add the following `<script>` tag to the `<head>` of your page:

```
<script src="~/Scripts/jquery-1.9.1.min.js"></script>
```

Bundles, on the other hand, require some more work. Bundling is a feature in ASP.NET that allows developers to combine multiple files into a single file. Another benefit is automatic minification. JavaScript and CSS files will also be minified to reduce the size of the resulting file. Having a single (minified) file to download means there is only one (really optimized) HTTP request for the file to load. This greatly reduces the page's loading time. You normally create bundles for JavaScript, CSS, and image files.

To create a bundle, you use the ScriptBundle and StyleBundle classes. They have a method called Include() that enables you to add files to the bundle. Bundles are added in the BundleConfig class located in the App_Start/BundleConfig.cs file. This class has a static method named RegisterBundles() that accepts a parameter of type BundleCollection to which you add your bundles.

For example, the BundleConfig class includes the following bundle for the jQuery library:

```
using System.Web;
using System.Web.Optimization;

namespace HaveYouSeenMe
{
    public class BundleConfig
    {
        public static void RegisterBundles(BundleCollection bundles)
        {
            bundles.Add(new ScriptBundle("~/bundles/jquery")
                                .Include("~/Scripts/jquery-{version}.js")
                        );

            bundles.Add(new StyleBundle("~/Content/css")
                                .Include("~/Content/site.css")
                        );
            ...
        }
    }
}
```

To use the bundles in the pages, you use the Scripts and Styles classes as follows:

```
@Scripts.Render("~/bundles/jqueryval")
@Styles.Render("~/Content/css")
```

Once you have the jQuery library (and all your libraries) loaded in the page, you are able to start working with it. You can use either the jQuery namespace or its alias $ (which is a valid JavaScript name). For jQuery to work, the page must be in a state where all the HTML elements have been loaded. You know when this state has been reached by handling the ready event with one of the following equivalent syntaxes:

```
$(document).ready(handler)
```

Or

```
$().ready(handler)
```

Or

```
$(handler)
```

The following is an example of the event handler:

```
$(document).ready(function() {
        // Add JavaScript code here
});
```

Or

```
$(function() {
        // add JavaScript code here
});
```

jQuery Selectors

To work with HTML elements, you first need to locate them. These are the target elements. To search for the target elements you use what is called a *selector*. A selector is a search string, similar to what you use in CSS 3 style rules. The most commonly used selectors are listed in Table 8-1.

Table 8-1. *Common CSS Selectors*

Selector	Description
$("#menu")	Finds the element with an id of menu
$(".selected")	Finds the elements with the class name of selected
$("h1")	Finds all the <h1> elements
$("#menu ul")	Finds all the <ul> elements that are descendants of the element with id menu

Let's say, for example, that you want to find what the user has entered in a form field with an id of MyName and then display it in a browser alert window. You would use the following code to achieve that:

```
var myName = $("#MyName").val();
alert(myName);
```

What is happening in the example is that jQuery is using the DOM to find an HTML element with id MyName. If it finds one, it uses the method val() to read the value of the element. Note that we haven't specified whether it is a text box, a drop-down list box, or any type of form field. jQuery will attempt to find the element using the given selector. If jQuery finds the element, it retrieves its current value based on which type of element it is. If it can't find any element with that id, then the method val() is not executed and the value in the variable myName is undefined. The keyword undefined means that the variable myName has not been assigned any value.

Event Handling with jQuery

Handling events using jQuery is simple; you only need to know the name of the event you want to handle and the HTML element for which you want the event to be handled.

As an example, imagine you have a page that has both a field for the user to enter an e-mail address and a button for the user to submit the address entered. You want to verify that the user actually entered something in the field. Doing this verification on the client side not only is faster but also saves a round trip to the server just to know whether information is missing. Also, in case the user didn't enter anything, you can let the user know about it almost instantly. The code in Listing 8-1 accomplishes all of this.

Listing 8-1. Handling Events with jQuery

```
@using (Html.BeginForm()){
    @Html.Label("email", "Email:");
    @Html.TextBox("email");
     <input type="submit" id="submitButton" value="Send" />
}

<script>
    $(document).ready(function () {
        $("#submitButton").on("click", function (e) {
            var email = $("#email").val();
            if (email == "") {
                e.preventDefault();
                alert("Please enter your email address first.");
            }
        });
    });
</script>
```

The first part of the code is very simple: you create an HTML form that has a text box for entering the e-mail address and a submit button for submitting it. Then, when the HTML elements are loaded, you tell jQuery to find the submit button using the selector of the element with id "submitButton". If it's found, then you use the on() method to attach an anonymous function to the click event. The event handler function has one parameter, which is the event object. When you run the application and click the button on the form, the click-event handler function is executed. The function gets the value from the "email" text box. If the text box is empty, the statement e.preventDefault() prevents the form from being submitted to the server.

Understanding Unobtrusive JavaScript

In the time before jQuery (and other modern JavaScript libraries), the most common way to implement event handlers was to use *inline declaration*. With inline declaration, developers added the event they wanted to handle to HTML elements as attributes. These attributes were named with the event name and the prefix "on" (for example, onclick). As an example to point out the differences between inline declaration and unobtrusive JavaScript, suppose we want to do something when the user clicks a button. Traditionally, developers would have to write something like the code shown in Listing 8-2.

Listing 8-2. Old-Fashioned Way to Handle the Click Event in JavaScript

```
<input id="doSomethingButton"
       type="button"
       value="Do Something"
       onclick="javascript:doSomething();"
/>

<script type="text/javascript">
        function doSomething() {
                var x = 5;
                var y = 3;
                var z = x * y;
                alert(z);
        }
</script>
```

The code in Listing 8-2 instructs the browser to execute the function doSomething() when the user clicks the button. You might be wondering what is so wrong with this code. There are a few things, actually:

- There is a mixture of HTML code and JavaScript code, which makes the code difficult to read (especially for novice developers).

- You cannot reuse the code in the doSomething() function in other pages, only in the same page.

- There is no actual restriction on the code that defines the event handler. The code can quickly deteriorate to having a full inline implementation of the event handler. For example:

```
<input id="doSomethingButton" type="button" value="Do Something"
        onclick="javascript:var x = 5; var y = 3; var z = x * y; alert(z);" />
```

By implementing unobtrusive JavaScript with jQuery, we achieve two main benefits:

- The JavaScript code for the event handler is implemented separately from the HTML (it even can be in a separate file that is referenced in the page).

- With code and markup separated, we can make changes to the code without affecting the markup, and vice versa.

To implement unobtrusive JavaScript with jQuery in the code from Listing 8-2, first we remove the onclick attribute from the button declaration. Then we create a new file named (for example) event-handlers.js, to move the JavaScript code there (this is not required but will bring other benefits such as better performance for the page, especially if bundling and minification are used). This is shown in Listing 8-3. This code is the same as the code in Listing 8-2, only now it is implemented using jQuery syntax.

The $(document).ready(function() {}) declaration instructs the browser to execute the code inside the curly brackets as soon as the DOM is ready—that is, after the HTML web page has been fully loaded. Then it binds the click event of the button with id doSomethingButton to a function (note that the function doesn't have a name, known as *anonymous function*). The code in this function will be executed whenever the user clicks the button.

You have to be careful with the selectors. If you make a mistake with the selector and jQuery cannot find the element you intend to use, then the code won't be executed. The anonymous function has the same code as the doSomething() function in Listing 8-2.

Listing 8-3. Contents of the scripts/event-handlers.js File

```
$(document).ready(function() {
        $("#doSomethingButton").on("click", function(e) {
                var x = 5;
                var y = 3;
                var z = x * y;
                alert(z);
        });
});
```

The modified definition of the button and the script reference is shown in Listing 8-4.

Listing 8-4. Modified Button Declaration and External JavaScript File Reference

```
<html>
<head>
   @Scripts.Render("~/bundles/jqueryval")
   <script src="scripts/event-handlers.js"></script>
</head>
```

```
<body>
    <input id="doSomethingButton" type="button" value="Do Something" />
</body>
```

What have we gained with these changes? First, code readability. The HTML definition of the button is now clear of any JavaScript code. Next, we now have the ability to create a bundle for this file (and other JavaScript files), thus improving the page's loading time. Finally, the code is now centralized, so when we do maintenance, any change we make to the event handler is automatically propagated to any element that implements it.

Working with Ajax

Traditionally, when a page needs to update its content, an element in the page (e.g. a button) triggers a request to the server. Once the server finishes processing the request, a new page is sent back to the browser. This behavior is known as a *full page refresh*. There are many negative consequences of this model, such as:

- Slow page refresh, particularly if the page has a lot of content

- Increased load for the server, because it needs to produce a new page on every request, even if the update is small

Ajax introduced a new paradigm to improve how pages update their content. Some of the benefits of using Ajax to update the page's content are as follows:

- Requests are made asynchronously. This allows the page to remain usable for the user.

- The server's response is very small. It produces only the necessary information that was requested, not an entire new page.

- The server's response is quicker. Producing the response is faster than producing a new page.

- The page can be updated only in the area that needs the update.

Triggering Ajax Calls

Ajax requests can be initiated by any user interaction. For example, an Ajax request can be initiated when a user clicks a button, when a user leaves one field to enter another, or when a user presses a key while the cursor is in a text box. Listing 8-5 shows how an Ajax request is issued when the user leaves a field with id `txtName`. The event's actual name is blur. Once the Ajax request completes successfully, an HTML element with id `result` is updated with the response from the server.

Listing 8-5. Ajax Request Initiated When the User Leaves a Field

```
$("#txtName").blur(function(e) {
    var name = $(this).val();
    var _url= "/Account/SendName/" + name;
    $.ajax({
        url:_url,
        type: "Post",
        success: function (data) {
            $("#result").html(data);
        }
    });
});
```

In the example shown in Listing 8-5, the jQuery function `$.ajax()` is used to make an Ajax request. The parameter `url` defines the URL to which the request will be sent. In the example, the request will be sent to the action method `SendName` in the `AccountController` class. The parameter `type` determines the HTTP method to use, in this case HTTP Post. The parameter `success` is a callback function that is to be executed when the request finishes successfully.

ASP.NET MVC 4 includes features that facilitate the usage of Ajax through the `@Ajax` property in the Razor view object. The `@Ajax` property is of type `System.Web.Mvc.AjaxHelper`. This property provides the implementation of HTML helper methods for forms and hyperlinks. The HTML helper methos in the `@Ajax` property are similar to those in the `@Html` property, the difference is that the ones in the `@Ajax` property work asynchronously using Ajax. For example, a traditional hyperlink would be created using

```
@Html.ActionLink("This is a regular link","actionName","controllerName")
```

With the @Ajax property, this hyperlink would be created like this:

```
@Ajax.ActionLink("This is an Ajax link", "actionName", "controllerName", ajaxOptions)
```

You may have noticed the additional parameter, `ajaxOptions`, in the declaration of the `@Ajax.ActionLink()` helper method. This parameter is an object of type `System.Web.Mvc.Ajax.AjaxOptions`. What the `AjaxOptions` parameter does is supply information on how to process the request using Ajax. An example of using this property follows:

```
<div id="resultDiv"> </div>
@Ajax.ActionLink("This is an Ajax link", "actionName", "controllerName",
                 new AjaxOptions
                     {
                         Confirm = "Are you sure?",
                         HttpMethod = "Post",
                         UpdateTargetId = "resultDiv",
                         InsertionMode = InsertionMode.Replace
                     })
```

In the preceding example, the `AjaxOptions` class includes the following properties:

- `Confirm`: This is a string property whose value will be displayed in a browser dialog to ask the user if it should continue or not. If the user clicks the "OK" button (or "Accept" button, depending on the browser), then the request is processed; otherwise it is cancelled.

- `HttpMethod`: This property indicates the type of HTTP method to use for the request. In this case we are specifying to use HTTP Post.

- `UpdateTargetId`: This property defines the id of an HTML element that will be used to display the results of the Ajax request. In the example, when the request completes successfully, the returned data will be inserted inside the `<div>` with id `resultDiv`.

- `InsertionMode`: This property determines how the returned data will be added to the HTML element defined in the `UpdateTargetId` property. The possible values are in the enumeration `InsertionMode` and are `InsertAfter`, `InsertBefore`, and `Replace`. These values indicate if the returned data should be inserted after or before the existing content in the target element, or if the existing content should be replaced with the returned data.

In addition to the previous properties, the following other properties for the AjaxOptions class are useful to process an Ajax request:

- OnBegin, OnComplete, OnSuccess, and OnFailure: These four properties for event callbacks are used to handle the events when the request begins and completes, and when the request is successful or failed. (These will be discussed later in the chapter, in the section "Implementing Ajax Callbacks.")

- LoadingElementId and LoadingElementDuration: These two properties define an HTML element that will be displayed while the request is processing and the duration (in milliseconds) it will be displayed. You could, for example, create a <div> that has an animated image such as the one shown in Figure 8-2.

Figure 8-2. *Animated image to indicate the request is processing*

- Url: This property defines the URL to make the request to.

Creating Ajax Forms

In this section, we'll take the HaveYouSeenMe application form used to send messages to pet owners, previously described in Listing 7-3 in Chapter 7, and modify it to be an Ajax form. What this means is that, instead of making a synchronous request to the server to send the message, the form will now send an asynchronous request. The new modification is shown in Listing 8-6. The following modifications need to be done:

- Enclose the <form> in a <div> element and set the id of the <div> to be messageForm. What we want to achieve with this is to replace the <form> with the data returned from the request execution when the request completes successfully. This <div> will be used in the UpdateTargetId property of the AjaxOptions parameter.

```
<div id="messageForm">
    <form>
        ...
    </form>
</div>
```

- After the messageForm <div>, add another <div> with id "loading". This will be the HTML element to be shown while the request is being processed. Add the text "Sending Message..." to the loading div and set the display style to "none" so it is hidden by default.

```
<div id="loading" style="display: none">
    Sending Message...
</div>
```

- Change the definition of the form from Html.BeginForm() to Ajax.BeginForm(). This will change the behavior of the form so that it processes the request asynchronously.

- Add an AjaxOptions object to the Ajax.BeginForm() call with the following settings to process the request:

  - Add a confirmation message.

  - Set the HTTP method to Post.

  - Set the InsertionMode property to Replace.

  - Set the LoadingElementId property to loading.

  - Set the UpdateTargetId property to messageForm. The objective is to replace the entire form with the response from the server.

Listing 8-6. Form from Listing 7-3 Updated to Be an Ajax Form

```
@model HaveYouSeenMe.Models.MessageModel

@{
    ViewBag.Title = "Send Message";
}

<div id="messageForm">

<h2>Send Message</h2>

@using (Ajax.BeginForm(new AjaxOptions
                       {
                           Confirm = "Are you sure you want to send this message?",
                           HttpMethod = "Post",
                           InsertionMode = InsertionMode.Replace,
                           LoadingElementId = "loading",
                           UpdateTargetId = "messageForm"
                       }))
{
    @Html.AntiForgeryToken()
    @Html.ValidationSummary(true)

    <fieldset>
        <legend>MessageModel</legend>

        <div class="editor-label">
            @Html.LabelFor(model => model.From)
        </div>
        <div class="editor-field">
            @Html.EditorFor(model => model.From)
            @Html.ValidationMessageFor(model => model.From)
        </div>

        <div class="editor-label">
            @Html.LabelFor(model => model.Email)
        </div>
</fieldset>
```

```
        <div class="editor-field">
            @Html.EditorFor(model => model.Email)
            @Html.ValidationMessageFor(model => model.Email)
        </div>

        <div class="editor-label">
            @Html.LabelFor(model => model.Subject)
        </div>
        <div class="editor-field">
            @Html.EditorFor(model => model.Subject)
            @Html.ValidationMessageFor(model => model.Subject)
        </div>

        <div class="editor-label">
            @Html.LabelFor(model => model.Message)
        </div>
        <div class="editor-field">
            @Html.EditorFor(model => model.Message)
            @Html.ValidationMessageFor(model => model.Message)
        </div>

        <p>
            <input type="submit" value="Send Message" />
        </p>
    </fieldset>
}
</div>

<div id="loading" style="display:none">
    Sending Message...
</div>

@section Scripts {
    @Scripts.Render("~/bundles/jqueryval")
}
```

In order to complete the functionality, we need to make one more change in the controller: render the ThankYou view as a partial view instead of a full view. The ThankYou() action method was used to return a view with specific markup to thank the user for sending a message. The reason we want to change its behavior to render only a partial view is that we only need to send the HTML that will replace the form, as described above, when the message is sent successfully. The modification is shown in Listing 8-7.

Listing 8-7. Modified ThankYou Action Method

```
public PartialViewResult ThankYou()
{
    return PartialView();
}
```

Note in Listing 8-7 that the action method was changed to return a `PartialViewResult` object. As explained in Chapter 4, `PartialViewResult` inherits from `ActionResult`, so it can be used as the return type of an action method. The only restriction when using `PartialViewResult` is that the returned object must be an actual partial view, not any action result object, and that is why the return statement uses `PartialView()`.

When sending a message now, the form first displays the confirmation dialog shown in Figure 8-3. Once the user clicks "OK," the loading message is displayed at the bottom of the form, as shown in Figure 8-4. After the request is processed, the message is displayed in the partial view `ThankYou`, as shown in Figure 8-5.

Figure 8-3. *Confirmation dialog when sending a message in the Ajax form*

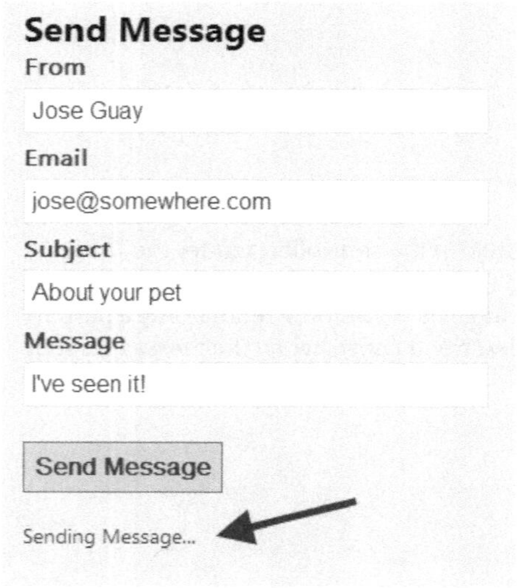

Figure 8-4. *Loading element shown during request processing*

122

Thank You

Your message has been sent

Figure 8-5. *ThankYou partial view returned from request and inserted in the target HTML element*

Creating Ajax ActionLinks

Creating Ajax links is a similar process to creating Ajax forms. Basically, all you need to do is

- Use Ajax.ActionLink() instead of Html.ActionLink()

- Add the AjaxOptions parameter to the Ajax.ActionLink() method

To see how this works, let's build an Ajax link. In the Send Message form, imagine we want to show a link to display the image of the pet. Remember, the main function of the Send Message form is to contact the pet owner about a sighting of his or her pet. It would be nice to able to see the image of the pet before sending the message, just to be sure it is the same one.

The code in Listing 8-8 shows the definition of the Ajax.ActionLink(). Note that the link is inside a <div> with id "petPhoto". The idea is that, when clicked, the link will be replaced with the pet's image. This code should be placed right after the closing bracket of the form so that the link is shown just below the Send Message button.

Listing 8-8. Ajax Link to Load the Pet Photo in the Send Message View

```
<div id="petPhoto">
@Ajax.ActionLink("Display pet picture", "GetPhoto", "Pet",
                 new RouteValueDictionary { {"id",ViewBag.PetName } },
                 new AjaxOptions
                     {
                         HttpMethod = "Post",
                         InsertionMode = InsertionMode.Replace,
                         LoadingElementId = "loadingPhoto",
                         UpdateTargetId = "petPhoto"
                     })
</div>
<div id="loadingPhoto" style="display:none">
    Loading Pet...
</div>
```

The Ajax.ActionLink() method also includes a RouteValueDictionary object, the purpose of which is to send the name of the pet so that the action method knows which pet the request is about. The value in the ViewBag.PetName property is set in the Send() action method when the request to send a message is processed (for example, /Message/Send/Fido). This is shown in Listing 8-9.

Listing 8-9. Send Action Method in the Message Controller

```
public ActionResult Send()
{
    var name = (string)RouteData.Values["id"];
    ViewBag.PetName = name;
    ViewBag.IsSent = false;
    return View();
}
```

The GetPhoto action method in the PetController class is shown in Listing 8-10. All these changes produce the result shown in Figure 8-6.

Listing 8-10. GetPhoto Action Method in the Pet Controller and the Partial View

```
public ActionResult GetPhoto()
{
    var name = (string)RouteData.Values["id"];
    ViewBag.Photo = string.Format("/Content/Uploads/{0}.jpg", name);

    return PartialView();
}
```

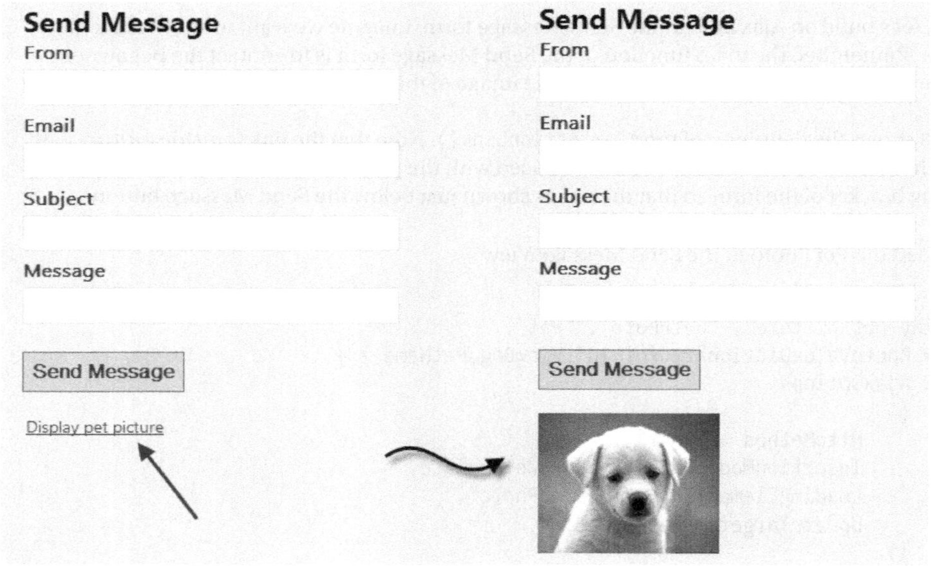

Figure 8-6. *Ajax link to load the pet photo*

The GetPhoto partial view is as follows:

```
<img src="@ViewBag.Photo" style="width:150px;height:120px" />
```

Implementing Ajax Callbacks

The AjaxOptions parameter also includes properties that define JavaScript functions to be called during the Ajax request life cycle. These are called event callback functions.

The Ajax request life cycle can be defined by the diagram in Figure 8-7. The life cycle is quite simple. When the request begins, the OnBegin callback function is executed. After the request completes but before the page is updated, the OnComplete callback function executes. At this point, if the request has completed successfully, the OnSuccess callback function is executed; otherwise, the OnFailure callback function is executed.

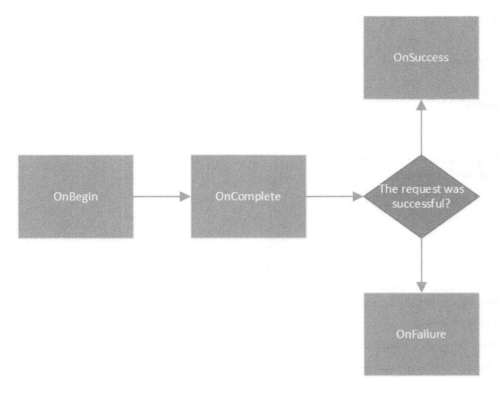

Figure 8-7. *Ajax request life cycle*

Let's use callback functions to further improve our Send Message form to prevent users from clicking the Send Message button multiple times. To do so, after the confirmation window, we will hide the form so that the only element visible is the loading `<div>`.

When the request is complete, we want to show the `messageForm` div again to display the result from the server. Modify the form definition to include the `OnBegin` and `OnComplete` callbacks functions, as follows:

```
@using (Ajax.BeginForm(new AjaxOptions
                    {
                        Confirm = "Are you sure you want to send this message?",
                        HttpMethod = "Post",
                        InsertionMode = InsertionMode.Replace,
                        LoadingElementId = "loading",
                        UpdateTargetId = "messageForm",
                        OnBegin = "beginRequest",
                        OnComplete = "endRequest"
                    }))
```

Now modify the @scripts section at the bottom of the form as follows:

```
@section Scripts {
    @Scripts.Render("~/bundles/jqueryval")

    <script>
        function beginRequest() {
            $("#messageForm").hide();
        }

        function endRequest(request, status) {
            $("#messageForm").show();
        }
    </script>
}
```

Figure 8-8 shows the result of these changes. Now the flow of sending a message is as follows:

1. The user completes the form and clicks the Send Message button.

2. The confirmation window is shown. When the user clicks OK, the OnBegin callback fires and the <form> disappears.

3. The loading <div> is shown.

4. After the request completes, the OnComplete callback fires.

5. The messageForm <div> is shown again with the result of the request.

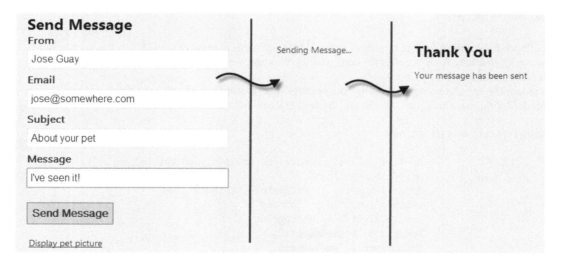

Figure 8-8. *Using callbacks to improve the Send Message form*

Making Ajax Requests Directly with jQuery

jQuery has methods that allow you to make Ajax requests directly. Under the covers, the Ajax.BeginForm() and Ajax.ActionLink() methods are translated into jQuery Ajax calls. jQuery needs specific information about the request. The information in the AjaxOptions object provides jQuery with everything it needs to produce the correct Ajax call. The settings in the AjaxOptions parameter tell MVC how to render the jQuery call in the HTML page.

The definition of the Ajax call in jQuery has many parameters and can be found at http://api.jquery.com/jQuery.ajax/. In addition to the $.ajax() function, jQuery provides two other specialized functions, called $.post() and $.get(). They perform the same functionality as $.ajax() but implement a specific HTTP method, as indicated by their names.

A simplified $.ajax() definition is as follows:

```
$.ajax ({
        url : "",
        type: ""
        data: "",
        dataType: "",
        beforeSend: handler,
        complete: handler,
        success: handler,
        error: handler
});
```

The parameters are listed and described in Table 8-2.

Table 8-2. *Parameters in the jQuery Ajax Call*

Event	Description	Supplied by AjaxOptions
url	Defines the URL to which the request is sent.	AjaxOptions.Url or BeginForm action method
type	Defines the HTTP method (Post, Get, Delete, or Put	AjaxOptions.HttpMethod
data	Data to send to the server. If the type is Get, then the fields are appended to the QueryString; otherwise they are placed in the Post payload.	Form fields
dataType	The data type expected from the server. It can be xml, json, jsonp, script, text, or html.	
beforeSend	Defines the JavaScript function that will be called immediately before the page is updated.	AjaxOptions.OnBegin
complete	Defines the JavaScript function that will be called when response data has been instantiated but before the page is updated.	AjaxOptions.OnComplete
error	Defines the JavaScript function that will be called if the page update fails.	AjaxOptions.OnFailure
success	Defines the JavaScript function that will be called if the page is successfully updated.	AjaxOptions.OnSuccess

Using the jQuery ajax() method gives you full control over the request, with the only drawback being that it involves a bit more work (but nothing significant). Let's see how we can use the jQuery ajax() method to replace the Ajax link we created to load the pet's photo. The code is implemented in Listing 8-11.

Listing 8-11. Implementing jQuery ajax() Method to Load the Pet Photo

```
<div id="petPhoto">
    <a href="#" id="getPhoto">Display pet picture</a>
</div>

<script>
    $(document).ready(function () {
        $("#getPhoto").on("click", function (e) {
            e.preventDefault();
            $.ajax({
                url: "/Pet/GetPhoto/Fido",
                type: "Post",
                dataType: "html",
                beforeSend: function () {
                    $("#loadingPhoto").show();
                },
                complete: function() {
                    $("#loadingPhoto").hide();
                },
                success: function (data) {
                    $("#petPhoto").html(data);
                }
            });
        });
    });
</script>
```

Working with JSON

JSON stands for JavaScript Object Notation, which is an open standard for data interchange that is language independent. There are many parsers for different languages. You can represent JavaScript objects in JSON format and send them as part of an Ajax request. Likewise, if you return a C# (or VB, etc.) object from an action method in your controller class, MVC is capable of converting the object into JSON format to be returned to the browser.

Using JSON is usually preferred over using XML for data interchange between the browser and the server because JSON can represent most of the data structures that XML can represent, but can do so with a much smaller payload. The same object can be presented in XML and JSON, but the JSON representation will most likely be much smaller in size, thus making it a better solution to transmit the object to the browser. Also, working with JSON in your JavaScript code is much easier than working with XML.

ASP.NET MVC includes features that make sending objects using JSON very easy. In the examples thus far, we have been using partial views to send responses back to the browser. Sending HTML in response to a request can be limiting because the data cannot be easily manipulated at the browser. A better approach would be to send just the data and create the HTML in the browser.

Returning JSON from an Action Method

Using an action method to return JSON is a very simple implementation. All you need to do is the following:

- Set the action method's return type to JsonResult.

- Create the object and return it using the Json object to serialize the object to JSON.

The example in Listing 8-12 shows an MVC action method that returns a Pet object in JSON format.

Listing 8-12. Returning JSON from an Action Method

```
public JsonResult GetInfo()
{
    var name = (string)RouteData.Values["id"];
    var pet = PetManagement.GetByName(name);

    return Json(pet);
}
```

CAUTION: AVOID RETURNING JSON WITH HTTP GET

Returning JSON from action methods is, by default, enabled only for HTTP Post requests. Using HTTP Get is not recommended in situations where sensitive data is being sent, because the possibility exists that a malicious user could use a technique called *JSON hijacking* to gain access to the information being sent. An excellent article by Phil Haack explaining this vulnerability can be found at http://bit.ly/JSON-Hijacking.

If you absolutely must use HTTP Get, then you have to pass a second parameter to the Json serialization call with the value JsonRequestBehavior.AllowGet. For example:

```
public JsonResult GetInfo()
{
    var name = (string)RouteData.Values["id"];
    var pet = PetManagement.GetByName(name);

    return Json(pet, JsonRequestBehavior.AllowGet);
}
```

Using JSON in the Browser

Now that we have a JSON object being returned by the action method, let's display some data in the browser. First, let's add a form that will request the pet information from the action method created in Listing 8-12. Replace the GetPhoto code in Listing 8-10 with the code shown in Listing 8-13. Note that I have added a hidden field to illustrate passing the parameter using HTTP Post.

Listing 8-13. Ajax Form to Get a JSON Object from the Action Method in Listing 8-12

```
<div id="petDetails">
    @using (Ajax.BeginForm("GetInfo", "Pet",
                new AjaxOptions
                    {
                        HttpMethod = "Post",
                        InsertionMode = InsertionMode.Replace,
                        LoadingElementId = "loadingDetails",
                        OnSuccess = "showPetDetails"
                    }))
    {
        <input type="hidden" value="Fido" id="name" name="name" />
        <button type="submit">Get Pet Details</button>
    }
</div>
<div id="loadingDetails" style="display: none">
    Loading Pet...
</div>
```

The definition of the AjaxOptions object doesn't include the UpdateTargetId property this time. This is because we are getting only the data, so the response is not quite ready to be rendered upon arrival. That's why we've added a handler for the OnSuccess callback. If we get a response successfully, it will be a JSON object with the information about the pet.

The callback function showPetDetails() is shown in Listing 8-14. First the function verifies that the response is not null; a null value would mean the pet was not found. If the pet was not found, a message indicating so will be displayed. If the pet is found and we get a proper JSON object, then we will use it to create a table with the information. The result is shown in Figure 8-9.

Listing 8-14. Using the JSON Object to Display Data

```
<script>

    function showPetDetails(petData) {
        var target = $("#petDetails");
        target.empty();

        if (!petData) {
            target.append("<em>The pet was not found...</em>");
        }
        else {
            var lastSeenOn = new Date(parseInt(petData.LastSeenOn.substr(6)));
            var lastSeen = lastSeenOn.getMonth() + 1 + "/"
                            + lastSeenOn.getDate() + "/"
                            + lastSeenOn.getFullYear();
            var age = petData.PetAgeYears + " years and "
                            + petData.PetAgeMonths + " months";
            var photo = "<img src='/Content/Uploads/" + petData.PetName
                            + ".jpg' style='width:150px;height:120px' />";
            target.append("<table>");
            target.append("    <tr><td>Name:</td><td>" + petData.PetName + "</td></tr>");
            target.append("    <tr><td>Age:</td><td>" + age + "</td></tr>");
            target.append("    <tr><td>Status:</td><td>" + petData.Status.Description
                                                    + "</td></tr>");
```

```
            target.append("    <tr><td>Last Seen On:</td><td>" + lastSeen
                                          + "</td></tr>");
            target.append("    <tr><td>Last Seen Where:</td><td>"
                                          + petData.LastSeenWhere + "</td></tr>");
            target.append("    <tr><td>Photo:</td><td>" + photo + "</td></tr>");
            target.append("</table>");
        }
    }

</script>
```

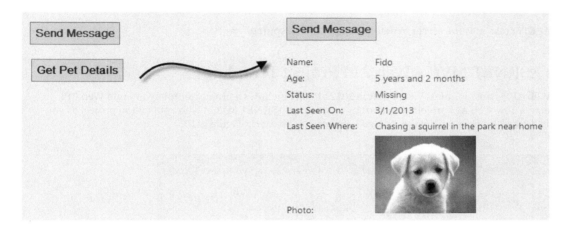

Figure 8-9. *Using JSON to display information in the browser*

Introducing Web API

Web API is a technology that allows you to easily create services that provide an API for clients using the HTTP protocol. While the idea behind Web API and its first implementations were developed inside ASP.NET MVC, the actual implementation is at the framework level, so it is available to all types of ASP.NET applications, not just MVC. The Web API classes are located inside the System.Web.Http namespace, which is different from the MVC namespace (System.Web.Mvc).

Because Web API works with HTTP, it can be used to create RESTful APIs. A *RESTful API* is a web API that is built using HTTP but also follows the principles of Representational State Transfer (REST). The architecture of REST consist of clients and servers. Clients initiate requests to servers; servers process requests and return appropriate responses. Requests and responses are built around the transfer of representations of resources. A resource can be essentially any coherent and meaningful concept that may be addressed. The following are the key goals of REST:

- Scalability of component interactions
- Generality of interfaces
- Independent deployment of components
- Intermediary components to reduce latency, enforce security, and encapsulate legacy systems

While REST was first defined in the context of HTTP, it is not limited to that protocol. It can be used on any protocol that provides a rich and uniform vocabulary that can be sent in the request from the client to the server. Each verb in the vocabulary presents a meaningful representational state; in other words, it tells the server how to treat the request to produce a response.

In HTTP there are many verbs (referred to in previous chapters as *request methods*) that can be included in requests to the server. The following are the most widely used verbs:

- GET: Instructs the server to return the specified resource. For example, if you request /api/Pet/Fido, the server should find the information about Fido and return such information—and do nothing more.

- POST: Instructs the server to accept the information of the resource included in the request. This verb is used to send any type of information to the server, such as a blog post, a new comment, a file to be uploaded, etc.

- PUT: Similarly to POST, instructs the server to accept the information of the resource in the request. If the resource already exists, it can be updated; otherwise it can be created.

- DELETE: Instructs the server to delete the specified resource.

Using the ASP.NET MVC 4 Web API Project Template

Working with Web API is not complex. Visual Studio 2012 already includes a project template to build Web API projects. To create a new Web API project, you start by creating an ASP.NET MVC 4 web application project as you would normally do, and then you select the Web API template as shown in Figure 8-10.

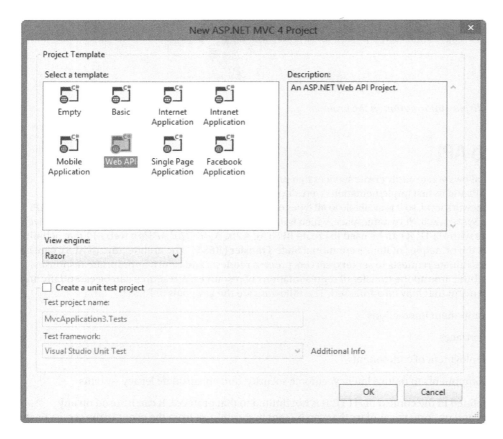

Figure 8-10. *Creating a new Web API project in Visual Studio 2012*

The structure of the project is quite similar to a typical ASP.NET MVC 4 web application. The difference is that this project includes a new type of controller that is based on the System.Web.Http.ApiController class, as opposed to the regular controllers that inherit from the System.Web.Mvc.Controller class. You can see the structure in Figure 8-11.

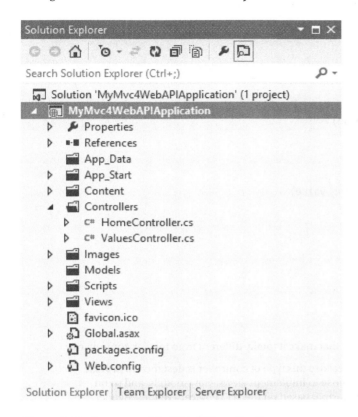

Figure 8-11. *Structure of the Web API application*

The Controllers/ValuesController.cs file is shown in Listing 8-15. Note that the controller includes some sample action methods for each of the four common HTTP verbs.

Listing 8-15. Content of the ValuesController Class in the Controllers/ValuesController.cs File

```csharp
using System;
using System.Collections.Generic;
using System.Linq;
using System.Net;
using System.Net.Http;
using System.Web.Http;

namespace MyMvc4WebAPIApplication.Controllers
{
    public class ValuesController : ApiController
    {
        // GET api/values
        public IEnumerable<string> Get()
```

```
        {
            return new string[] { "value1", "value2" };
        }

        // GET api/values/5
        public string Get(int id)
        {
            return "value";
        }

        // POST api/values
        public void Post([FromBody]string value)
        {
        }

        // PUT api/values/5
        public void Put(int id, [FromBody]string value)
        {
        }

        // DELETE api/values/5
        public void Delete(int id)
        {
        }
    }
}
```

This new type of controller has two characteristics that make it totally different from regular controllers:

- The action methods return objects only. Because this type of controller is designed to provide data services over HTTP, it doesn't make sense to implement views, view models, and so on. The objects are returned in JSON or XML format based on the HTTP Accept request header.

- The names of the action methods can be (or can include) the actual HTTP method used in the request.

Additionally, a few other characteristics of Web API are worth mentioning. The first one is related to how the JSON representation is generated. In action methods returning a JsonResult from regular controllers, the JSON object is created using the built-in JSON serializer, whereas action methods in Web API controllers use the library Json.NET for serialization. This is important because the Json.NET library has implemented some improvements over the built-in JSON serializer, such as in dealing with dates. A DateTime value would be serialized to milliseconds in the form of \/Date(1362117600000)\/. Using Json.NET, the same date would be serialized to the standard ISO 8016 format as 2013-03-01T00:00:00 -06:00.

Another (probably more important) characteristic is that Web API can choose which format to return automatically (e.g., XML) based on the HTTP Accept header from the client. A request using jQuery's ajax() function would look like this:

```
$.ajax({
    url: "/api/sample/Info",
    type:"Get",
    accepts:"application/xml",
    success:function(data) {
      // process returned xml data
    }
});
```

Creating Web API Controllers

At this point, you may have noticed that the Internet Application template used in our sample application (HaveYouSeenMe) doesn't include any Web API controllers. This type of controller is very simple to create. Follow these steps to create a Web API controller to serve the data for pets:

1. Right-click the "Controllers" directory and choose Add ➤ Controller, as shown in Figure 8-12. Alternatively, use the keyboard shortcut Ctrl+M, Ctrl+C.

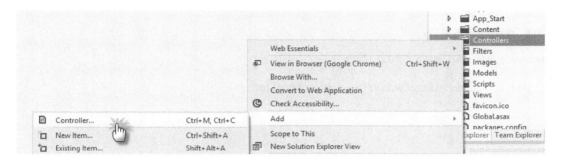

Figure 8-12. *Creating a new controller*

2. In the Add Controller dialog, name the controller **PetDataController**, select "Empty API controller" in the Template drop-down list, as shown in Figure 8-13, and click "Add."

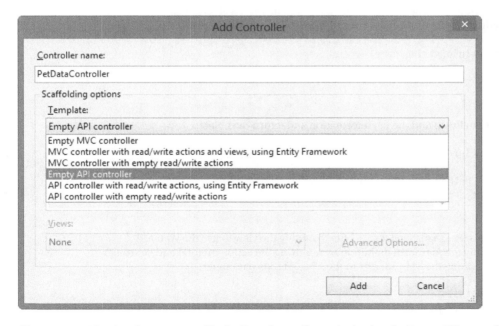

Figure 8-13. *Naming the new controller PetDataController and selecting the Empty API controller template*

You have now created your first Web API controller. The generated code should be similar to the one presented in Listing 8-16.

Listing 8-16. Empty Web API Controller

```
using System;
using System.Collections.Generic;
using System.Linq;
using System.Net;
using System.Net.Http;
using System.Web.Http;

namespace HaveYouSeenMe.Controllers
{
    public class PetDataController : ApiController
    {
    }
}
```

3. To add the GetInfo() action method, first import the Models and Models.Business namespaces with the following statements:

    ```
    using HaveYouSeenMe.Models;
    using HaveYouSeenMe.Models.Business;
    ```

4. Add an action method named GetInfo(). This action method will return an object of type Pet. The method should take a parameter of type string with the name name.

    ```
    public Pet GetInfo(string name)
    {

    }
    ```

5. Add the functionality to find the pet information and return the object:

    ```
    public Pet GetInfo(string name)
    {
        var pet = PetManagement.GetByName(name);
        return pet;
    }
    ```

6. Open the /Views/Message/Send.cshtml file to modify the view to use the Web API controller. Modify the Ajax form definition by removing the action method and controller definition and adding the Url property to the AjaxOptions parameter:

    ```
    <div id="petDetails">
        @using (Ajax.BeginForm(
                    new AjaxOptions
                        {
                            Url = "/api/PetData/Info",
                            HttpMethod = "Get",
                            InsertionMode = InsertionMode.Replace,
    ```

```
                        LoadingElementId = "loadingDetails",
                        OnSuccess = "showPetDetails"
                }))
    {
        <input type="hidden" value="Fido" id="name" name="name" />
        <button type="submit">Get Pet Details</button>
    }
</div>
```

Note that the HttpMethod property is set to Get and the Url property is set to /Api/ PetData/Info. These two properties instruct the form to make the request to the GetInfo action method in the PetData controller.

The api part in the Url property is defined by a route. This route is created in the App_ Start/WebApiConfig.cs class. This was added by default in the Visual Studio template we used for the web application:

```
config.Routes.MapHttpRoute(
    name: "DefaultApi",
    routeTemplate: "api/{controller}/{id}",
    defaults: new { id = RouteParameter.Optional }
);
```

7. Change how the date is handled in the OnSuccess callback:

```
// Old code for dates serialized with built-in Json serializer
// var lastSeenOn = new Date(parseInt(petData.LastSeenOn.substr(6)));

// New code for dates serialized with Json.NET
var lastSeenOn = new Date(petData.LastSeenOn);
```

When you execute the web site and make the request, you get a result similar to the one shown previously in Figure 8-7.

Using Web API has many advantags over regular controllers to present data to clients. I would suggest using it when you want to control the return data format (XML or JSON) without actually writing the specific serialization. Also, if you need to implement an API following the principles of REST because it is actually designed with that goal in mind.

Summary

In this chapter you have seen how to work with Ajax and jQuery. ASP.NET MVC includes helper methods that make working with Ajax very easy. jQuery is supported by Microsoft and is included in all the web application templates in Visual Studio.

The unobtrusive JavaScript features in ASP.NET MVC are built on top of jQuery. They allow you to have cleaner code by separating the markup from the client-side code.

Ajax allows you to make asynchronous requests to the server and update the page with updated information. The configuration options for Ajax forms and links allow you to set the Url, HTTP method, callback functions, and more.

ASP.NET MVC includes support for JSON format with the built-in Json serializer class implemented by action methods in regular controllers that return a JsonResult.

Web API is a technology that allows you to easily create services that provide an API for clients using the HTTP protocol. It can be used to create RESTful APIs. With a RESTful API, you can use the HTTP verb in the request to identify how to process the request in the server. The most common HTTP verbs are Get, Post, Put, and Delete.

To start with Web API, you can create a new ASP.NET MVC 4 project and select the Web API template, or you can create API controllers in your existing application that inherit from System.Web.Http.ApiController. The action methods in this type of controller can be (or can include) the HTTP verb in the name so that they are automatically recognized and executed.

CHAPTER 9

Security

Securing a web application is a very important task. Security cannot be taken lightly. It must be implemented to prevent the stored information from being compromised. Developers need to ensure that certain security measures have been implemented to keep the web site working and in compliance with the expected level of service. Also, access to sensitive parts of the web site should be restricted to only certain users, such administrators.

ASP.NET MVC is built on top of ASP.NET and has access to the security features in the framework. In this chapter you will see how to secure your ASP.NET MVC 4 application. We are going to explore the different authentication methods and how to implement security measures to avoid threats such as cross-site scripting (XSS) and cross-site request forgery (CSRF). We'll also look at how to properly authorize users to perform only the tasks they are authorized to do.

Additionally, we are going to examine certain techniques to prevent SQL injection and HTML injection attacks. By the end of the chapter you will be able to secure your application by applying security best practices.

Authentication and Authorization

In a web application, the process of *authentication* refers to identifying who the user is, whereas *authorization* refers to determining what the user is allowed do. In addition to users, *roles* is another concept that is often implemented to identify groups of users. Instead of assigning permissions to individual users, permissions are assigned to roles, and all users within the same role inherit such permissions.

ASP.NET MVC is capable of working with different schemes of authentication. The two most relevant are Windows Authentication and Forms Authentication. Windows Authentication is used in applications where all user accounts are stored in Windows Active Directory (AD). In this scenario, web applications rely on Internet Information Services (IIS) to authenticate the requests. If the request is valid, then IIS transfers the request to ASP.NET for processing. This authentication method is great for developers because they don't have to deal with user management; everything is managed through the AD administrators.

Forms authentication, on the other hand, is suitable for Internet-facing applications where users identify themselves with a username and a password. Alternatively, users can authenticate using the OAuth protocol to link and use their third-party accounts (Facebook, Twitter, Google, etc.).

Using Windows Authentication

Implementing Windows Authentication is relatively simple. First you need to enable Windows Authentication in the web application. To enable this setting, create a new ASP.NET MVC 4 application using the Intranet Application project template. The following steps will guide you through the process:

1. Open Visual Studio.

2. Create a new ASP.NET MVC 4 application (as described in Chapter 2).

3. Select the Intranet Application project template. For this example, you can omit the creation of a test project.

4. Open the Web.config file in the root of the application.

5. The authentication method is defined in the <authentication> section. Add the <authentication> section with the property mode as follows:

```
<configuration>
    <system.web>
        <authentication mode="Windows" />
    </system.web>
</configuration>
```

While the web site is being developed, you would normally use IIS Express to run and test the functionality. IIS Express can also be configured to run Windows Authentication. All you need to do is

1. Right-click the web application in Visual Studio and choose the option "Properties" at the bottom of the context menu.

2. In the Properties window, scroll down until you see the option Windows Authentication.

3. Select "Enabled" from the drop-down list, as shown in Figure 9-1.

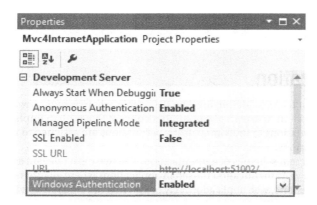

Figure 9-1. *Enabling Windows Authentication in IIS Express*

When you run the application, IIS Express (or IIS) will identify the currently logged-in user in the computer. In the example shown in Figure 9-2, it is the Windows user. In a corporate environment where there is an Active Directory domain, it will be the domain account of the user.

Figure 9-2. *Web application with Windows Authentication enabled*

When the application is ready for production, we move it from IIS Express to a full installation of IIS. We also need to modify the configuration in IIS for Windows Authentication. To make this modification, we need to either open the IIS Manager program located in the Administrative Tools folder in the Control Panel or execute `inetmgr` from the Run command window (which you access by pressing Windows Key+R).

IIS Manager is the tool that you use to administer IIS. You can create web sites, create application pools, and configure all aspects of IIS in a graphical user interface. IIS Manager is basically composed of three panes. The left pane is the navigation tree for all the options that can be managed. The center pane is where all the configuration options are located. For web sites, for example, you can find in the center pane options for ASP.NET applications such as the version of .NET Framework, connection strings, and application settings. The center pane also includes IIS configuration settings such as authentication options and error messages. The right pane is where you see the available actions when an option is selected in the center pane. To enable Windows Authentication in IIS using IIS Manager use the following steps:

1. In the left pane of the IIS Manager window, expand the [Server Name] ➤ Sites node to display the available web sites.

2. Select "Default Web Site."

3. In the Home pane in the middle of the window, double-click "Authentication" under IIS. The options are shown in Figure 9-3. Note that these options are available only if they were installed when IIS was configured.

Figure 9-3. *IIS Authentication options*

4. By default, the Windows Authentication option at the bottom is disabled. To enable it, select it and click "Enable" in the Actions pane to the right of the window, as shown in Figure 9-4.

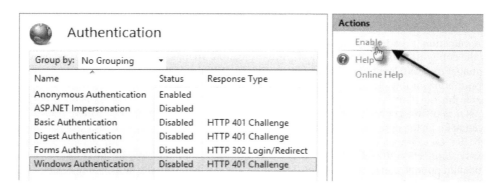

Figure 9-4. *Enabling Windows Authentication in IIS*

5. Disable Anonymous Authentication by selecting it and clicking "Disable" in the Actions pane.

Anonymous authentication is the form of authentication used to allow users to visit the web site without identifying themselves. If a user visits the web site, by default that user is an anonymous user because no credentials have been sent to the server. If we hadn't disabled anonymous authentication in the preceding step, the web site would be open to all users, whereas we want to ensure users identify themselves with an account.

Using Forms Authentication

For scenarios where Active Directory is not available, developers need to implement a different mechanism to authenticate users. Forms Authentication allows developers to create a simple login page that validates who a user is based on the username and password the user enters. After the user is validated, an HTTP cookie is created to store information about the user. The information in the cookie is passed with every request by the browser so that the server knows who the user is. The cookie name is .ASPXAUTH. The information in the cookie is encrypted, as shown in Figure 9-5. Forms Authentication takes care of this cookie management and transport automatically. You don't need to do anything to make it work.

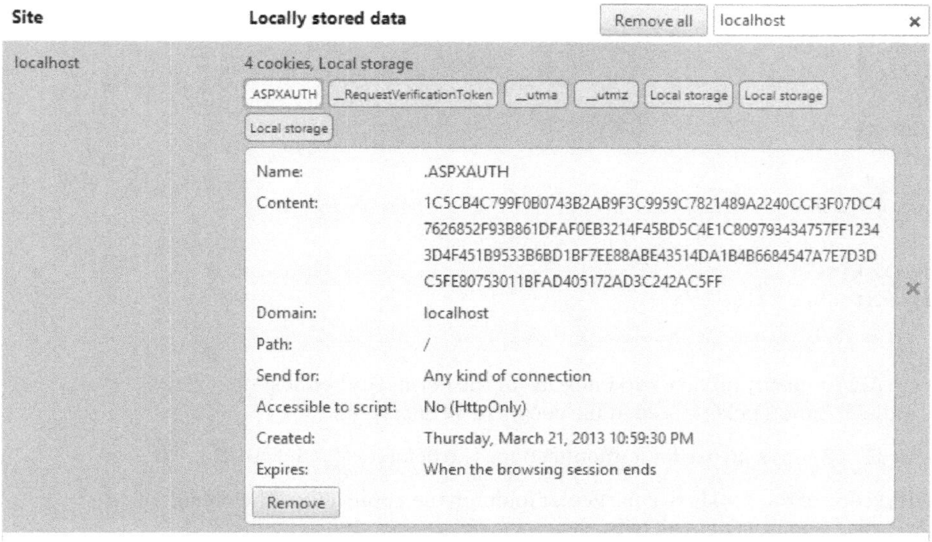

Site	Locally stored data			Remove all	localhost	×
localhost	4 cookies, Local storage					

ASPXAUTH _RequestVerificationToken __utma __utmz Local storage Local storage
Local storage

Name:	.ASPXAUTH
Content:	1C5CB4C799F0B0743B2AB9F3C9959C7821489A2240CCF3F07DC4
	7626852F93B861DFAF0EB3214F45BD5C4E1C809793434757FF1234
	3D4F451B9533B6BD1BF7EE88ABE43514DA1B4B6684547A7E7D3D
	C5FE80753011BFAD405172AD3C242AC5FF
Domain:	localhost
Path:	/
Send for:	Any kind of connection
Accessible to script:	No (HttpOnly)
Created:	Thursday, March 21, 2013 10:59:30 PM
Expires:	When the browsing session ends

Remove

Figure 9-5. *.ASPXAUTH cookie content as seen in Google Chrome*

To enable Forms Authentication, you need to set the authentication mode to `Forms` in the `Web.config` file and identify where the login page is, as shown in Listing 9-1.

Listing 9-1. Forms Authentication Configuration in the Web.config File

```
<authentication mode="Forms">
  <forms loginUrl="~/Account/Login" timeout="2880" />
</authentication>
```

The ASP.NET MVC 4 Internet Application project template includes Forms Authentication as the default mechanism to authenticate users. The template includes an `AccountController` class, which contains several action methods to deal with all the necessary authentication-related view pages (e.g., log in, log out, change password, etc.). You can customize the code in these action methods, if you like.

Visual Studio also generates various model classes that contain authentication-related information (e.g., `LoginModel`, `RegisterModel`, and `ExternalLogin`). Visual Studio also generates default view pages that correspond to these action methods. You can customize the UI of these view pages, if you like.

Listing 9-1 includes two properties to configure the behavior of Forms Authentication:

- `loginUrl`: Tells ASP.NET where the login page is to redirect the user when a request is made to access a secured area. You should place the login page in a folder that requires Secure Sockets Layer (SSL). This helps ensure the integrity of the credentials when they are passed from the browser to the web server.

- `timeout`: Used to specify a limited lifetime for the Forms Authentication session. The default value is 30 minutes. If a persistent Forms Authentication cookie is issued, the `timeout` attribute is also used to set the lifetime of the persistent cookie.

There are more configuration properties for Forms Authentication. The following is the list of the properties included in the Internet Application project template. You can find the complete list of properties that can be used to configure Forms Authentication at `http://bit.ly/FormsAuthSettings`.

```
<authentication mode="Forms">
    <forms loginUrl="/Account/Login"
           protection="All"
           timeout="2880"
           name="AppNameCookie"
           path="/FormsAuth"
           requireSSL="false"
           slidingExpiration="true"
           defaultUrl="/"
           cookieless="UseCookies"
           enableCrossAppRedirects="false" />
</authentication>
```

- protection: Set to All to specify privacy and integrity for the Forms Authentication ticket. This causes the authentication ticket stored in the cookie to be encrypted.

- name: Specifies the HTTP cookie to use for authentication. The default is ".ASPXAUTH".

- path: Specifies the scope of the cookie to a particular folder in the application. The default of "/" indicates the cookie is to be sent in all requests.

- requireSSL: Set to false, which means that authentication cookies can be transmitted over channels that are not SSL-encrypted. You should consider setting requireSSL to true to minimize the probability of a session-hijacking attack.

- slidingExpiration: Set to true to enforce a sliding session lifetime. This means that the session timeout is periodically reset as long as a user stays active on the site.

- defaultUrl: Set to the home page for the application.

- cookieless: Set to UseDeviceProfile to specify that the application use cookies for all browsers that support cookies. If a browser that does not support cookies accesses the site, then Forms Authentication packages the authentication ticket on the URL. Other values are UseCookies, to always use cookies, UseUri, to never use cookies, and AutoDetect, which specifies that cookies are used if the device profile supports cookies; otherwise, cookies are not used.

- enableCrossAppRedirects: Set to false to indicate that Forms Authentication does not support automatic processing of tickets that are passed between applications on the query string or as part of a form POST.

The ~/Account/Login view for the HaveYouSeenMe sample application is shown in Listing 9-2. It is a strongly typed view using the LoginModel view model. You can customize the look and feel of the page view to match the design of your web site.

Listing 9-2. Content of the ~/Account/Login View Included in the Internet Application Project Template

```
@model HaveYouSeenMe.Models.LoginModel

@{
    ViewBag.Title = "Log in";
}

<hgroup class="title">
    <h1>@ViewBag.Title.</h1>
</hgroup>
```

```
<section id="loginForm">
<h2>Use a local account to log in.</h2>
@using (Html.BeginForm(new { ReturnUrl = ViewBag.ReturnUrl })) {
    @Html.AntiForgeryToken()
    @Html.ValidationSummary(true)

    <fieldset>
        <legend>Log in Form</legend>
        <ol>
            <li>
                @Html.LabelFor(m => m.UserName)
                @Html.TextBoxFor(m => m.UserName)
                @Html.ValidationMessageFor(m => m.UserName)
            </li>
            <li>
                @Html.LabelFor(x=>x.Password)
                @Html.PasswordFor(m => m.Password)
                @Html.ValidationMessageFor(m => m. Password)
            </li>
            <li>
                @Html.CheckBoxFor(m => m.RememberMe)
                @Html.LabelFor(m => m.RememberMe, new { @class = "checkbox" })
            </li>
        </ol>
        <input type="submit" value="Log in" />
    </fieldset>
    <p>
        @Html.ActionLink("Register", "Register") if you don't have an account.
    </p>
}
</section>

<section class="social" id="socialLoginForm">
    <h2>Use another service to log in.</h2>
    @Html.Action("ExternalLoginsList", new { ReturnUrl = ViewBag.ReturnUrl })
</section>

@section Scripts {
    @Scripts.Render("~/bundles/jqueryval")
}
```

Securing Controllers and Action Methods

One of the most important (and common) aspects of securing applications is to allow access to certain sections in the application only to specific users (or groups of users). This can be achieved only after users have been authenticated. In the world of ASP.NET MVC, these application sections are identified by action methods and controllers, rather than actual URLs.

To allow only authenticated users to access certain sections in the application, you need to specify those sections with the [Authorize] attribute. You can make a single action method or a controller accessible to only authenticated users. If you added the [Authorize] attribute to a controller, all action methods in the controller will be accessible only to authenticated users, however, you can allow certain action methods to not require authentication by decorating them with the [AllowAnonymous] attribute.

After the controllers and action methods are set to require users to be authenticated to access them, the framework will redirect to the login page all requests made by anonymous users (that is, users who have not yet entered their authentication information). After the user is properly authenticated on the page, the MVC framework will redirect them back to the original, intended destination. This is done using a parameter in the URL named ReturnUrl that instructs the login page where to go after the user is authenticated.

When we created our HaveYouSeenMe sample application, we used the Internet Application template. We used this template with the goal of providing specific areas for members and administrators. These areas are intended to be accessible to authenticated users and members of the Administrators role, respectively. To achieve this functionality, we are going to create two controllers now: MembersController and AdminController. These controllers will be used, respectively, for the members section and the administration section of our web site. They will need to be accessible only to authenticated users. We'll use basically the same steps to create a controller as outlined in Chapter 4, the only difference being that we will decorate the controllers with the [Authorize] attribute, as shown in Listings 9-3 and 9-4.

Listing 9-3. MembersController Class

```
using System;
using System.Collections.Generic;
using System.Linq;
using System.Web;
using System.Web.Mvc;

namespace HaveYouSeenMe.Controllers
{
    [Authorize]
    public class MembersController : Controller
    {
        //
        // GET: /Members/

        public ActionResult Index()
        {
            return View();
        }

    }
}
```

Listing 9-4. AdminController Class

```
using System;
using System.Collections.Generic;
using System.Linq;
using System.Web;
using System.Web.Mvc;

namespace HaveYouSeenMe.Controllers
{
    [Authorize]
    public class AdminController : Controller
```

```
    {
        //
        // GET: /Members/

        public ActionResult Index()
        {
            return View();
        }

    }
}
```

We need to add a view for the action methods in each of the controllers. Don't worry about the content of the view for now; just create the view. If you now make a request to those controllers (for example, /Members), ASP.NET MVC automatically redirects you to the login page, as shown in Figure 9-6.

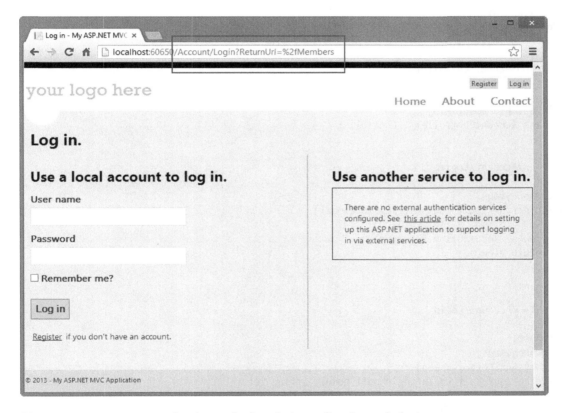

Figure 9-6. *Access to a secured action method results in a redirection to the login page*

Note in Figure 9-6 that the actual destination URL is defined in the ReturnUrl parameter in the query string. If the user enters a valid username and password in the login page, ASP.NET MVC will automatically redirect the browser to the intended URL (as specified in the ReturnUrl query string parameter).

As noted before, you can allow certain action methods in a secured controller to be accessible to all users, not just the authenticated ones. For this purpose, you use the [AllowAnonymous] attribute in the action method. For example, the Login() action method in the Account controller (in the Controllers/AccountController.cs file) is defined this way, as shown in Listing 9-5.

Listing 9-5. Partial Listing of the Account Controller Class

```
using System;
using System.Collections.Generic;
using System.Linq;
using System.Transactions;
using System.Web;
using System.Web.Mvc;
using System.Web.Security;
using DotNetOpenAuth.AspNet;
using Microsoft.Web.WebPages.OAuth;
using WebMatrix.WebData;
using HaveYouSeenMe.Filters;
using HaveYouSeenMe.Models;

namespace HaveYouSeenMe.Controllers
{
    [Authorize]
    [InitializeSimpleMembership]
    public class AccountController : Controller
    {
        //
        // GET: /Account/Login

        [AllowAnonymous]
        public ActionResult Login(string returnUrl)
        {
            ViewBag.ReturnUrl = returnUrl;
            return View();
        }

        //
        // POST: /Account/Login

        [HttpPost]
        [AllowAnonymous]
        [ValidateAntiForgeryToken]
        public ActionResult Login(LoginModel model, string returnUrl)
        {
            if (ModelState.IsValid &&
                WebSecurity.Login(model.UserName,
                                  model.Password,
                                  persistCookie: model.RememberMe))
            {
                return RedirectToLocal(returnUrl);
            }
```

```
            // If we got this far, something failed, redisplay form
            ModelState.AddModelError("", "The user name or password provided
                                        is incorrect.");
            return View(model);
        }
...

}
```

Authenticating with External Sources

The ASP.NET MVC 4 Internet Application project template also includes support for authentication using the Open Authentication protocol (OAuth). This functionality is based on the DotNetOpenAuth open source library (see www.dotnetopenauth.net). The project template includes all the necessary pieces to enable users with Twitter, Facebook, Google, or Microsoft accounts to use their accounts as a mean to authenticate.

Providing the ability to authenticate users using these well-established services is great for web applications because:

- Users don't need to authenticate themselves again (separately) in your application.

- Users therefore don't need to remember a separate set of username/password details in order to use your app (which means they're more likely to use it!).

- You don't have to worry about storing (and securing) the credentials for all these users in your application.

Note in Figure 9-6 that the right section of the page is an area designated to host the available external sources for authentication. It also includes a link to a detailed article that describes the steps you have to follow as a developer to configure support for external authentication sources in the application.

To enable your application to support authentication with external sources, you first need to tell the application which sources you will be using. You do this in the App_Start/AuthConfig.cs file. The initial content of the file (that is, as generated by Visual Studio) is provided in Listing 9-6.

Listing 9-6. Content of the App_Start/AuthConfig.cs File

```
using System;
using System.Text;
using Microsoft.Web.WebPages.OAuth;
using HaveYouSeenMe.Models;

namespace HaveYouSeenMe
{
    public static class AuthConfig
    {
        public static void RegisterAuth()
        {
            // To let users of this site log in using their accounts
            // from other sites such as Microsoft, Facebook, and Twitter,
            // you must update this site. For more information visit
            // http://go.microsoft.com/fwlink/?LinkID=252166
```

```
            //OAuthWebSecurity.RegisterMicrosoftClient(
            //    clientId: "",
            //    clientSecret: "");

            //OAuthWebSecurity.RegisterTwitterClient(
            //    consumerKey: "",
            //    consumerSecret: "");

            //OAuthWebSecurity.RegisterFacebookClient(
            //    appId: "",
            //    appSecret: "");

            //OAuthWebSecurity.RegisterGoogleClient();
        }
    }
}
```

As you can see, to enable an external source, you just need to uncomment the source in the AuthConfig.cs file and add the appropriate credentials. We are going to use all four external sources. For Google accounts to work, we don't need any configuration setting; we simply need to uncomment the last line in the file. For Microsoft, Facebook, and Twitter, we need to obtain identification keys.

Getting Keys from Facebook and Twitter for OAuth

The following information for getting keys from Facebook and Twitter is based on the Microsoft Development Network (MSDN) article "OAuth/OpenID Support for Web Forms, MVC and Web Pages," by Pranav Rastogi, available at http://bit.ly/MVC-OAuth-Config.

Steps to Get Keys for Facebook

Follow these steps to get keys for Facebook:

1. Go to the Facebook Developers site, at http://developers.facebook.com/apps.

2. If you have a Facebook account, log in (if you're not already logged in). If you do't have an account you will need to create one.

3. Click the "Create New App" button in the top right corner as shown in Figure 9-7, and then follow the prompts to name and create the new application.

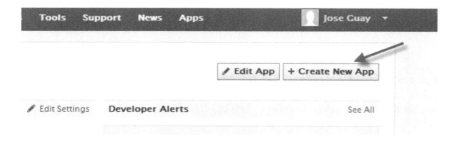

Figure 9-7. Create New App button in the Facebook Developers site

4. In the section "Select how your app will integrate with Facebook," choose "Website with Facebook Login" section as shown in figure 9-8.

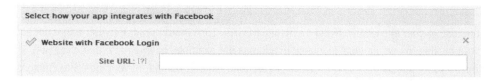

Figure 9-8. *Website with Facebook Login option*

5. Fill in the Site URL field with the URL of your site (for example, `http://www.example.com`). The Domain field is optional; you can use this to provide authentication for an entire domain (such as `example.com`).

■ **Note**   If you are running a site on your local computer with a URL like `http://localhost:12345` (where the number is a local port number), you can add this value to the Site URL field for testing your site. However, any time the port number of your local site changes, you will need to update the Site URL field of your application.

---

6. Click the "Save Changes" button.

7. Click the Apps tab again, and then view the start page for your application.

8. Copy the App ID and App Secret values for your application and paste them into a temporary text file. You will pass these values to the Facebook provider in your website code.

9. Exit the Facebook Developers site.

Steps to Get Keys for Twitter

Follow these steps to get keys for Twitter:

1. Browse to the Twitter Developers site at `https://dev.twitter.com/apps`.

2. Sign in with your username and password. If you don't have a Twitter account you must create one.

3. Click the "Create a new application" button as shown in figure 9-9.

Figure 9-9. *Creating a new application in Twitter*

4. On the Create an Application form, fill in the Name and Description fields.

5. In the WebSite field, enter the URL of your site (for example, `http://www.example.com`).

■ **Note**   If you're testing your site locally (using a URL like `http://localhost:12345`), Twitter might not accept the URL. However, you might be able to use the local loopback IP address (for example, `http://127.0.0.1:12345`). This simplifies the process of testing your application locally. However, every time the port number of your local site changes, you'll need to update the WebSite field of your application.

---

6. In the Callback URL field, enter a URL for the page in your web site that you want users to return to after logging in to Twitter. For example, to send users to the home page of the Starter Site (which will recognize their logged-in status), enter the same URL that you entered in the WebSite field.

7. Accept the terms and click the "Create your Twitter application" button.

8. On the My Applications landing page, choose the application you created.

9. On the Details tab, scroll to the bottom and click the "Create My Access Token" button.

10. On the Details tab, copy the Consumer Key and Consumer Secret values for your application and paste them into a temporary text file. You'll pass these values to the Twitter provider in your website code.

11. Exit the Twitter Developers site.

Getting Keys from Microsoft for OAuth

The following instructions are based on the MSDN article "Configuring your ASP.NET application for Microsoft OAuth account," also by Pranav Rastogi, available at `http://bit.ly/ms-oauth`.

1. Create a new ASP.NET MVC/Web Forms or Web Pages application.

   - Build and run the web site.

2. Use a test domain.

   - You need to use a domain other than localhost since Microsoft accounts cannot redirect back to localhost.

   - Some folks have graciously reserved `localtest.me` for local testing of domains so you do not have to mess with host files. Go to `http://readme.localtest.me/` for more information.

   - You can use `Foo.localtest.me` as a test domain. (Make sure `Foo` is unique. The article's author, Pranav Rastogi, recommends prefixing it with something unique, such as `Foo<MyName>.localtest.me`). For the purpose of this example, use `Foo.localtest.me`.

   - Pinging `Foo.localtest.me` should revert to the local machine.

3. Edit firewall rules for port 80 to receive external requests.

   - Follow the guidelines at `http://maximumpcguides.com/windows-7/open-a-port-in-windows-7s-firewall/` (these work for Windows 8 as well).

4. Configure the Microsoft Application Management portal:

    a. Open the link https://manage.dev.live.com/AddApplication.aspx. Log in using your Microsoft account. If you don't have a Microsoft account you must create one.

    b. Type in the application name and select the application's language.

    c. Read the terms of use and privacy statement. If you agree to them click "I accept."

    d. You should be now in the API Settings page of your application. If you are not, In the Live Connect Developer Center:

        •   Click My Apps at the top of the page.

        •   Then click in the name of your application.

        •   Click on Edit Settings.

        •   Click on API Settings.

    e. In the Redirect Domain field, enter the domain name you previously created (for example, http://Foo.localtest.me).

    f. Click "Save" and the changes should be saved.

5. Map the test domain to your application.

    You need to add mapping for the domain name to be redirected to your application created in step 1. The steps are given for IIS Express first and then for IIS (7.0 and later).

    For IIS Express:

    a. Open applicationHost.config in %Documents%\IISExpress\config.

    b. Locate the binding for the web application in the file. It will be defined in the <site> tag. For example:

    ```
    <site name="WebApplication5" id="6">
    <application path="/" applicationPool="Clr4IntegratedAppPool">
    <virtualDirectory path="/" physicalPath="pathtoapplication\WebApplication5" />
    </application>
    <bindings>
    <binding protocol="http" bindingInformation="*:46178:localhost" />
    </bindings>
    </site>
    ```

    c. Add a new binding for port 80 and the domain name to this web application under the <bindings>:

    ```
    <binding protocol="http" bindingInformation="*:80:Foo.localtest.me " />
    ```

    d. Restart IIS Express and relaunch the web site. Test the above setting by opening Foo.localtest.me in the browser. It should open the web application created.

For IIS (7.0 and later):

    a.   Host you application in IIS.

    b.   Open IIS Manager, locate and select your web application under the Sites list, and select "Bindings" from the Actions menu on the right. Add a binding for your chosen hostname (e.g., Foo.localtest.me).

  6.   Run the site to see it in action.

    a.   Make sure you are running Visual Studio as an admin, which is required for this to work.

    b.   Launch the application, either hosted in IIS Express or hosted in IIS.

    c.   Browse to the test domain Foo.localtest.me.

    d.   Navigate to the Login page and log in using your Microsoft account. Login should be successful.

Configuring the Application to Use the Keys

Once you have the keys for all the external sources, you need to add them to the AuthConfig.cs file, as shown in Listing 9-7.

Listing 9-7. App_Start/AuthConfig.cs File After Adding Keys for Connecting to External OAuth Sources

```
using System;
using System.Text;
using Microsoft.Web.WebPages.OAuth;
using HaveYouSeenMe.Models;

namespace HaveYouSeenMe
{
    public static class AuthConfig
    {
        public static void RegisterAuth()
        {
            // To let users of this site log in using their accounts from
            // other sites such as Microsoft, Facebook, and Twitter,
            // you must update this site. For more information visit
            // http://go.microsoft.com/fwlink/?LinkID=252166

            OAuthWebSecurity.RegisterMicrosoftClient(
                clientId: "00000000400EF579",
                clientSecret: "6KQc3wk1Gbapkqt5taQTnu5kghaX5yz0");

            OAuthWebSecurity.RegisterTwitterClient(
                consumerKey: "DkHHXTnfqeeVs36LsEDznQ",
                consumerSecret: "FLM48v3AnwhyRWlJd82x9asLrgFUYKhYkcnzYiEBCg");

            OAuthWebSecurity.RegisterFacebookClient(
                appId: "234957339982566",
                appSecret: "a68e8c9fc57dec9283dde2c3f4f2d20e");
```

```
            OAuthWebSecurity.RegisterGoogleClient();
        }
    }
}
```

■ **Caution** The keys shown in Listing 9-7 can be used in your application, but keep in mind they were created for the sole purpose of demonstrating the OAuth configuration in this book. Please don't use them for any purpose other than testing your application.

Now build and run the application, and you should see your login screen, similar to the one shown in Figure 9-10.

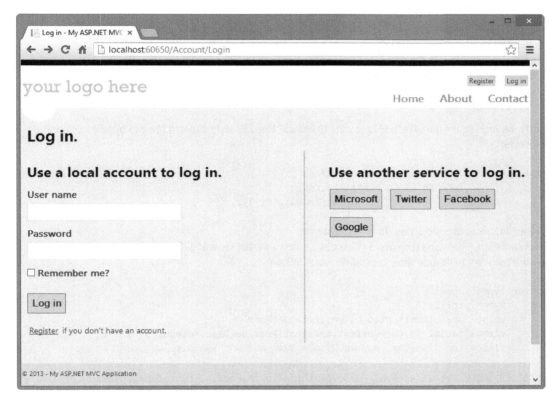

Figure 9-10. *Login page after enabling and configuring external sources*

CUSTOMIZING THE EXTERNAL LOGIN BUTTONS

You can customize the look and feel of the login buttons to make them look nicer. For example, using CSS to customize the buttons can be a simple task using the many available (and mostly free) styles found on the Internet.

One CSS style that I've found to be very simple to use and also good looking is the set of 42 Zocial CSS social buttons (from Sam Collins, at `http://zocial.smcllns.com/`). To use these buttons, all you need to do is follow these steps:

1. Download the Zocial CSS social buttons CSS style sheet and images from GitHub at `https://github.com/samcollins/css-social-buttons/`.

2. The download file is a compressed Zip file. Uncompress the file to a temporary folder in your computer.

3. The temporary folder includes a subfolder called `css`. Add the `zocial.css` style sheet file from the `css` subfolder to the `Content` folder in the application (either drag and drop the `zocial.css` file to the `Content` folder of the application in Visual Studio or right-click the `Content` folder in Visual Studio and select Add ➤ Existing Item and then browse for the `zocial.css` file).

4. Modify the `App_Start/BundleConfig.cs` file to include the CSS style sheet in the `css` bundle as follows:

```
bundles.Add(new StyleBundle("~/Content/css")
            .Include("~/Content/site.css,
                      "~/Content/zocial.css"));
```

5. Tell the buttons to use the styles. To do so, open the `Views/Account/_ExternalLoginsListPartial.cshtml` partial view and modify the `<button>` tag to include the `class` attribute as follows:

```
<button type="submit"
        name="provider"
        value="@p.AuthenticationClient.ProviderName"
        class="zocial @p.AuthenticationClient.ProviderName.ToLower()"
        title="Log in using your @p.DisplayName account">@p.DisplayName</button>
```

6. Repeat step 5 in the `Views/Account/_RemoveExternalLoginsPartial.cshtml` partial view.

7. Save all the files, rebuild the solution, and run the application. In the login page, you should see the new login buttons, as shown next.

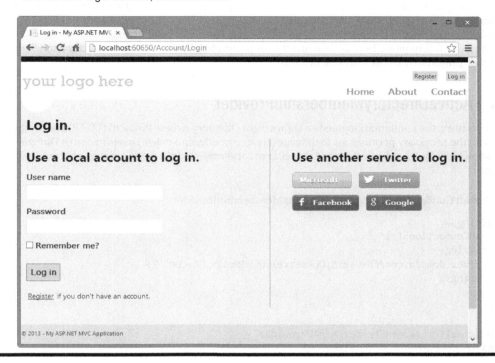

Implementing Membership and Roles

The ASP.NET Membership System is a feature included in ASP.NET that provides secure credential storage for application users. It also provides an API that simplifies the task of validating user credentials when used with Forms Authentication.

Membership providers abstract the underlying store used to maintain user credentials. ASP.NET includes two membership providers, ActiveDirectoryMembershipProvider and SqlMembershipProvider. Additionally, you can develop your own membership provider by implementing the MembershipProvider abstract class.

In addition to ActiveDirectoryMembershipProvider and SqlMembershipProvider, there is a simpler membership system in ASP.NET. This system is SimpleMembership, which was introduced in Chapter 3, where we created the database tables that handle users authenticated locally (with username and password) and externally (with services such as Facebook and Twitter).

Configuring ASP.NET Membership and Roles

To configure ASP.NET Membership, you first need to define where to store the user profiles. In our HaveYouSeenMe sample application, this happens in a LocalDB database. Because we are using SimpleMembership, users are stored in the UserProfile and webpages_Membership tables, or the webpages_OAuthMembership table for externally authenticated users. Roles are stored in the webpages_Roles table.

If the users will be stored in Active Directory, then you need ActiveDirectoryMembershipProvider. If users will be stored in a SQL Server database, then you need SqlMembershipProvider or SimpleMembership. If users will be stored in a different system (e.g., a NoSQL database such as MongoDB), you will need to create a custom membership provider implementing the MembershipProvider class.

Additionally, to use either of the membership providers described, you need to remove the configuration for SimpleMembership. This is required because the membership providers based on Active Directory and SQL Server are different, and the application can use only one of them.

Configuring ActiveDirectoryMembershipProvider

To use Active Directory, the configuration needs a Lightweight Directory Access Protocol (LDAP) connection and a user account with the necessary permissions to manage (create, modify, and delete) users in Active Directory. The code in Listing 9-8 shows a default configuration for ActiveDirectoryMembershipProvider in the Web.config file of the application.

Listing 9-8. Default Configuration for ActiveDirectoryMembershipProvider

```
<connectionStrings>
  <add name="ADConnectionString"
  connectionString=
    "LDAP://server.domain.com/CN=Users,DC=server,DC=domain,DC=com" />
</connectionStrings>

<system.web>
 ...
 <membership defaultProvider="MembershipADProvider">
  <providers>
    <add
      name="MembershipADProvider"
      type="System.Web.Security.ActiveDirectoryMembershipProvider, System.Web,
            Version=2.0.0.0, Culture=neutral, PublicKeyToken=b03f5f7f11d50a3a"
                connectionStringName="ADConnectionString"
                connectionUsername="<domainName>\administrator"
                connectionPassword="password"/>
   </providers>
 </membership>
 ...
</system.web>
```

The LDAP connection string to the Active Directory user store is in the following format:

LDAP://*server/userdn*

where:

- server is the name (or IP address) of the server that is hosting the directory.

- userdn is the distinguished name (DN) of the Active Directory user store. This consists of /CN=Users, which is the user store container name, followed by the partition, which is derived from the fully qualified domain name.

Configuring SqlMembershipProvider

Before you can use SqlMembershipProvider, you need to configure the SQL Server database that will store the user accounts. To create the supporting database, tables, and stored procedures, use the following steps:

1. Open the Developer Command Prompt for Visual Studio 2012. Based on your operating system use the following instructions:

    *   In Windows 7, go to Start ➤ All Programs ➤ Microsoft Visual Studio 2012 ➤ Visual Studio Tools ➤ Developer Command Prompt for VS 2012.

    *   In Windows 8, press Windows Key+F (or just Windows Key) to open the search box. Type **Developer Command Prompt** and select "Apps."

2. Run the following command:

    ```
    aspnet_regsql.exe -E -S localhost -A m
    ```

where:

*   -E indicates to authenticate using the Windows credentials of the currently logged-in user.

*   -S (server) indicates the name of the server where the database will be installed or is already installed.

*   -A m indicates to add membership support. This creates the tables and stored procedures required by the membership provider.

■ **Note**   The aspnet_regsql.exe tool is also used to install database elements for other ASP.NET features, such as Role Management, Profile, Web Parts Personalization, and Web Events. Other command-line arguments perform database operations for these other features. You can use aspnet_regsql.exe without any command-line arguments to use a wizard that allows you to specify connection information for your SQL Server database and install or remove the database elements for all of the supported features.

In the Web.config file, you need to add the configuration in Listing 9-9. Note that you need a connection string for the target database (where the tables and stored procedures were created).

Listing 9-9. Configuration of SqlMembershipProvider in Web.config

```
<connectionStrings>
  <add name="MySqlConnection" connectionString="Data Source=MySqlServer;Initial
Catalog=aspnetdb;Integrated Security=SSPI;" />
</connectionStrings>
<system.web>
...
  <membership defaultProvider="SqlProvider" userIsOnlineTimeWindow="15">
    <providers>
      <clear />
      <add
        name="SqlProvider"
        type="System.Web.Security.SqlMembershipProvider"
        connectionStringName="MySqlConnection"
```

```
            applicationName="MyApplication"
            enablePasswordRetrieval="false"
            enablePasswordReset="true"
            requiresQuestionAndAnswer="true"
            requiresUniqueEmail="true"
            passwordFormat="Hashed" />
        </providers>
    </membership>
```

The properties to configure `SqlMembership` are as follows:

- `applicationName`: Specifies the unique identifier for the web application.

- `enablePasswordRetrieval`: Defines whether passwords can be retrieved by users.

- `enablePasswordReset`: Defines whether users can reset their passwords.

- `requiresQuestionAndAnswer`: Indicates whether the provider is configured to require the user to answer a password question for password reset and retrieval.

- `requiresUniqueEmail`: Defines whether user account e-mail addresses must be unique.

- `passwordFormat`: Can be either "Hashed," "Encrypted", or "Clear." Clear passwords are stored in plain text. This improves the performance of password storage and retrieval, but it is less secure because passwords are easy to read if your data source is compromised. Encrypted passwords are encrypted when stored and can be decrypted for password comparison or password retrieval. This requires additional processing for password storage and retrieval, but it is more secure because passwords are not easy to determine if the data source is compromised. Hashed passwords are hashed using a one-way hash algorithm and a randomly generated salt value when stored in the database. When a password is validated, it is hashed with the salt value in the database for verification. Hashed passwords cannot be retrieved.

You can add additional properties to enforce the strength of passwords, such as `MaxInvalidPasswordAttempts`, `MinRequiredNonAlphanumericCharacters`, `MinRequiredPasswordLength`, and `PasswordAttemptWindow`.

Configuring SimpleMembership

`SimpleMembership` was introduced with ASP.NET Web Pages and WebMatrix to simplify the task of authenticating users. The idea behind it is to use a minimalistic schema that can be easily customized to fit the needs of any application. With `SimpleMembership`, developers overcome the issues of the full Membership System, such as being limited to SQL Server or Active Directory, the rigid schema, and the extreme difficulty of integrating with external sources (e.g., OAuth and OpenID).

To use `SimpleMembership`, all you need is a connection string pointing to the database that will store the user accounts. As discussed in Chapter 3, the configuration of `SimpleMembership` happens automatically with the first request to the `AccountController` class. Chapter 3 also pointed out that the `AccountController` class is decorated with the `[InitializeSimpleMembership]` attribute. Under the hood, the `[InitializeSimpleMembership]` attribute is calling the following command:

```
WebSecurity.InitializeDatabaseConnection("DefaultConnection", "UserProfile", "UserId",
"UserName", autoCreateTables: true);
```

You can find this code can in the `Filters/InitializeSimpleMembershipAttribute.cs` file, which implements the `[InitializeSimpleMembership]` attribute.

The InitializeDatabaseConnection() method instructs the web application to use the database configured in the DefaultConnection connection string defined in the Web.config file. In our HaveYouSeenMe sample application, the connection string points to the LocalDB database we are using. The second and third parameters in the InitializeDatabaseConnection() call are the table and primary key column where user accounts will be stored. The fourth parameter is the column in the table that stores the username that identifies each user account. The fifth and final parameter defines whether the SimpleMembership tables will be created if they are absent in the database.

Using the ASP.NET SimpleMembership API

ASP.NET SimpleMembership includes an API that can be used to programmatically execute operations on user accounts, such as creating or deleting accounts. These operations are encapsulated in methods located in the WebSecurity class in the WebMatrix.WebData namespace.

Visual Studio has already created the code that handles common operations such as validating user credentials and changing passwords in the AccountController class. Remember that the Internet Application project template we used for our HaveYouSeenMe sample application implements SimpleMembership by default. This is why the action methods in the AccountController class use the methods in the WebSecurity class to handle all these operations.

The methods that handle the most common tasks for user accounts using SimpleMembership are listed and described in Table 9-1. You can find more information about the WebSecurity class at http://bit.ly/WebSecurityClass.

Table 9-1. *Common Methods in the ASP.NET SimpleMembership API*

Method	Parameters	Notes
CreateUserAndAccount()	string userName string password Object propertyValues bool requireConfirmationToken	Creates a new user. The propertyValues parameter is a dictionary of additional properties to fill for the user account (for example, first and last names). The requireConfirmationToken parameter indicates if the user account must be confirmed. If set to true, the user account must be confirmed. The default is false.
ChangePassword()	string userName string currentPassword string newPassword	Changes the password for the specified user.
Login()	string userName string password bool persistsCookie	Validates a user's credentials. Returns true if the credentials are valid, and returns false if they are not. If they are valid, an authentication cookie is created and the user logs in. If persistCookie is true, then the cookie will be saved even if the browser is closed.
Logout()		Logs out the user from the application.
UserExists()	string userName	Returns true if the user exists in the database.

(continued)

Table 9-1. (*continued*)

Method	Parameters	Notes
GeneratePasswordResetToken()	string userName int tokenExpirationInMinutesFromNow	Generates a password reset token that can be sent to a user via e-mail.
ResetPassword()	string passwordResetToken string newPassword	Changes the password for the user with the specific reset token.
InitializeDatabaseConnection()	string connectionStringName string userTableName string userIdColumn string userNameColumn bool autoCreateTables	Initializes SimpleMembership by connecting to a database specified in the connectionStringName parameter. The user accounts table is defined in the userTableName parameter. The userIdColumn and userNameColumn parameters indicate the unique id column in the table and username column. If the tables are not present in the database but the autoCreateTables parameter is set to true, then the tables will be created.

To validate user credentials using SimpleMembership, you use the Login() method in the WebSecurity class, as shown in Listing 9-10. The Login() method takes three parameters: the username, the password, and a Boolean parameter that defines the behavior of the authentication cookie.

Listing 9-10. Validating User Credentials Using ASP.NET SimpleMembership

```
[HttpPost]
[AllowAnonymous]
[ValidateAntiForgeryToken]
public ActionResult Login(LoginModel model, string returnUrl)
{
    if (ModelState.IsValid &&
                WebSecurity.Login(model.UserName,
                                  model.Password,
                                  persistCookie: model.RememberMe))
    {
        return RedirectToLocal(returnUrl);
    }

    // If we got this far, something failed, redisplay form
    ModelState.AddModelError("", "The user name or password provided is incorrect.");
    return View(model);
}
```

Using the ASP.NET Membership API

ASP.NET membership has a more complex and rigid schema than SimpleMembership. Once configured, you can use the Membership API to manage user accounts (for example, create and delete accounts, assign accounts to roles, etc.). The ASP.NET Membership API is defined by the methods in the Membership class in the System.Web.Security namespace. Because the default membership provider in the Internet Application template is now SimpleMembership, Visual Studio doesn't generate any code that implements this API.

As usual, you would implement the user functionality in action methods from a controller. The code is somewhat similar to the code implemented with SimpleMembership; the method names and parameters are a little different, as you will see in a moment.

Table 9-2 lists and describes the most commonly used methods in the Membership class. You can find more information about the Membership class at http://bit.ly/MembershipClass.

Table 9-2. *Common Methods in the ASP.NET Membership class*

Method	Parameters	Notes
CreateUser()	string username string password string email string passwordQuestion string passwordAnswer bool IsApproved object providerUserKey out MembershipCreateStatus status	Creates a new user.
DeleteUser()	string username bool removeAllRelatedData	Removes a user identified by the supplied username. Returns true if the user was deleted or false if the user was not found.
FindUsersByName()	string usernameToMatch int pageIndex int pageSize	Returns a collection of users where the string parameter passed matches part of the username. Wildcard support depends on how each data store handles characters such as "*," "%," and "_."
FindUsersByEmail()	string emailToMatch int pageIndex int pageSize out int totalRecords	Returns a collection of users whose e-mail address matches any part of the string parameter passed. Wildcard support depends on how each data store handles characters such as "*," "%," and "_."
GeneratePassword()	int length int numberOfNonAlpha NumericCharacters	Returns a password of the specified length that contains the specified number of nonalphanumeric characters.
GetAllUsers()	int pageIndex int pageSize out int totalRecords	Returns a subset of users from the collection of all users. The subset is based on the pageIndex and pageSize methods.

(continued)

163

Table 9-2. *(continued)*

Method	Parameters	Notes
GetNumberOfUsersOnline()	None	Returns a count of all the users who are currently online. The Active Directory provider does not implement this functionality.
GetUserNameByEmail()	string email	Return a member's username.
UpdateUser()	MembershipUser user	Updates a member's properties (for example, an e-mail address).
ValidateUser()	string username string password	Validates a user's credentials. Returns true if the credentials are valid and false if they are not. With Active Directory, regardless of the configured connection credentials, the provider connects to the directory with the username and password parameters as the connection credentials.

Following is the typical process that occurs when a user logs in to the application:

1. In the login page, the user enters his or her username and password.

2. The login page posts the entered credentials to the server.

3. The server validates the credentials against the user account database.

4. If a match is found, a cookie with the security ticket is issued; if no match is found, an error is returned to the user.

Using the ASP.NET Membership API, the code is a bit different. You use the ValidateUser() method in the Membership class. The ValidateUser() method takes two parameters, the username and password, and returns a Boolean value indicating whether the validation was successful or not. If the validation was successful, the previous authentication cookie is removed (if there was any) and a new authentication cookie is created using the SetAuthCookie() method in the FormsAuthentication class. The code shown in Listing 9-11 implements the ASP.NET Membership API to validate the user credentials.

Listing 9-11. *Validating User Credentials Using the ASP.NET Membership API*

```
[HttpPost]
[AllowAnonymous]
[ValidateAntiForgeryToken]
protected ActionResult Login(LoginModel model, string returnUrl)
{
   if (ModelState.IsValid && Membership.ValidateUser(model.UserName, model.Password))
   {
      Response.Cookies.Remove(FormsAuthentication.FormsCookieName);
      FormsAuthentication.SetAuthCookie(model.UserName, model.RememberMe);
      return RedirectToLocal(returnUrl);
   }
```

```
        // If we got this far, something failed, redisplay form
        ModelState.AddModelError("", "The user name or password provided is incorrect.");
        return View(model);
    }
```

To create users, you use the `CreateUser()` method. The method returns an object of type `MembershipUser`. For example:

```
MembershipUser u = Membership.CreateUser(model.UserName, model.Password, model.Email);
u.FirstName = model.FirstName;
u.LastName = modelLastName;
Membership.UpdateUser(u);
```

If you are using the `SimpleMembership` API, the `WebSecurity` class has a `CreateUserAndAccount()` method that allows you to create a new user and account as follows:

```
WebSecurity.CreateUserAndAccount(model.UserName, model.Password,
            new { FirstName = model.FirstName,
                  LastName = model.LastName,
                  Email = model.Email },
            false);
```

In this case, we are passing the additional properties (FirstName, LastName and Email) as an anonymous object to the `CreateUserAndAccount()` method so the database table is filled with the information.

In the case of `Membership.CreateUser()`, the method returns a `MembershipUser` object. We need to use this object to set the values in the FirstName and LastName properties. Finally, we call the `Membership.UpdateUser()` to save the values to the database.

Using Roles

Roles define groups of users. In large environments where there are many different types of users, it is easier to manage permissions for roles and then assign users to roles so that they inherit the roles' permissions. In ASP.NET, the task of managing roles is delegated to a feature called Role Manager. Role Manager includes an API that allows you to create roles, delete roles, and assign roles to and remove roles from users.

With `SimpleMembership`, the storage for roles is in the `webpages_Roles` and `webpages_UsersInRoles` tables. This is a much cleaner approach than that of the Membership System, whose complex schema also includes views and stored procedures. With `SimpleMembership`, it is also a lot easier to manage roles for users authenticated with external sources such as OAuth and OpenID.

The configuration of Role Manager is very simple. Similarly to ASP.NET Membership, the configuration of Role Manager is specified in the `Web.config` file. ASP.NET by default includes support for three different role providers:

- `SqlRoleProvider`: Roles are stored in SQL Server.

- `WindowsTokenRoleProvider`: This is a read-only provider that retrieves role information for a Windows user account based on the account's Windows security group membership. You cannot create, add to, or delete roles with this provider.

- `AuthorizationRoleStoreProvider`: This provider is used if your application uses Authorization Manager (AzMan). With AzMan, the roles are stored in an XML file, in Active Directory, or in Active Directory Application Mode (ADAM). It is typically used in an intranet or extranet scenario where Windows Authentication and Active Directory are used for authentication.

For example, to use SqlRoleProvider, you would add the following to the Web.config file:

```
<roleManager enabled="true" defaultProvider="SqlRoleManager">
  <providers>
    <add name="SqlRoleManager"
         type="System.Web.Security.SqlRoleProvider"
         connectionStringName="SqlRoleManagerConnection"
         applicationName="MyApplication" />
  </providers>
</roleManager>
```

A single SQL Server database can be used to store membership and role information for multiple applications. The connectionStringName and applicationName parameters define the database where users and roles will be stored for an application. To work correctly, the values in both parameters must be the same in the membership and Role Manager configuration. This will ensure that users in an application are not mixed with roles in another application.

Creating roles is also a simple operation. For example, use the following to create a role called Administrators:

```
Roles.CreateRole("Administrators");
```

This code works for ASP.NET Membership or SimpleMembership. Now, adding users to roles is also as simple as

```
Roles.AddUserToRole(model.UserName, "Administrators");
```

Or, to add a user to multiple roles:

```
Roles.AddUserToRoles(model.UserName, new string[] {"Administrators","Managers"});
```

Finally, to verify if a user belongs to a role (e.g., Administrators) in ASP.NET SimpleMembership:

```
if (User.IsInRole("Administrator"))
{
  ...
}
```

To test for a particular user in ASP.NET SimpleMembership, you use

```
ff (User.Identity.Name == "Joe")
{
  ...
}
```

In ASP.NET Membership, you use

```
MembershipUser u = Membership.GetUser(model.UserName);
if (u.IsInRole("Administrators"))
{
  ...
}
```

In action methods that were secured using the [Authorize] attribute, you can ask for specific users or roles; for example:

```
[Authorize(Users="Jose")]
```

Or

```
[Authorize(Roles="Administrators")]
```

The Users and Roles parameters also accept multiple users or roles, respectively. To define multiple users or roles, you separate them with commas. For example:

```
[Authorize(Users="Jose,Ewan,Ana")]
```

Or

```
[Authorize(Roles="Administrators,Managers")]
```

Securing ASP.NET MVC Applications Against External Attacks

As users begin to use a web application, it becomes susceptible to attacks. Malicious users, accidental misuses, compromised browsers, and more can expose vulnerabilities in the web application. Such vulnerabilities can be exploited, causing all kinds of problems. In the end, developers need to make sure their web applications are as secure as possible by implementing security best practices.

To help us secure our web applications, ASP.NET MVC 4 includes many features that help prevent the most common types of attacks. These attacks aim to exploit some vulnerabilities in the application such as cross-site scripting (XSS) and cross-site request forgery (CSRF).

Preventing Cross-Site Scripting

Cross-site scripting is a vulnerability in web applications that allows an attacker to inject JavaScript code in form fields whose values are not sanitized properly (or at all). These values are then either saved to the database, to be executed later when they are used in other areas of the application, or displayed immediately in the page. As defined by The Open Web Application Security Project (OWASP), these two types of attacks are classified as *stored XSS* and *reflected XSS*, respectively (see http://bit.ly/OWASP-XSS).

To help you better understand XSS, let's take a look at an example. In our HaveYouSeenMe sample application, we allow users to send messages to pet owners. At this point, if a user tries to add HTML tags to the message, the user gets an error, as shown in Figure 9-11. This is because ASP.NET verifies all input fields to prevent XSS and, by default, doesn't allow users to post any HTML tags.

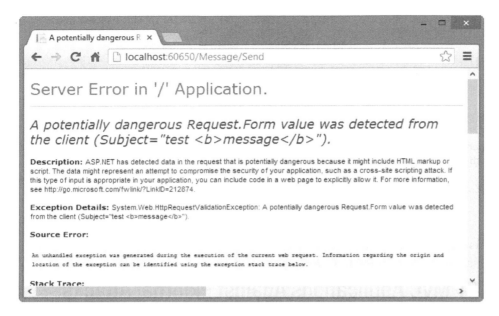

Figure 9-11. *ASP.NET default XSS prevention mechanism disallowing HTML to be posted to the server*

Now, if we really want to allow users to post HTML in the messages, we can modify the behavior by adding the [ValidateInput(false)] attribute to the Send action method in the MessageController class, as shown in Listing 9-12. The problem with this approach is that it will disable all XSS validation for all fields in the model.

Listing 9-12. Disabling All XSS Validation in the Send Action Method

```
[HttpPost]
[ValidateInput(false)]
public ActionResult Send(MessageModel model)
{
    if (ModelState.IsValid)
    {
        //Send message
        ViewBag.IsSent = true;
        return View(model);
    }

    ModelState.AddModelError("", "One or more errors were found");
    return View(model);
}
```

A better approach is to allow HTML tags only in specific fields of our choosing. In this example, the only field in which we will allow HTML tags is the Message field. To achieve this, we need to remove the [ValidationInput(false)] attribute from the action method and add the [AllowHtml] attribute to the field in the MessageModel view model, as shown in Listing 9-13. I have modified the Send view to show the values posted after the user has sent the message (see Listing 9-14). When a user sends a message, you now get the result shown in Figure 9-12.

Listing 9-13. Allowing HTML Tags in the Message Field from the MessageModel View Model

```
public class MessageModel
{
    [Required(ErrorMessage="Please type your name")]
    [StringLength(150, ErrorMessage="You can only add up to 150 characters")]
    [FullName(ErrorMessage="Please type your full name")]
    public string From { get; set; }

    [Required(ErrorMessage="Please type your email address")]
    [StringLength(150, ErrorMessage = "You can only add up to 150 characters")]
    [EmailAddress(ErrorMessage="We don't recognize this as a valid email address")]
    public string Email { get; set; }

    [StringLength(150, ErrorMessage = "You can only add up to 150 characters")]
    public string Subject { get; set; }

    [Required(ErrorMessage="Please type your message")]
    [StringLength(1500, ErrorMessage = "You can only add up to 1500 characters")]
    [AllowHtml]
    public string Message { get; set; }
}
```

Listing 9-14. Modified Send View That Displays the Posted Values

```
@model HaveYouSeenMe.Models.MessageModel

@{
    ViewBag.Title = "Send";
}

<h2>Send</h2>
@if (ViewBag.IsSent) {
        <fieldset>
            <div class="editor-label">
                @Html.LabelFor(model => model.From)
            </div>
            <div class="editor-field">
                @Model.From
            </div>

            <div class="editor-label">
                @Html.LabelFor(model => model.Email)
            </div>
            <div class="editor-field">
                @Model.Email
            </div>

            <div class="editor-label">
                @Html.LabelFor(model => model.Subject)
            </div>
```

```
            <div class="editor-field">
                @Model.Subject
            </div>

            <div class="editor-label">
                @Html.LabelFor(model => model.Message)
            </div>
            <div class="editor-field">
                @Model.Message
            </div>

            <h2>
                Message sent...
            </h2>
        </fieldset>

}
else{
    using (Html.BeginForm()) {
        @Html.ValidationSummary(true)

        <fieldset>
            <legend>MessageModel</legend>

            <div class="editor-label">
                @Html.LabelFor(model => model.From)
            </div>
            <div class="editor-field">
                @Html.EditorFor(model => model.From)
                @Html.ValidationMessageFor(model => model.From)
            </div>

            <div class="editor-label">
                @Html.LabelFor(model => model.Email)
            </div>
            <div class="editor-field">
                @Html.EditorFor(model => model.Email)
                @Html.ValidationMessageFor(model => model.Email)
            </div>

            <div class="editor-label">
                @Html.LabelFor(model => model.Subject)
            </div>
            <div class="editor-field">
                @Html.EditorFor(model => model.Subject)
                @Html.ValidationMessageFor(model => model.Subject)
            </div>

            <div class="editor-label">
                @Html.LabelFor(model => model.Message)
            </div>
```

```
            <div class="editor-field">
                @Html.EditorFor(model => model.Message)
                @Html.ValidationMessageFor(model => model.Message)
            </div>

            <p>
                <input type="submit" value="Create" />
            </p>
        </fieldset>
    }
}
<div>
    @Html.ActionLink("Back to List", "Index")
</div>

@section Scripts {
    @Scripts.Render("~/bundles/jqueryval")
}
```

Send

From
Jose Guay

Email
some@email.com

Subject
test

Message
test message

Message sent...
Back to List

Figure 9-12. *Form that accepts HTML tags in the Message field*

Note in Figure 9-12 that the HTML tags are displayed as they were entered. This is because Razor automatically encodes all output in the view by adding, for example, @Model.Message to output the value in the Message field. To see the message correctly, we would have to change the view to display the HTML tags as HTML and not as text:

```
@Html.Raw(Model.Message)
```

After the change, the message displays as shown in Figure 9-13, with the HTML tags interpreted correctly in the browser.

Send
From
Jose Guay
Email
jose@somewhere.com
Subject
test
Message
test message
Message sent...
Back to List

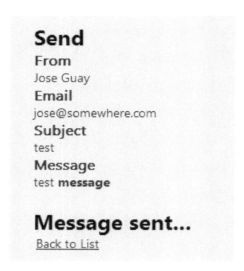

Figure 9-13. *Send view displaying HTML tags as HTML and not as text*

The application has now opened one door to let users enter HTML tags, including `<script>` tags. If, for example, the user enters `<script type="text/javascript">alert("Evil Script");</script>`, the result is as shown in Figure 9-14.

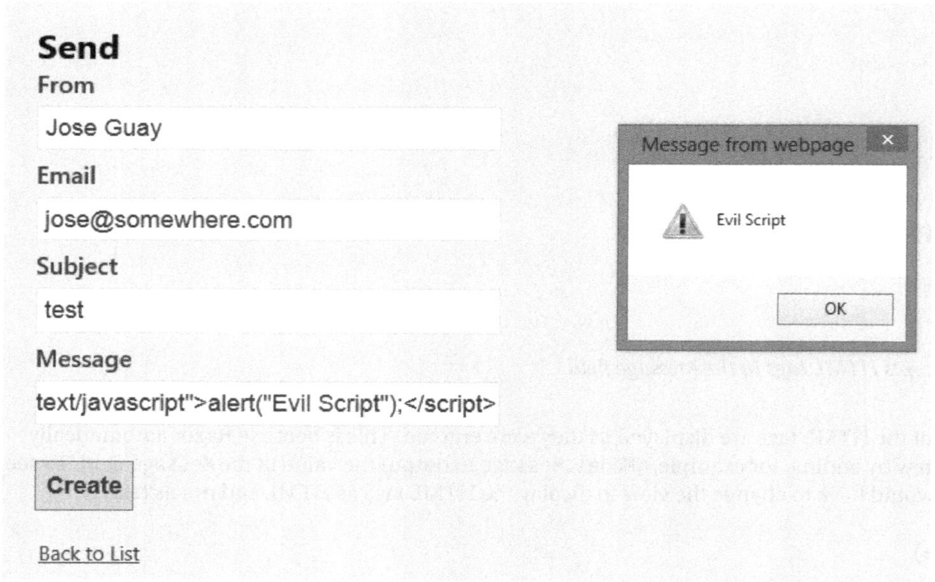
Send
From
Jose Guay
Email
jose@somewhere.com
Subject
test
Message
text/javascript">alert("Evil Script");</script>
Create
Back to List
Message from webpage
Evil Script
OK

Figure 9-14. *JavaScript injected in the Message field using Internet Explorer*

WebKit-based browsers such as Google Chrome and Apple Safari have an integrated XSS validation module, called XSS Auditor, that can prevent execution of <script> tags. The Chromium Blog article "Security in Depth: New Security Features" (found at http://bit.ly/ChromiumBlog) describes the behavior of XSS Auditor (at the time known as XSS filter) as follows:

> The XSS filter is similar to those found in Internet Explorer 8 and NoScript. Instead of being layered on top of the browser like those filters, our XSS filter is integrated into WebKit, which Google Chrome uses to render webpages. Integrating the XSS filter into the rendering engine has two benefits: (1) the filter can catch scripts right before they are executed, making it easier to detect some tricky attack variations, and (2) the filter can be used by every WebKit-based browser, including Safari and Epiphany.

In the same blog article, the Google Chrome team also acknowledges that there are some ways to bypass the XSS filter (XSS Auditor). However, the team is always improving this technology, so over time these scenarios should be avoided by default.

For example, in Google Chrome, the message entered previously produces an error in the developer tools console, as shown in Figure 9-15.

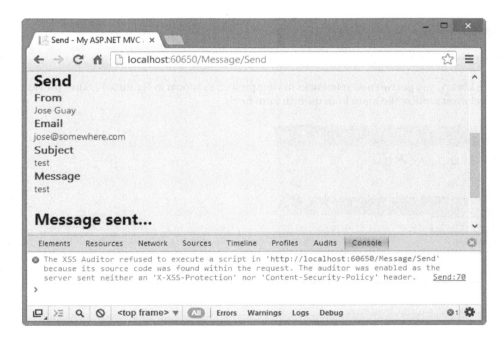

Figure 9-15. *XSS Auditor module in Google Chrome*

Using the AntiXSS Library

One of the best solutions to prevent XSS attacks is to use the AntiXSS library from Microsoft. It is part of the Microsoft Web Protection Library (WPL) hosted at CodePlex (http://wpl.codeplex.com/). The AntiXSS library provides a set of encoding functions for user input, including HTML, HTML attributes, XML, CSS, and JavaScript. You can download it via NuGet, as shown in Figure 9-16. (See Chapter 6 for further information about using NuGet.)

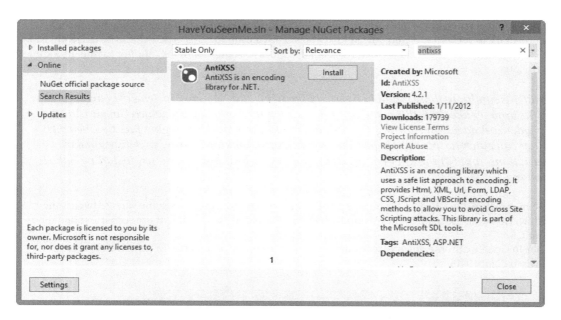

Figure 9-16. *NuGet package library download of AntiXSS library*

After you install the AntiXSS library, you get two new references in your project, as shown in Figure 9-17. They provide the encoding functions to help you sanitize the input from users in form fields.

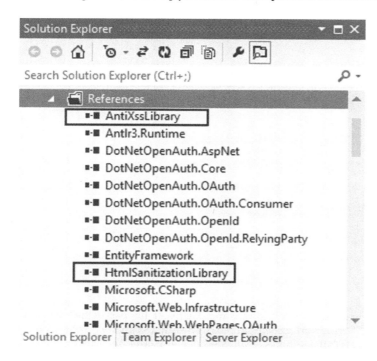

Figure 9-17. *References added by the AntiXSS library*

To help clean the input, we can use the sanitization library to validate whatever input we get in the Message field. This is done in the server prior to sending the message. The sanitization library is accessed by using the Sanitizer class. For example, use the Sanitizer.GetSafeHtmlFragment() method in the Send(MessageModel model) action method from the MessageController class as follows:

```
model.Message = Sanitizer.GetSafeHtmlFragment(model.Message);
```

After building the application, we get the result in Chrome shown in Figure 9-18. Notice that the XSS Auditor module no longer shows up in the developer tools console at the bottom of the browser window. This is because the action method took care of cleaning the input before it got to the browser. Also, if you run the code in Internet Explorer, you won't get the alert dialog box shown earlier in Figure 9-18 to simulate a rogue JavaScript code injected by the user.

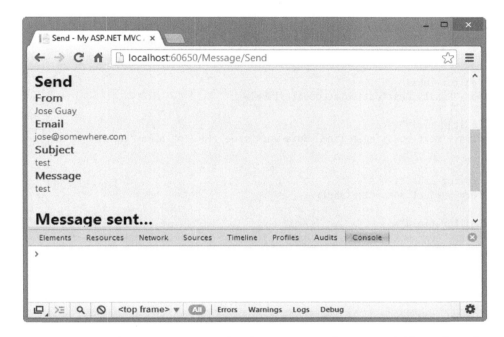

Figure 9-18. *Result in Google Chrome after the user input in the Message field was cleaned*

Preventing Cross-Site Request Forgery

Cross-site request forgery (CSRF; also known as XSRF) is a different type of XSS attack in which a logged-in user (someone who has been authenticated and for whom a security cookie/token has been issued) is tricked into going to a malicious web site where their credentials are used to perform an unauthorized action.

The Open Web Application Security Project (OWASP) defines CSRF as follows (http://bit.ly/OWASP-CSRF):

Cross-Site Request Forgery (CSRF) is an attack that tricks the victim into loading a page that contains a malicious request. It is malicious in the sense that it inherits the identity and privileges of the victim to perform an undesired function on the victim's behalf, like change the victim's e-mail address, home address, or password, or purchase something. CSRF attacks generally target functions that cause a state change on the server but can also be used to access sensitive data.

How does it work, exactly? Imagine the scenario where a user logs in to her bank's online system and accesses a page where she can transfer money from one account to another. This is a very typical scenario; however, suppose for the sake of this example that the bank's web developers were not careful to take extra steps to prevent CSRF attacks. The code in Listing 9-15 shows a portion of the transfer page.

Listing 9-15. Portion of the Transfer Page Showing the <form> Tag

```
<form action="/Operation/Transfer" method="post">
<fieldset>
            <legend>MessageModel</legend>

            <div class="editor-label">
                <label for="From">Source account:</label>
            </div>
            <div class="editor-field">
                <input class="text-box single-line" data-val="true" id="From" name="From"
type="text" value="" />
            </div>
            <div class="editor-label">
                <label for="Email">Destination account:</label>
            </div>
            <div class="editor-field">
                <input class="text-box single-line" data-val="true" id="To" name="To"
type="text" value="" />
            </div>
            <div class="editor-label">
                <label for="Subject">Amount</label>
            </div>
            <div class="editor-field">
                <input class="text-box single-line" data-val="true" id="Amount" name="Amount"
type="text" value="" />
            </div>
            <p>
                <input type="submit" value="Transfer the money" />
            </p>
        </fieldset>
</form>
```

An attacker can see here (the same as you) all the pieces needed to make a request to transfer money from one account to another. All the input fields are clearly identified, as are the target URL and the HTTP method to use.

After the user has logged in to the bank system, she turns her attention to an e-mail she just received in her e-mail client. The e-mail contains a link, which the user just trusts she can click. This is no ordinary link, though; the attacker has prepared it, with all the information needed to perform a money transfer. When the user clicks the link, it opens a page in a new tab of the user's browser. The page may even look like the bank's application. This page makes a request to transfer money from the user's account to the attacker's account by using the user's credentials that were shared between browser tabs, and the transfer is successful.

To prevent this type of attack, ASP.NET MVC 4 includes the [ValidateAntiForgeryToken] attribute. This attribute is added to the action method so that a security token is saved to a cookie. Additionally, you need to modify the view to include an anti-forgery token field with the @Html.AntiForgeryToken() helper method. The helper method creates a hidden field with the same token saved in the cookie. When the form is submitted, ASP.NET MVC compares the value in the hidden field to the value in the cookie, and the request is only accepted if both match.

As an example in the context of our HaveYouSeenMe sample application, I have modified the Send action method from Listing 9-12 to include the anti-forgery token, as shown in Listing 9-19. Also, the Send view includes the HTML helper method to include the anti-forgery token field, as shown in Listing 9-17. If, for example, the token is not sent with the request, then ASP.NET generates an error, as shown in Figure 9-16.

Listing 9-16. Send Action Method with Anti-Forgery Token

```
[HttpPost]
[ValidateAntiForgeryToken]
public ActionResult Send(MessageModel model)
{
    if (ModelState.IsValid)
    {
        //Send message
        model.Message = Sanitizer.GetSafeHtmlFragment(model.Message);
        ViewBag.IsSent = true;
        return View(model);
    }

    ModelState.AddModelError("", "One or more errors were found");
    return View(model);
}
```

Listing 9-17. Send View with the Anti-Forgery Token Field

```
@model HaveYouSeenMe.Models.MessageModel

@{
    ViewBag.Title = "Send";
}

<h2>Send</h2>
@if (ViewBag.IsSent) {
        <fieldset>
            <div class="editor-label">
                @Html.LabelFor(model => model.From)
            </div>
            <div class="editor-field">
                @Model.From
            </div>

            <div class="editor-label">
                @Html.LabelFor(model => model.Email)
            </div>
            <div class="editor-field">
                @Model.Email
            </div>

            <div class="editor-label">
                @Html.LabelFor(model => model.Subject)
            </div>
```

```
            <div class="editor-field">
                @Model.Subject
            </div>

            <div class="editor-label">
                @Html.LabelFor(model => model.Message)
            </div>
            <div class="editor-field">
                @Html.Raw(Model.Message)
            </div>

            <h2>
                Message sent...
            </h2>
        </fieldset>

}
else{
    using (Html.BeginForm()) {
        @Html.AntiForgeryToken()
        @Html.ValidationSummary(true)

        <fieldset>
            <legend>MessageModel</legend>

            <div class="editor-label">
                @Html.LabelFor(model => model.From)
            </div>
            <div class="editor-field">
                @Html.EditorFor(model => model.From)
                @Html.ValidationMessageFor(model => model.From)
            </div>

            <div class="editor-label">
                @Html.LabelFor(model => model.Email)
            </div>
            <div class="editor-field">
                @Html.EditorFor(model => model.Email)
                @Html.ValidationMessageFor(model => model.Email)
            </div>

            <div class="editor-label">
                @Html.LabelFor(model => model.Subject)
            </div>
            <div class="editor-field">
                @Html.EditorFor(model => model.Subject)
                @Html.ValidationMessageFor(model => model.Subject)
            </div>

            <div class="editor-label">
                @Html.LabelFor(model => model.Message)
            </div>
```

```
            <div class="editor-field">
                @Html.EditorFor(model => model.Message)
                @Html.ValidationMessageFor(model => model.Message)
            </div>

            <p>
                <input type="submit" value="Create" />
            </p>
        </fieldset>
    }
}
<div>
    @Html.ActionLink("Back to List", "Index")
</div>

@section Scripts {
    @Scripts.Render("~/bundles/jqueryval")
}
```

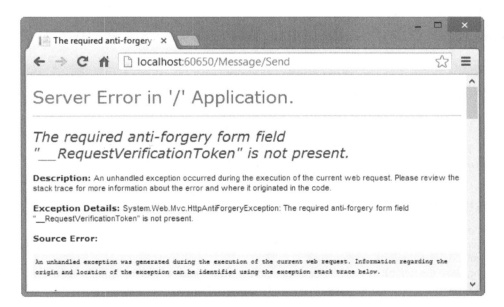

Figure 9-19. *Exception thrown when the anti-forgery token is not present in the view*

Additionally, you should always validate that HTTP Post requests have originated from within the application and not from any other source. This is to ensure that the request was properly built using all the security mechanisms that our application requires. For example, it would be very difficult for a third-party web site to post information and have a valid anti-forgery token in the HTML form since the token was not generated by our application.

Preventing Other Types of Attacks

XSS and CSRF attacks are just a few of the myriad types of attacks that are launched against web sites. For example, attackers can also steal cookies, manipulate forms to include additional fields the web site is not expecting, or even redirect users to a different, nefarious web site. This section looks at how to prevent these types of attacks. Covering all the possible types of attacks is beyond the scope of this book.

Preventing Cookie-Stealing Attacks

While cookies are not normally accessed through JavaScript, by default, they can be. However, an XSS vulnerability exists (because developers didn't secure the application properly), a malicious user can gain access to cookies, and then use the information stored in them to perform actions in the name of another user who is the real owner of the cookies. Making a simple modification to how cookies are treated can make a big difference in preventing them from being stolen. Basically, you need to configure the cookie to be accessible only in HTTP calls, and not in scripts. You do this by setting the cookie's `HttpOnly` property to `true` when you first create the cookie in your action method code (which is server-side code). You should do this whenever you create cookies, regardless of the HTTP method (`GET` or `POST`) used in the request. For example:

```
Request.Cookies["SomeCookie"].HttpOnly = true;
```

If you want to configure this setting for the entire web site, add the following line to the `Web.config` file:

```
<system.web>
...
<httpCookies httpOnlyCookies="true" requireSSL="true" />
...
</system.web>
```

To fully protect your cookies, you should also ensure that they are transferred from the server to the client, and vice versa, using SSL. To do so, set the `requireSSL` property to `true` as shown in the previous example.

Preventing Over-Posting Attacks

A malicious user can alter a form in a page (or can simulate a form with network tools) to include more fields that it was originally intended. When this happens in a strongly typed view, there is the possibility to modify values of objects represented by the view model. This is known as over-posting.

Over-posting happens because the default model binder doesn't know which fields you actually included in the form and will try to map all the values in the request to an object. Imagine that you have a view to display product information, and that the view model looks like the one shown in Listing 9-18.

Listing 9-18. View Model for a Product

```
public class ProductModel {
    public int ProductID { get; private set; }
    public string ProductName { get; set; }
    public string ProductImage { get; set; }
    public bool IsActive { get; set; }
}
```

Now, the view displays the product information and accepts updates to the product name, as shown in Listing 9-19. Note that the view uses only the ProductName and ProductImage properties.

Listing 9-19. Part of the Product View That Uses a <form> to Update the Product's Name

```
using (Html.BeginForm()) {
    @Html.AntiForgeryToken()
    @Html.ValidationSummary(true)

    <fieldset>
        <legend>Product</legend>

        <div class="editor-label">
            @Html.LabelFor(model => model.ProductID)
        </div>
        <div class="editor-field">
            <span>@Model.ProductID</span>
        </div>

        <div class="editor-label">
            @Html.LabelFor(model => model.ProductName)
        </div>
        <div class="editor-field">
            @Html.EditorFor(model => model. ProductName)
            @Html.ValidationMessageFor(model => model. ProductName)
        </div>

        <div class="editor-label">
            <img src="@Model.ProductImage" />
        </div>
        <p>
            <input type="submit" value="Create" />
        </p>
    </fieldset>
}
```

Using any type of web developer tool, an attacker can use this form to add an additional field to the query string or form post data and add, for example, IsActive=false as part of the request. The default model binder will not know the difference, and the product will be deactivated once the mapping is complete and the update is processed. Although most likely the attacker will not know all the properties in your model, he can guess that it includes a property named IsActive and, after a few tries, discover that it can be exploited.

To prevent this type of attack, you can add an annotation to the ProductModel class to allow binding only on the ProductName field, as shown in Listing 9-20. You can set the annotation to *include* certain fields in the binding (a.k.a. white list) or to *exclude* certain fields from the binding (a.k.a. black list). To specify multiple fields, separate them with commas. Alternatively, as shown in Listing 9-21, you can apply the binding in the action method itself. This is useful if you need different binding schemes based on the action method that is handling the request.

Listing 9-20. Allowing Binding on Only Specific Fields of the View Model

```
[Bind(Include="ProductName")]
public class ProductModel {
    public int ProductID { get; private set; }
```

```
    public string ProductName { get; set; }
    public string ProductImage { get; set; }
    public bool IsActive { get; set; }
}
```

Listing 9-21. Allowing Binding on Specific Fields per Action Method

```
public ActionResult Update([Bind(Include="ProductName")]ProductModel model)
{
...
}
```

Preventing Open Redirection Attacks

When a user is taken to a different web site as a result of calling the Redirect() method in an action method, then we have an Open Redirection attack . The problem with this is that users might be taken to a web site that can be used to steal information from them, such as credit card numbers or passwords. The method accepts a string that is the address of the web site to which the user will be taken. In ASP.NET MVC 4 you can prevent open redirection attacks by analyzing the destination address before allowing the redirection. The System.Web.Mvc.Url helper class includes a method called IsLocalUrl(string address) that returns true if the address is within the web site and returns false if it is an external address. You use the method as follows:

```
if (IsLocalUrl(address))
{
    Redirect(address);
}
else
{
    // Open Redirection detected
}
```

The Internet Application project template that we used for our HaveYouSeenMe sample application includes a helper method in the AccountController class to identify if a redirection is to a different web site. The Login action method uses this helper method to validate whether the address in the returnUrl query string parameter is a local address (within the application) or an external address. This is shown in Listing 9-22.

Listing 9-22. RedirectToLocal Action Method

```
private ActionResult RedirectToLocal(string returnUrl)
{
    if (Url.IsLocalUrl(returnUrl))
    {
        return Redirect(returnUrl);
    }
    else
    {
        return RedirectToAction("Index", "Home");
    }
}
```

SECURING CONNECTION STRINGS IN WEB.CONFIG

Database connection strings are typically stored in the `Web.config` configuration file, which is an XML-based file that stores the information in clear text. Having connection strings that include passwords in clear text is normally not a good practice, of course, because if an attacker is able to steal the file, the attacker then has the necessary information to locate the database and the credentials to access it.

The `connectionStrings` section in the `Web.config` file looks like this:

```
<connectionStrings>
  <clear />
  <add name="DefaultConnection" connectionString="Data Source=(LocalDb)\v11.0;
Initial Catalog=aspnet-MvcApplication1-20130225235623;Integrated Security=SSPI;
AttachDBFilename=|DataDirectory|\aspnet-MvcApplication1-20130225235623.mdf"
    providerName="System.Data.SqlClient" />
  <add name="Entities".
connectionString="metadata=res://*/Models.Model1.csdl|res://*/Models.Model1.
ssdl|res://*/Models.Model1.msl;provider=System.Data.SqlClient;provider connection
string=&quot;data source=(LocalDb)\v11.0;attachdbfilename=|DataDirectory|\
aspnet-MvcApplication1-20130225235623.mdf;initial catalog=aspnet-MvcApplication1-
20130225235623;integrated security=True;MultipleActiveResultSets=True;
App=EntityFramework&quot;"
    providerName="System.Data.EntityClient" />
</connectionStrings>
```

It is possible, though, to encrypt sections of the configuration file so that connection strings are not easily accessible if someone steals the file. To perform that encryption, you can use the `aspnet_regiis.exe` utility program installed with Visual Studio. Additionally, you can programmatically encrypt the configuration file.

By default, the utility program uses the RSA algorithm and the value in the `machineKey` property of the `Web.config` file to do the encryption.

To encrypt the `connectionStrings` section in the configuration file using the `aspnet_regiis.exe` utility:

1. Open the Visual Studio tools command window with administrator permissions.

2. Execute the following command:

    ```
    aspnet_regiis.exe -pef "connectionStrings" [path to web.config file]
    ```

3. Open the `Web.config` file in a text editor. You will notice the following in the place where the connection strings were:

    ```
    <connectionStrings configProtectionProvider="RsaProtectedConfigurationProvider">
      <EncryptedData Type="http://www.w3.org/2001/04/xmlenc#Element"
        xmlns="http://www.w3.org/2001/04/xmlenc#">
        <EncryptionMethod Algorithm="http://www.w3.org/2001/04/xmlenc#tripledes-cbc" />
        <KeyInfo xmlns="http://www.w3.org/2000/09/xmldsig#">
          <EncryptedKey xmlns="http://www.w3.org/2001/04/xmlenc#">
            <EncryptionMethod Algorithm="http://www.w3.org/2001/04/xmlenc#rsa-1_5" />
            <KeyInfo xmlns="http://www.w3.org/2000/09/xmldsig#">
    ```

```
            <KeyName>Rsa Key</KeyName>
        </KeyInfo>
        <CipherData>
```

```
<CipherValue>AqHWVHPQRia6jjEOtqzMOWCezMDUf6XOhY98O55UAmy6mlPDAMDAvqa
QIVoLWOfvBX8RPdeD6Pex17R2/NqahU9APBR8GivUWbUGORWWvavROyCVRgwbJnc72Ny+
vSKOuJJf2fDTvvTy2HzcbFTeAl/6DsuCWxLGWwKJyLj471OTQP/gdsaZyb+UTJmYpslX
Az7Vjr4YL3RAuIZgrY9/U5LTiE9Q8AFuwvBNtbqN2WwmIjHBU+BLr15wBUA/c5ppPBuuymz
IaOufbev9STV3rBO+l38Jr2+LKqvoceAU6eLJIkvOse6wir+qCKWn1OvJ8HEiiA3N9a9O2up9
Tw6OnQ==</CipherValue>
        </CipherData>
    </EncryptedKey>
</KeyInfo>
<CipherData>
```

```
<CipherValue>2MpcPC+Rk/q55GDvEQ58xeONT4fLnGVaP6OBsZtOs6SgYjM87Ws83KepeJvq8MAp+
SNcDX76N61VZvqJL7RWZmdMJ7mhmh+32OIRbrvn9iL+/+wXFj6v9Hwk6UVHObHK9LTqzilsVNysx
fETZn2NdEUQx6/Yq3BS/ckhzFGy+p3Sc4YZIdQcXLbkXDboFOCZC2K5h5z8sbbhDCHF9gOr
c9HqkXIlYS1CfAwabjWP+thL32sOsghY78Ht3p+H2UHXMpGfE6jwSGK5bmDecfm5FRM2QG/
VD15uR7TXqlBMa4LD3QHz9+TRkPVHvvRJ+GOF/MOjB9my97Pe9NNK6DuvHxr8xulKOEsJdOc2m
Sg9nEwD/YJ37ixq5D7sRvl+hjGdOnkiEISTf9PJoOU3L7EHtdNSYsM5R1tt9N1oXTx3fTzkuj8Q8FNJwj
H4US9vkPVrUgT5lxOiRTfbS7iW6geMm6Ae5p6fJAR4Eavbqn6wlttTOZyAurtiDW275Bl8GUKz
NU1D4kazqYKI+YnbTITNTcYf+u4DJtvBNsVYmVxJeXEhOesolJB8itBFQDBthUn3Kpu+
mB4fIeILRiHrb5Onu32nmcdw/wgD+KKk5Mt3vkoSY+nNRHMF8W16oeOBe1+PWdytvItODZ+
inCNJJCxfqvkogIbdJMtmHOyTHasseSe+9yi214PpXxrlxaxrY2VM3XkCPpx1P1Yaudn5oT+
5BxQOs7nYT4hg/GXfluzlplqEsOjwYesCN/CMdCh3gutSbn9QJS4XnXOvpuxPy4eHbNi+/
OiSYzn56ZmfCWQryQy8ZfCfZ7fp85BQLxoR2LT6N7qWkHtT84ELjQUmIBmom7jKfEMV4XfjLBx
7DpVJupTUippPIWlVBNhzBsO4fF36JjrYzbUtdMufSiOae8yZ2QFP1HO14UG/OWNvq9Cq6qc8506j
Ra99Lmu2NY6+PHLDwCIsbXKju4DmBhNtvHQ2Iaa2ICQ3TRLzVykA1sikE8ZjctES/
QfxvjO+9Y11Dw6cn3/OOM3wWbGOSQMkL7vnQ2UAv8O4CRHBegcCVAsqoTJVxtg/hQD7GEf+l4e8+
kc8ARfdAztqmU=</CipherValue>
        </CipherData>
    </EncryptedData>
</connectionStrings>
```

And there you have it. The connection strings are now encrypted. The best part about this process is that you don't have to handle the decryption in order to use the connection strings in your application. The decryption happens automatically and is handled by ASP.NET at runtime.

Finally, if you need to change your connection strings, you can decrypt the information with the following command:

```
aspnet_regiis.exe -pdf "connectionStrings" [path to web.config file]
```

This should give you a secure starting point when handling connection strings and passwords stored in the application's configuration file.

Summary

In this chapter you have seen the different elements that you can use in your application to make it more secure and to protect your users and their information. You can take advantage of the default security features ASP.NET MVC 4 provides to easily prevent malicious users from exploiting vulnerabilities present in every web application.

You also learned about the different authentication schemes you can use: Windows Authentication, Forms Authentication, and OAuth. Your choice of authentication method should be based on where the information about users is stored. Windows Authentication uses Active Directory to store and validate users, while Forms Authentication uses virtually any type of storage, such as the SQL Server family of databases or other (relational or even NoSQL) databases. With OAuth the users catalog is stored in the external service database (for example Twitter or Facebook) and the application just keeps a reference to the account.

As you also learned, with ASP.NET SimpleMembership, ASP.NET Membership, and Role Manager, you can manage users and roles stored in Active Directory or SQL Server, and you can also create your own membership provider. You can also authorize users or roles to access certain areas of your application, and require them to log in with proper credentials to gain access to those areas.

Finally, you discovered that ASP.NET MVC 4 includes features to prevent external attacks, such as cross-site scripting (XSS) and cross-site request forgery (CSRF), and that you can implement simple changes to your view models and cookies to avoid compromising the integrity of the data they represent.

In the next chapter we will explore the routing engine in detail. You will learn how to use it properly to make your application's URLs easy to manage and use.

CHAPTER 10

Routing

ASP.NET routing allows developers to create a logical set of URLs that is independent of the folder structure of the web application on the server. This is a fundamental concept in ASP.NET MVC, because it allows the MVC routing engine to map URLs to action methods in controller classes.

With ASP.NET routing, the URLs can be as descriptive as necessary, making them more user-friendly. In addition, the URLs can be examined more easily by search engines, thus enhancing the visibility of the application in search engines' results. This is a key component of search engine optimization (SEO).

Chapter 4 provided a brief introduction to the routing engine and how routes work. In this chapter we'll dive deeper into the routing engine and its concepts. We will look at when routing is used and when it is not, and how to take control of this setting. Finally, we will examine the options to generate links and URLs and how you can use these options in the HaveYouSeenMe sample application.

Routing Concepts

To understand routing fully, you first need to understand a few important concepts about routing. Some of these concepts were introduced in Chapter 4 but others are new.

URL Pattern

A *URL pattern* is the definition of the segments that compose a URL request. Each segment is composed of one or more placeholders separated by literal values. The most common literal value is the hyphen (-). Segments are separated by the slash (/) character. Placeholders are defined by a name surrounded by braces (e.g., {controller}). Some examples of URL patterns are listed in Table 10-1.

Table 10-1. *Examples of URL Patterns*

URL Pattern	Matching URL Request
{controller}/{action}/{id}	/Pet/Display/Fido
{section}/{language}-{country}/{operation}	/Admin/en-US/Users
blog/{postYear}-{postMonth}-{postDay}/{postName}	/blog/2013-04-15/MissingPetsSummary

An example of an invalid URL pattern would be person/{firstName}{lastName}. The problem with this URL pattern is that the two placeholders {firstName} and {lastName} are not separated by a literal, so the routing engine won't know where the first name finishes and where the last name starts.

Routes

A *route* is a URL pattern that is mapped to a handler. In a file-based application such as a Web Forms application, the handler is an .aspx file. In an MVC application, the handler is an action method in a controller class.

Each route in an MVC application is represented by a Route object (the Route class is defined in the System.Web.Routing namespace). ASP.NET MVC applications have a collection of such Route objects, known as the *routing table*. The creation and configuration of the routing table happens when the application first starts. There is an event handler in the Global.asax.cs file called Application_Start. This event handler calls the RegisterRoutes() method in the static class RouteConfig located in the App_Start folder. The code in Listing 10-1 shows the Application_Start() event handler in the Global.asax.cs file.

Listing 10-1. Application_Start() Event Handler in the Global.asax.cs File

```
using System;
using System.Web.Http;
using System.Web.Mvc;
using System.Web.Optimization;
using System.Web.Routing;
using System.Web.WebPages;

namespace HaveYouSeenMe
{

    public class MvcApplication : System.Web.HttpApplication
    {
        protected void Application_Start()
        {
            AreaRegistration.RegisterAllAreas();

            WebApiConfig.Register(GlobalConfiguration.Configuration);
            FilterConfig.RegisterGlobalFilters(GlobalFilters.Filters);
            RouteConfig.RegisterRoutes(RouteTable.Routes);
            BundleConfig.RegisterBundles(BundleTable.Bundles);
            AuthConfig.RegisterAuth();
        }
    }
}
```

The default route configuration when you use the ASP.NET MVC 4 Internet Application project template is shown in Listing 10-2. As described earlier in this section, this is defined in the RouteConfig class located in the App_Start/RouteConfig.cs file.

Listing 10-2. Default Routing Configuration in the ASP.NET MVC 4 Internet Application Project

```
using System;
using System.Collections.Generic;
using System.Linq;
using System.Web;
using System.Web.Mvc;
using System.Web.Routing;
```

```
namespace HaveYouSeenMe
{
    public class RouteConfig
    {
        public static void RegisterRoutes(RouteCollection routes)
        {
            routes.IgnoreRoute("{resource}.axd/{*pathInfo}");

            routes.MapRoute(
                name: "Default",
                url: "{controller}/{action}/{id}",
                defaults: new { controller = "Home",
                                action = "Index",
                                id = UrlParameter.Optional }
            );
        }
    }
}
```

The code in Listing 10-2 shows a route named `Default`. Naming routes is not recommended because ASP.NET MVC has a feature that allows an HTML helper method to generate URLs based on route names, which breaks one of the core principles of the MVC pattern: separation of concerns. If you create a URL based on a route, you give the view knowledge about elements from the routing engine. The routing engine is part of the controller's world and as such, you are creating a dependency between views and controllers. With this dependency, you no longer have separation of concerns.

The suggested best practice is to never create URLs based on routes. Instead, URLs should be based only on controllers and action methods. If you follow this best practice, then there is no need to give names to routes, apart from documentation and debugging purposes, and you can just set the parameter to an empty string (or `null`) when creating routes. For example:

```
routes.MapRoute(
    name: "",
    url: "{controller}/{action}/{id}",
    defaults: new { controller = "Home",
                    action = "Index",
                    id = UrlParameter.Optional });
```

The parameter `defaults` in the `MapRoute()` method is an object that should include all the segments in the URL pattern. All segments in a route are required, unless you define them as `UrlParameter.Optional`, which makes them optional and can be omitted when making requests. In Listing 10-2, the `{id}` segment has been defined as optional.

Defining a segment as optional is different from having a default value for the segment. When a default value is defined for a segment, the default value is passed in the request for that segment when an explicit value is not specified in the URL of a request. On the other hand, when a segment is defined as optional, no value is passed in the request for the segment if an explicit value is not specified in the URL of a request. To better understand the difference between default values and optional segments, take a look at the examples in Table 10-2.

Table 10-2. *Differences Between Default Values for Route Segments and Optional Segments*

Route Definition	Request (Home Page)	Values for Segments

routes.MapRoute(
  name: "",
  url: "{controller}/{action}/{id}",
  defaults:
    new { controller = "Home",
    action = "Index",
    id = "0" }
	/	controller = "Home"
		action = "Index"
		id = "0"

routes.MapRoute(
  name: "",
  url: "{controller}/{action}/{id}",
  defaults:
    new { controller = "Home",
    action = "Index",
    id = UrlParameter.Optional }
	/	controller = "Home"
		action = "Index"
		id = ""

Creating Custom Routes

URL requests can be easily matched to action methods in controller classes using the default route. If your application, however, needs to accept URL requests with a different structure, then you can easily create new routes by using the MapRoute() extension method in the RouteConfig class (shown previously in Listing 10-2).

Imagine, for example, that we want to allow users of the HaveYouSeenMe sample application to see pictures of pets by just making a request to /ShowMe/{name of the pet}. The route to handle that request is shown in Listing 10-3.

Listing 10-3. Custom Route to Handle Requests /ShowMe/{name of the pet}

```
using System;
using System.Collections.Generic;
using System.Linq;
using System.Web;
using System.Web.Mvc;
using System.Web.Routing;

namespace HaveYouSeenMe
{
    public class RouteConfig
    {
        public static void RegisterRoutes(RouteCollection routes)
        {
            routes.IgnoreRoute("{resource}.axd/{*pathInfo}");

            routes.MapRoute(
                name: "",
                url: "ShowMe/{id}",
                defaults: new { controller = "Pet",
                                action = "GetPhoto",
                                id = "Fido" }
            );
```

```
        routes.MapRoute(
            name: "Default",
            url: "{controller}/{action}/{id}",
            defaults: new { controller = "Home",
                            action = "Index",
                            id = UrlParameter.Optional }
        );
    }
  }
}
```

After rebuilding the application, you could make the request, for example, /ShowMe/Fido, and you would get the result shown in Figure 10-1.

Figure 10-1. *Result from a custom route*

A final, very important note regarding adding custom routes: *The order in which routes are created does matter.* In the code from Listing 10-3, if we were to add the new custom route after the default route, the new custom route would never be used, as all requests would be picked by the default route. In that scenario, the values for the segments would be

```
controller = "ShowMe"
action = "Fido"
id = ""
```

Because there is no controller named ShowMe, an error would be thrown.

Creating a Catch-all Segment

When the routing engine attempts to match a URL request to a route, it uses the segments defined in the route's URL pattern. For example, the request /Message/send/Fido will be matched to the URL pattern {controller}/{action}/{id} from the default route.

191

If a different request is made, such as /Message/Send/Fido/Bubba, the routing engine will try to find a route with a URL pattern that has four segments. If the routing engine can't find one, then the request cannot be handled and a 404 HTTP error will be thrown, as shown in Figure 10-2.

Figure 10-2. *Error when no route can be matched to a request*

ASP.NET routing provides a mechanism to include a *catch-all* segment in URL patterns. The catch-all segment must be defined as the last segment in the URL pattern. It will contain all the values in the URL request after the last specific segment. This is useful if you want to allow requests with a variable number of parameters.

To add the catch-all segment to a route, all you need to do is add a segment that includes an asterisk in the name; for example: {*MoreValues}. Listing 10-4 shows how this would be applied to the default route from Listing 10-1.

Listing 10-4. Catch-all Parameter Added to the Default Route

```
routes.MapRoute(
    name: "Default",
    url: "{controller}/{action}/{id}/{*MoreValues}",
    defaults: new { controller = "Home",
                    action = "Index",
                    id = UrlParameter.Optional });
```

After making the modification in Listing 10-4, the route will accept requests with any number of parameters. At this point, it will be the responsibility of the action method to handle the values in the catch-all segment. Table 10-3 provides some examples of requests and how they are handled by a route with a catch-all segment.

Table 10-3. *Requests Handled by a Route with a Catch-all Segment*

Request	{controller}	{action}	{id}	{*MoreValues}
/Pet/Display	Pet	Display		
/Pet/Display/Fido	Pet	Display	Fido	
/Pet/Display/Fido/Bubba	Pet	Display	Fido	Bubba
/Pet/Display/Fido/Bubba/Penny	Pet	Display	Fido	Bubba/Penny
/Pet/Display/Fido/Bubba/Penny/Bolt	Pet	Display	Fido	Bubba/Penny/Bolt

Adding Constraints to Routes

The segments in a URL pattern can be further restricted by defining constraints. For example, a constraint would define that a particular segment has a fixed number of characters, or that it should be only digits. Constraints are defined by using regular expressions or by using objects that implement the IRouteConstraint interface.

Imagine we want to add a constraint in which the length of the {id} segment in the custom route added in Listing 10-3 is exactly four characters. We would modify the route as follows:

```
routes.MapRoute(
    name: "",
    url: "ShowMe/{id}",
    defaults: new { controller = "Pet", action = "GetPhoto", id = "Fido" },
    constraints: new { id = ".{4}" }
);
```

When you make the request to /ShowMe/Fido, it will work as expected, but if you use /ShowMe/Bubba, it will throw an error because Bubba does not conform to the specified constraint for the segment.

Understanding When Routing Is Not Applied

In the following scenarios, routing is not used to handle requests. While these are special conditions in the application, you can control how they work and alter the behavior to match your application's requirements.

- A physical file is found that matches the URL pattern
- Routing is explicitly disabled for a URL pattern

A Physical File Is Found that Matches the URL Pattern

If a request that matches a URL pattern also happens to match a physical file, then the physical file is served to the client. For example, a request such as /Home/About/Terms-And-Conditions.html matches the URL pattern {controller}/{action}/{id}. Under normal circumstances, routing should be used to handle this request, but if there is a physical file in the application that exactly matches the request, then the file will be sent to the client, and routing will not be used.

This behavior is controlled by the RouteExistingFiles property in the application's RouteCollection object. By default, the property is set to false, which instructs routing to verify if a physical file matches the request and, if one does, to serve the file. Setting the property to true instructs routing to not check for physical files and to handle all requests.

To change this behavior, you would need to modify the RegisterRoutes() method in the RouteConfig class as shown in Listing 10-5.

Listing 10-5. Modification to Use Routing for All Requests

```
public static void RegisterRoutes(RouteCollection routes)
{
    routes.RouteExistingFiles = true;

    routes.IgnoreRoute("{resource}.axd/{*pathInfo}");
```

```
    routes.MapRoute(
        name: "Default",
        url: "{controller}/{action}/{id}/{*MoreValues}",
        defaults: new { controller = "Home",
                        action = "Index",
                        id = UrlParameter.Optional }
    );
}
```

Routing Is Explicitly Disabled for a URL Pattern

You can explicitly disable routing for certain URL patterns. For example, in Listing 10-3 we have the following:

```
routes.IgnoreRoute("{resource}.axd/{*pathInfo}");
```

This statement disables routing for all requests to resources with extension .axd and with any number of parameters. As explained in Chapter 4, these resources don't physically exist as files in the application; rather, they are HttpModules that load special content (such as images, scripts, CSS, etc.) that is embedded in DLL files so that it can be sent to the browser as part of the response.

You can use the method IgnoreRoute() to add more URL patterns that should not be handled by routing. For example, if you created an HttpModule that processes images and renders them to a file extension such as myimage.xyz, then you would disable routing for xyz resources as follows:

```
routes.IgnoreRoute("{resource}.xyz/{*pathInfo}");
```

ASP.NET Routing vs. URL Rewriting

URL rewriting was a very popular technique in Web Forms applications to clean and simplify URLs. It was widely used before the introduction of ASP.NET routing. It helped to improve SEO and allow users to easily remember specific URLs in the application.

The idea of URL rewriting was to have URLs that had structure and would be easy to use; for example: http://mysite/blog/articles/12345. This URL would in turn be changed internally to something like http://mysite/blog/article.aspx?id=12345, which is neither pretty nor easy to remember.

URL rewriting works at a higher level in the HTTP request process than ASP.NET routing. There are conceptual differences between both technologies, such as:

- URL rewriting is used to manipulate URLs before the request is handled by the web server. The URL rewriting module does not know which handler will eventually process the rewritten URL. In addition, the actual request handler might not know that the URL has been rewritten.

- ASP.NET routing is used to map a request to a handler based on the URL. As opposed to URL rewriting, the routing module knows about the handlers and selects the handler that should generate a response for the requested URL.

Normally, you do not need to use URL rewriting if you are using ASP.NET routing, and vice versa. Both technologies can be implemented side by side, and from a functional perspective, neither is better than the other. They just work differently and produce almost the same result.

Reading Parameters from the URL

Up to this point in the chapter, we have discussed how requests map to different segments and what the values for each segment would be based on the request (for example, see Table 10-3). Recall that in Listing 10-3, the route definition for the custom route we added explicitly defines default values for the controller and action segments, but those segments are not defined in the URL pattern. The {Controller} and {action} segments are required even if they are not defined in the URL pattern because they tell the routing engine which action method and controller will handle the requests that match the URL pattern. As you saw in Listing 10-3, all the requests that match /ShowMe/{id} will be processed by the GetPhoto() action method in the PetController class.

The values for the segments in the URL request can be read using the Page.RouteData property in the body of the action method that processes the request. The RouteData property is of type System.Web.Routing.RouteData. RouteData has a property named Values, of type System.Web.Routing.RouteValueDictionary, that contains all the values for the segments in the URL.

To read the values in the {id} segment of the default route in an action method, we would need to do the following:

```
object id = RouteData.Values["id"];
```

The variable id will now have the value specified in the URL request for the {id} segment. One important thing to consider is that the data type for the variable is object, so it should be cast to a specific data type in order to make it usable. To cast the value to a string, use

```
string id = (string)RouteData.Values["id"];
```

Generating Links and URLs

ASP.NET routing can be used to create links and URLs in views. The simplest and preferred way to create links and URLs is with the @Html.ActionLink() and @Html.Action() methods (or @Ajax.ActionLink() for Ajax-based links). Using these helper methods is preferred over using fixed links in the view because the helper methods use the parameters to render an HTML link properly, so you don't have to build it manually.

Using the helper methods also ensures the generated HTML links comply with the information from the URL patterns defined in the route collection; if you change the URL patterns, then the helper methods will follow the new patterns, causing minimal to no issues with the URLs in the application.

This example shows how to create a hyperlink in a view page, to map to the Index() method in the HomeController class:

```
@Html.ActionLink("Home", "Index", "Home")
```

It will render the following HTML:

```
<a href="/">Home</a>
```

In this case, the parameters for the @Html.ActionLink() method are the link text, action method, and controller. @Html.ActionLink() was designed to understand the definition of the default route. It determined that the {action} and {controller} segments have default values that exactly match the action method and controller specified as parameters in our ActionLink() call. That is why the resulting URL doesn't include them (in other words, there is no need for the generated URL to be as verbose as /Home/Index, because Home is the default controller and Index is the default action).

The following is another example of creating a hyperlink in a view page:

```
@Html.ActionLink("Contact", "Contact", "Home",
                new { id = 1 },
                new {style = "font-weight:bold" } )
```

We have added two new parameters to @Html.ActionLink(), one for specifying a route parameter value for the {id} segment, and another one to add HTML attributes, in this case the style attribute. This will render the following HTML:

```
<a href="/Home/Contact/1" style="font-weight:bold">Contact</a>
```

If we add a parameter that doesn't exist in the route, for example:

```
@Html.ActionLink("Contact", "Contact", "Home", new { id = 1, Name = "Jose" }, null)
```

it will be rendered as a query string parameter:

```
<a href="/Home/Contact/1?Name=Jose">Contact</a>
```

Additionally, an overload of @Html.ActionLink() can be used to generate fully qualified URLs. For example:

```
@Html.ActionLink("Contact", "Contact", "Home",
                "https", "www.missingpets.com", "company",
                new { id = 1 },null)
```

will create the following:

```
<a href="https://www.missingpets.com/Home/Contact/1#company">Contact</a>
```

Summary

This chapter presented the core concepts of ASP.NET routing. We have examined what exactly a route is and how to create URL patterns. Routes are created with the MapRoute() method from the RouteCollection object. To work properly, they must be created when the application starts. The values of the segments in a request are read using the Values dictionary of the page's RouteData property.

Routes can be created to handle a variable number of parameters. To do this, a catch-all segment must be defined in the URL pattern for the route. This segment is the last of the pattern and includes an asterisk (*) in the name.

There are a few (uncommon) scenarios in which routing is not used. One scenario is when a physical file exists that matches the URL pattern. This behavior can be controlled with the RouteExistingFiles property of the RouteCollection object. Another scenario is when a URL pattern is explicitly excluded using the method IgnoreRoute().

The recommended approach to create links and URLs in a view page is to use the ActionLink() and Action() helper methods. They will use the existing routes collection as a baseline for URL generation; therefore, if you change the URL patterns, the URLs generated by ASP.NET MVC will be updated accordingly.

CHAPTER 11

Testing the Application

Testing is one of the most important tasks for developers. Before you deliver your application to end users, you must test it thoroughly to ensure that you are providing the best quality possible. Proper testing of your application also helps you to uncover issues that might cause loss of data, miscalculations, and other such problems.

A technique known as *unit testing* helps you with this task by allowing you to create classes and methods to test specific functionality in your application. In Chapter 3, we created a test project at the same time we created our HaveYouSeenMe sample ASP.NET MVC 4 application (by checking the "Create a unit test project" check box). In this chapter, we take a closer look at that test project in the context of testing the sample application.

Many frameworks for unit testing area available, some of which are even free, such as NUnit. For our testing project, we are going to use Microsoft Test Framework, which is also free. Many concepts you are going to see here also work for other test frameworks, so you do not necessarily need to use Microsoft Test Framework.

One of the benefits of ASP.NET MVC is that it promotes unit testing. You can, for example, execute controller methods (action methods) in complete isolation (that is, within the test framework). This is in stark contrast to traditional ASP.NET Web Forms, where the code-behind files are runnable only within the context of a real HTTP request (and therefore do not lend themselves to unit testing).

Note   This chapter is not intended to be a complete guide on testing; rather, it serves as a starting point from which you can investigate the subject further.

Understanding Unit Testing

Unit testing is not a new concept; in fact, it's been around since the 1970s. The basic idea is to create a program (usually a method in a class) that will make certain assumptions about a specific piece of code in your application and determine if, based on those assumptions, the code produces an expected result.

Defining a Unit Test

The program that will perform the test is called a *unit test*. An excellent definition of a unit test is given by Roy Osherove in his book *The Art of Unit Testing* (Manning Publications, 2009):

> *A unit test is an automated piece of code that invokes the method or class being tested and then checks some assumptions about the logical behavior of that method or class. A unit test is almost always written using a unit-testing framework. It can be written easily and runs quickly. It's fully automated, trustworthy, readable, and maintainable.*

A key concept implicit in Osherove's definition is that each unit test must test one, and only one, behavior of the functionality being tested. Take, for example, a method that returns an object based on an id. The method can behave in either of two ways. If it finds the object with the specified id, then it should return that object. If it doesn't find the object, then (for example) it should return null. Because the method has two behaviors, we would write two unit tests: one to test the case where it finds an object, and one to test when it returns null. This can lead to writing many unit tests for a single piece of code. It is perfectly okay to have many unit tests—in fact, it is expected. Unit tests are executed automatically and are very fast, so it doesn't matter how many you have.

Also, you should not delete a unit test just because it succeeds. You should delete a unit test only if you have removed from the application the corresponding functionality being tested. This will ensure that you can run the test each time you add new functionality or make changes in the application, thereby ensuring nothing has been broken by the addition or change.

With Microsoft Test Framework, you create unit tests as methods that are decorated with the [TestMethod] attribute. The methods must be in a class that is decorated with the [TestClass] attribute.

Structure of Unit Tests

One of the most common patterns to follow when writing unit tests is the AAA pattern, in which you write your unit test in three parts:

- *Arrange*: Set up the unit test. For example, you initialize variables and objects so that they are ready to pass in code (functionality) to be tested.

- *Act*: Invoke the code you want to test. In reality, this typically means invoking a particular method that you're trying to test.

- *Assert*: Analyze the result produced in the Act part. For example, you might verify that the return value and any output parameters are what you expected.

Understanding Isolation

Another important aspect of unit testing is that it should accurately locate the source of problems when they arise. With unit testing, although you are testing only small pieces of code, you should do those tests in an isolated environment. It is important to isolate your code from external resources out of your control (e.g., databases, web services, the file system, etc.) because

- Those resources might fail for unpredictable reasons.

- The data yielded by such external resources might be unpredictable and nonrepeatable (which really ruins your unit tests).

- Those resources might not actually be available yet in your development project.

An additional benefit of testing in isolation is that you can test your code even if the external resources it should interact with are not ready yet. For example, suppose you are working as part of a team and your piece of code has a dependency on some piece of code from a colleague, but that colleague hasn't completed that piece of code yet. Or suppose your code has a dependency on a completely external component (e.g., from a third party or trading partner). In either case, by isolating your code, you don't need to worry about those dependencies. You can move forward with your development and be ready to go when the rest of the team is ready.

Naming Unit Tests

An often ignored aspect of creating a good unit test is its name. While nothing prevents you from naming your unit test something as generic as `Test1()`, this will hardly give you and others any useful information. A common practice is to name your unit test in a manner that gives developers as much information as possible when that test fails. A good pattern for naming unit tests is to concatenate the name of the method being tested, the key assumptions, and the expected result. For example, `UploadFile_ValidFileSpecificied_SizeOnServerOverZeroKb()`.

Correctly naming the test classes is also a best practice. You should use the same name as the class to be tested and the suffix `Test` (for example, `HomeControllerTest`—which raises an interesting MVC-related point: you can perform unit tests on controller classes).

Testing Frameworks

As previously mentioned, many testing frameworks are available, both commercial and free. Some of the most commonly used are the xUnit family of frameworks, most notably NUnit, xUnit.net, and MbUnit. Of the three, NUnit is probably the most widely used, because it has been available longer in the market and because of its extensibility (it supports plug-ins). You can easily download any of these frameworks from NuGet (http://nuget.org). Visual Studio allows you to use any of these frameworks seamlessly within the IDE so that you have a familiar interface to work with.

In addition to basic testing frameworks, there are also *mocking frameworks*, the purpose of which is to provide *mock objects*. Mock objects simulate (or mimic) the functionality of real objects. With mock objects, developers can simulate nonexistent functionality and external resources. In general, they provide a means to write unit tests following the principle of isolation, as described earlier in the chapter.

There are many freely available mocking frameworks, such as Moq, NUnit.Mocks, and RhinoMocks. You can download any of these directly from NuGet. Some of the commercial (not free) ones are JustMock from Telerik (http://bit.ly/JustMock) and Isolator from Typemock (http://bit.ly/TypemockIsolator). Microsoft Test Framework has a feature called *Fakes*, which is the equivalent of mock objects.

For the purpose of this chapter, we are using Microsoft Test Framework because it is included in Visual Studio and doesn't require any setup or configuration. That said, not all the features in Microsoft Test Framework are available in all versions of Visual Studio. For example, the Fakes feature to create mocking objects is only available in Visual Studio 2012 Premium and Ultimate. Therefore, for mocking objects, we are going to use a mocking framework called Moq.

Introducing Moq

Moq is a mocking framework that is really simple and easy to use. It has no dependencies (all you need is `Moq.dll`), and it is free. It is open source, and you can use it in all editions of Visual Studio, including the free ones.

Originally, Moq was designed to take advantage of C# 3.0, but it works very well with most recent versions of the language. It supports both mocking interfaces and classes. Internally, Moq uses Castle DynamicProxy (http://bit.ly/DynamicProxy) as the mechanism to enable mocking. This means that DynamicProxy helps Moq create a .NET proxy on-the-fly at runtime. With this proxy, Moq is able to intercept objects without modifying the code of the class. Once Moq intercepts the object, it can determine its behavior and can even add functionality to the object without modifying the object's code.

Using a proxy mechanism to mock objects is simple and fast, but it has a serious limitation: while both interfaces and classes can be proxied, only *virtual* members can be intercepted and thus mocked. In other words, if you have, for example, static classes or members, they cannot be mocked with Moq.

Setting Up Moq

The easiest way to set up Moq in your application is to install it via NuGet. To open NuGet, choose Tools ➤ Library Package Manager ➤ Manage NuGet Packages for Solution, as shown in Figure 11-1.

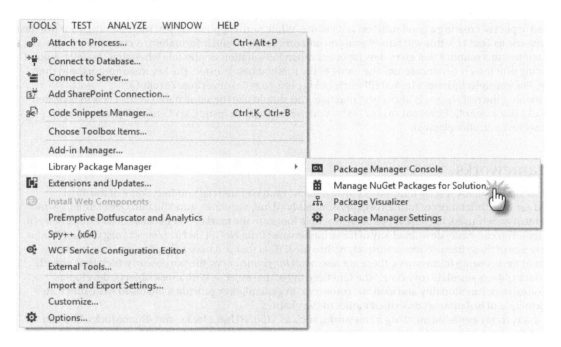

Figure 11-1. Opening the NuGet Package Manager window

Once the NuGet Package Manager window is open, type **moq** in the search box, and the results should appear as shown in Figure 11-2.

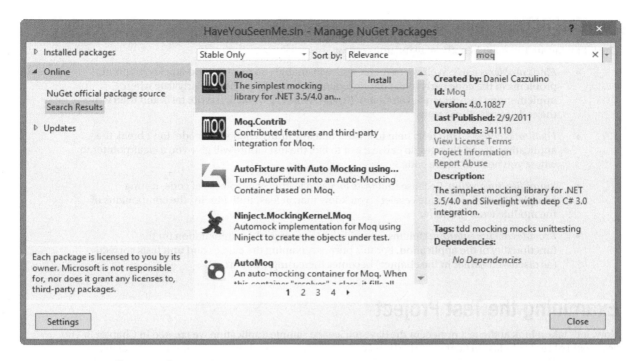

Figure 11-2. Installing Moq from NuGet

Click the "Install" button for Moq. In the Select Projects dialog that opens, check the box for the HaveYouSeenMe. Tests project, as shown in Figure 11-3, and click "OK." That is all it takes to set up Moq in your test project. You are now ready to use it.

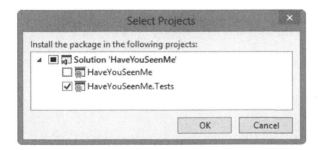

Figure 11-3. Selecting the project in which to install Moq

■ **Note**   You'd need to repeat this process to install Moq in another test project.

Benefits of Unit Testing

The following are the main benefits of using unit testing:

- *Finds problems early*: Well-written unit tests will enable you to easily and quickly pinpoint problems in the code early in the development process. This is particularly true when implementing test-driven development (TDD). With TDD, you first write tests and then write the code to pass those tests.

- *Facilitates change*: Unit tests help to ensure that any future changes to code don't break the application. If any changes do cause a test to fail, the test failure will give you a clear pointer to where you need to fix the code.

- *Simplifies integration*: Because unit tests focus on testing small pieces of code, testing complete modules becomes easier—you know that, at least individually, the components of the module work properly.

- *Provides documentation*: Unit tests provide a nice source of documentation for the functionality of the application. For this purpose, naming the classes and unit tests correctly (as discussed earlier in the chapter) becomes increasingly important.

Examining the Test Project

Now, let's take a look at the test project in the HaveYouSeenMe sample application we created in Chapter 3. The HomeControllerTest class in Controllers/HomeControllerTest.cs is shown in Listing 11-1. Note the reference to the Microsoft.VisualStudio.TestTools.UnitTesting namespace. This will provide all the features for testing. Also, we have two references to the HaveYouSeenMe and HaveYouSeenMe.Controllers namespaces, which will give the class access to the controllers in our application.

Listing 11-1. HomeControllerTest Class

```
using System;
using System.Collections.Generic;
using System.Linq;
using System.Text;
using System.Web.Mvc;
using Microsoft.VisualStudio.TestTools.UnitTesting;
using HaveYouSeenMe;
using HaveYouSeenMe.Controllers;

namespace HaveYouSeenMe.Tests.Controllers
{
    [TestClass]
    public class HomeControllerTest
    {
        [TestMethod]
        public void Index()
        {
            // Arrange
            HomeController controller = new HomeController();

            // Act
            ViewResult result = controller.Index() as ViewResult;
```

```
        // Assert
        Assert.AreEqual("Modify this template to jump-start your ASP.NET MVC application.",
                        result.ViewBag.Message);
    }

    [TestMethod]
    public void About()
    {
        // Arrange
        HomeController controller = new HomeController();

        // Act
        ViewResult result = controller.About() as ViewResult;

        // Assert
        Assert.IsNotNull(result);
    }

    [TestMethod]
    public void Contact()
    {
        // Arrange
        HomeController controller = new HomeController();

        // Act
        ViewResult result = controller.Contact() as ViewResult;

        // Assert
        Assert.IsNotNull(result);
    }
}
}
```

Note that there are three test methods (they are decorated with the [TestMethod] attribute), corresponding to the three action methods in the HomeController class. Each action method returns ViewResult, which the generated test code tests by using the Assert class from the Microsoft.VisualStudio.TestTools.UnitTesting namespace. The Assert class is used to verify conditions in unit tests. It is a static class that implements methods that return true or false by comparing the values in the parameters. The methods indicate the type of comparison. Table 11-1 shows some of the methods in the Assert class. You can find the complete list of methods in the Assert class at http://bit.ly/AssertClass.

Table 11-1. *Commonly Used Methods in the Assert Class*

Method	Parameters	Notes
AreEqual()	Object expected Object actual	Verifies that two objects are equal. One is the expected result, while the other is the actual result produced in the Act part of the unit test.
AreEqual<T>()	T expected T actual	Verifies that two generic type data are equal.
AreNotEqual()	Object notExpected Object actual	Verifies that two objects are not equal.
AreNotEqual<T>()	T notExpected T result	Verifies that two generic type data are not equal.
AreNotSame()	Object notExpected Object actual	Verifies that two object variables reference to different objects.
AreSame()	Object expected Object actual	Verifies that two object variables reference to the same object.
Equals()	Object objA Object objB	Verifies whether two objects are equal.
IsFalse()	bool condition	Verifies if the condition is false.
IsTrue()	bool condition	Verifies if the condition is true.
IsNull()	Object object	Verifies if the object is null.
IsNotNull()	Object object	Verifies if the object is not null.
IsInstanceOfType()	Object value Type expectedType	Verifies if the object is an instance of the specified type.

If you didn't create a test project in chapter 3 you will need to create a new one. The following section "Creating a Test Project" will guide you through the process of adding a new test project.

Creating a Test Project

If you didn't create a test project for the HaveYouSeenMe sample application in Chapter 3 for some reason, or if you need to create a test project for another application that doesn't have one, the steps to create one are very simple:

1. Open your solution in Visual Studio (if it's not already open).

2. Right-click the solution name in Solution Explorer and choose Add ➤ New Project, as shown in Figure 11-4. (Alternatively, you can select the solution name and choose File ➤ New Project.)

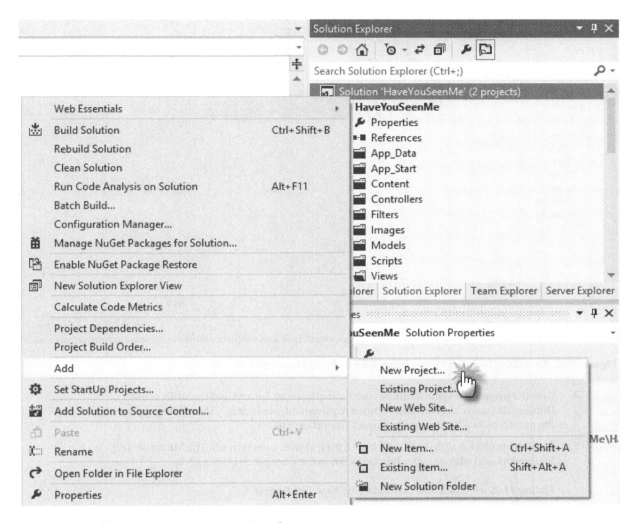

Figure 11-4. *Adding a new project to an existing solution*

3. In the Add New Project dialog, select Test in the left pane and then select Unit Test Project
   in the central pane, as shown in Figure 11-5.

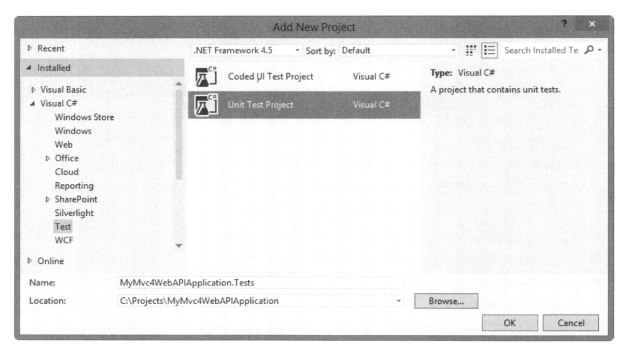

Figure 11-5. *Creating a Unit Test Project using Microsoft Test Framework*

4. Give the project the same name as your main project name and add the suffix `.Tests`. (Adding this suffix is a convention, not a requirement, but it clearly shows the purpose of the project by just looking at the name.) Then click "OK."

5. Once the project is added, you will have a project with a reference to The Microsoft Test Framework and with a single class as shown in the example in Listing 11-2.

Listing 11-2. Default Class Created in the New Test Project

```csharp
using System;
using Microsoft.VisualStudio.TestTools.UnitTesting;

namespace MyMvc4Application.Tests
{
    [TestClass]
    public class UnitTest1
    {
        [TestMethod]
        public void TestMethod1()
        {
        }
    }
}
```

6. To make your code accessible to the test project, you need to add a reference in the test project to your existing project. Right-click the References node under the test project in Solution Explorer and choose Add Reference, as shown in Figure 11-6.

Figure 11-6. *Adding a reference to the test project*

7. In the Reference Manager window, select Solution in the left pane, and in the center pane check the box corresponding to the project you want to test, as shown in Figure 11-7.

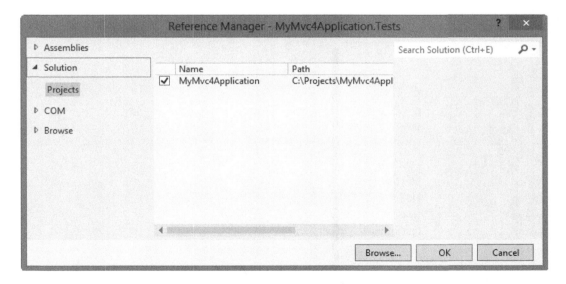

Figure 11-7. *Adding the main project as a reference to the test project*

Although the preceding process is not difficult, I strongly encourage you to create your test project at the same time that you create your MVC application. Simply check the "Create a unit test project" check box when choosing your project options. Visual Studio will automatically create a Unit Test project with methods to test your controller action methods. Figure 3-3 in Chapter 3 shows where this option is located when you are creating a new MVC web application.

Additionally, if you use the Empty project template or Test Project template in Visual Studio, you won't have any controllers, nor any corresponding test classes. Only if you use a more functional template (e.g., Internet Application or Intranet Application) you get the controllers and the corresponding test classes.

Also note that if you add a controller to an MVC project, it doesn't automatically add a test class in the test project. Similarly, if you add an action method in a controller class, it doesn't automatically add a test method in the test class.

Running Tests

Once you have your tests ready, it is time to execute them. There are a few ways to do so, but the most common is by choosing Test ➤ Run ➤ All Tests, as shown in Figure 11-8. Another way is to right-click in any of the code pages or test methods and select Run Tests, as shown in Figure 11-9.

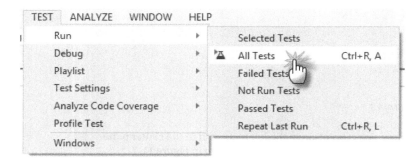

Figure 11-8. *Running all tests from the Test menu option*

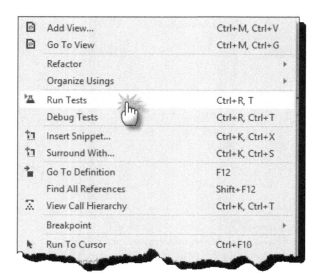

Figure 11-9. *Running tests from the context menu in a code file*

Either option runs all test methods (annotated with [TestMethod]). Also, the Test Explorer window opens, as shown in Figure 11-10, displaying the status and the results of all test methods.

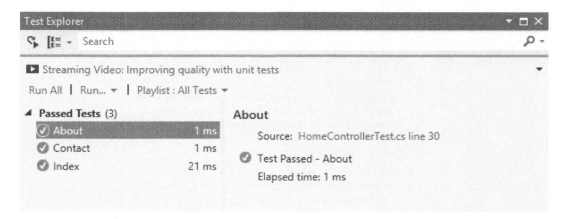

Figure 11-10. *Test Explorer window showing successful tests*

In Figure 11-10, the status of all the tests is "Passed," designated by a white check mark inside a green circle. When a test fails (e.g., by changing the message expected in the ViewBag in the Index() test method), it is labeled with a white X inside a red circle, as shown in Figure 11-11. A test may fail for any of several reasons:

- The method return value is not correct (as per our Assert statements)
- Output parameters are not correct
- An unexpected exception occurred
- An expected exception didn't occur
- A genuine bug exists in the test code

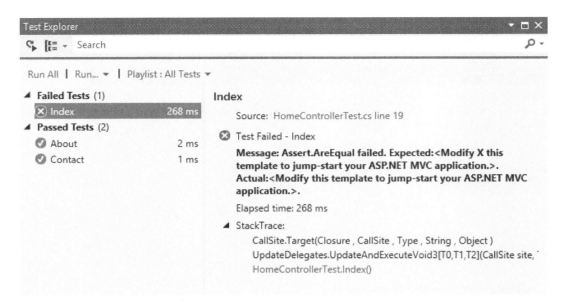

Figure 11-11. Test Explorer window showing a failed test

To see an example of how a test might fail, in the Index() test method in the HomeControllerTest class, change the expected string that represents the value in the ViewBag.Message property. Then compile the application and run the tests again.

Clicking the Run link in the Test Explorer window gives you more granular options to run tests, as shown in Figure 11-12.

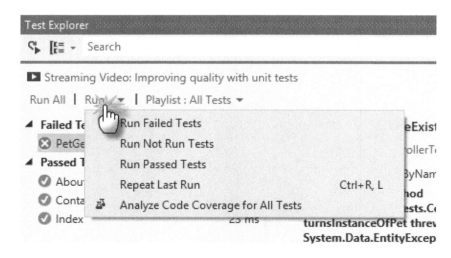

Figure 11-12. Options to run tests with the Run link

Testing Business Models

Unit tests are most commonly written for testing the functionality in the business models and action methods in controller classes. Unit tests for business models verify the functionality of the models to ensure they work as expected. For example, in a shopping cart application, we would write a unit test to verify the shipping calculation of a product based on the delivery ZIP code. We will examine unit tests for controllers in the next section.

Let's write some unit tests for our model. In our HaveYouSeenMe sample application, we have a business model called PetManagement. In the PetManagement class, we have a method called GetByName(), which takes as a parameter a string representing the name of the pet we want to find. What we are going to test now is whether the GetByName() method can return a the details for a pet we know exists in the system. If the pet is found, the method returns a Pet object. If the pet cannot be found, the method returns null. These are two different behaviors, so we are going to write two unit tests, one for each of them.

To start writing these tests, follow these steps:

1. Create a folder called Business in the test project. This gives us a place to store all the unit tests for the business models. This step is not required, but it will help us to organize our test classes.

2. If you created the test project at the same time you created the MVC project:

   a. Right-click the Business folder and select Add ➤ Unit Test. This creates a new class named UnitTest1 with the [TestClass] attribute. It also includes a method named TestMethod1() with the [TestMethod] attribute.

   b. Rename the class to PetManagementTest and rename the method to GetByName_ExistingPet_ReturnsPet(), as shown in Listing 11-3.

   Listing 11-3. PetManagementTest Class in Business/PetManagementTest.cs

```
using System;
using Microsoft.VisualStudio.TestTools.UnitTesting;
using HaveYouSeenMe;
using HaveYouSeenMe.Models.Business;

namespace HaveYouSeenMe.Tests.Business
{
    [TestClass]
    public class PetManagementTest
    {
        [TestMethod]
        public void GetByName_ExistingPet_ReturnsPet()
        {

        }
    }
}
```

If you added the test project after creating the MVC project:

    a.   Rename the existing UnitTest1 class to PetManagementTest and rename the method TestMethod1() to GetByName_ExistingPet_ReturnsPet().

    b.   Move the file to the Business folder to keep the test classes in the project organized.

  3.   Add the following namespaces to the PetManagementTest class:

```
using HaveYouSeenMe;
using HaveYouSeenMe.Models.Business;
```

  4.   The code in Listing 11-4 shows the test method content (note the AAA structure). It tests that GetByName() returns a Pet object when we pass in the name of an existing pet.

Listing 11-4. Unit Test to Verify GetByName() Returns an Object

```
[TestMethod]
public void GetByName_ExistingPet_ReturnsPet()
{
    // Arrange
    string petName = "Fido";

    // Act
    HaveYouSeenMe.Models.Pet result = PetManagement.GetByName(petName);

    // Assert
    Assert.IsNotNull(result); // The pet exists
}
```

Identifying External Dependencies

This unit test works, but it has a problem: the implementation of the GetByName() method depends on external code (a database), meaning it doesn't conform to the rules of isolation described earlier in the chapter. If the test fails, we cannot be entirely sure whether the problem is with the external resource or with the implementation of the code in the method itself. To fix this problem, we first need to examine the code in the GetByName() method. Listing 11-5 shows how the method was written.

Listing 11-5. Implementation of the GetByName() Method in the PetManagement Class

```
using System;
using System.Collections.Generic;
using System.Globalization;
using System.Linq;
using System.Web;

namespace HaveYouSeenMe.Models.Business
{
    public class PetManagement
    {
        public static Pet GetByName(string name)
        {
            Pet p = null;
            using (var db = new EntitiesConnection())
```

```
    {
        p = db.Pets.SingleOrDefault(x => x.PetName.Contains(name));
    }
    return p;
    }
}

}
```

As you can see in the code, this is a simple method that queries the database to retrieve a record in the Pet table where the pet name matches the value in the name parameter. The problem here is the direct dependency on the database. The method depends on the query to the database to obtain the record. If anything happens to the database (e.g., it is not available), then the method will just fail and throw an exception. This is what is called a *tightly coupled* implementation. This implementation is very difficult to test.

Separating your Code from External Dependencies

To fix this problem, we need to implement the same functionality but with a *loosely coupled* implementation. To do this, we need to separate the code that deals with the database information retrieval from the code that manipulates the information.

The first step is to create an interface that will expose which methods will interact with the database. This interface will be used to create a class that implements such methods. Listing 11-6 shows the interface called IRepository, which (for now) exposes one method, GetPetByName(). Add a class file in the /Models folder, name it IRepository.cs, and then add the code in Listing 11-6.

Listing 11-6. IRepository Interface in the Models/IRepository.cs File

```
using System;
using System.Collections.Generic;
using System.Linq;
using System.Web;

namespace HaveYouSeenMe.Models
{
    public interface IRepository
    {
        Pet GetByName(string name);
    }
}
```

Listing 11-7 creates a class that implements the IRepository interface. This class is called EFRepository. The name represents the implementation of the IRepository interface using a database accessed using Entity Framework. Create another class in the Models folder named EFRepository.cs and add the code in Listing 11-7.

Listing 11-7. EFRepository Class in the /Models/EFRepository.cs File

```
using System;
using System.Collections.Generic;
using System.Linq;
using System.Web;
```

```
namespace HaveYouSeenMe.Models
{
    public class EFRepository : IRepository
    {
        public Pet GetPetByName(string name)
        {
            Pet p = null;
            using (var db = new EntitiesConnection())
            {
                p = db.Pets.SingleOrDefault(x => x.PetName.Contains(name));
            }

            return p;
        }
    }
}
```

The great benefit of using the IRepository interface is that now we can create any number of different classes that implement the same methods (e.g., an Oracle-based implementation or an XML documents implementation). When the application utilizes these classes, it knows indistinctively that when a method is called, it will get an object regardless of where the information came from.

Now, how do we use this interface and class in the application? We need to change the PetManagement class to accept as a parameter a class that implements the IRepository interface. The easiest way to do this is to create a private variable of type IRepository and then, in the class constructor, set the variable with the class we want to use, as shown in Listing 11-8. You now see two constructors: one without a parameter, with defaults to the EFRepository class, and another one with a parameter used to set the value of the private variable. Alternatively we can use a technique called Dependency Injection (DI). With DI you define a container object with the knowledge of which class should be used in the code when you reference a specific interface. Then you just ask the container for the class by supplying the interface.

Listing 11-8. PetManagement Class Implementing a Parameter of Type IRepository

```
namespace HaveYouSeenMe.Models.Business
{
    public class PetManagement
    {
        private IRepository _repository;

        public PetManagement()
        {
            _repository = new EFRepository();
        }

        public PetManagement(IRepository repository)
        {
            _repository = repository;
        }
    }
}
```

We can then modify the GetByName() method to use the private _repository variable, as shown in Listing 11-9. Note in the code that the method is actually very simple. We could do some more processing with the object we get from the repository, but the idea of the method is to just obtain the object and return it.

Listing 11-9. Modified GetByName() Method That Implements the Private IRepository Value

```
public Pet GetByName(string name)
{
    Pet p = _repository.GetByName(name);
    return p;
}
```

There is just one more change we need to make in the application. We need to change the behavior of the GetByName() method so that is not static anymore. Because the method isn't static, we cannot call it using

```
PetManagement.GetByName()
```

Instead, we need to create an instance of the PetManagement class so that the method can be called:

```
PetManagement pm = PetManagement();
Pet p = pm.GetByName("name of pet");
```

With this implementation, we can now be sure that when the method is tested, the method's intended functionality will be tested, and not the external dependencies.

Mocking External Dependencies

Let's now fix the test we created in Listing 11-4. The proper way to test the GetByName() method is to create a mock object that will simulate the repository. The following steps guide you through the process of configuring Moq to create the mock object and to rewrite the test method:

1. Add the Moq namespace to the PetManagementTest class:

    ```
    using Moq;
    ```

2. Create a mock object using the IRepository interface. This will give us access to the methods the repository is supposed to implement.

    ```
    Mock<IRepository> _repository = new Mock<IRepository>();
    ```

3. Configure the behavior of the mock object using the Setup() method. We want to simulate that when the GetPetByName() method is called and the parameter passed is a string and exactly matches "Fido", then an object of type Pet is returned with a PetName property of "Fido" (this simulates getting a record from the database):

    ```
    _repository.Setup(x => x.GetPetByName(It.Is<string>(y=>y=="Fido")))
               .Returns(new Models.Pet { PetName = "Fido" });
    ```

4. Create an object of type PetManagement, and pass the mock object as a parameter in the constructor. Note that the actual mock object is in the Object property of the mock variable.

    ```
    var pm = new PetManagement(_repository.Object);
    ```

5. Call the GetByName() method using the PetManagement object

    ```
    var result = pm.GetByName(petName);
    ```

6. Verify that the result is what we expect, an actual object, representing the pet named Fido:

```
// The pet exists
Assert.IsNotNull(result);
// The pet name is "Fido"
Assert.AreEqual(petName, result.PetName);
```

The full test method is presented in Listing 11-10.

Listing 11-10. Unit Test for the GetByName() Method Using Mock Objects

```
[TestMethod]
public void GetByName_ExistingPet_ReturnsPet()
{
    // Arrange
    string petName = "Fido";
    Mock<IRepository> _repository = new Mock<IRepository>();
    _repository.Setup(x => x.GetPetByName(It.Is<string>(y=>y=="Fido")))
               .Returns(new Models.Pet { PetName = "Fido" });
    var pm = new PetManagement(_repository.Object);

    // Act
    var result = pm.GetByName(petName);

    // Assert
    // The pet exists
    Assert.IsNotNull(result);
    // The pet name is "Fido"
    Assert.AreEqual(petName, result.PetName);
}
```

Testing Controllers

One of the key features of ASP.NET MVC is that controller classes can be used outside the context of an HTTP web request. This means that you can write unit tests for controller classes, to ensure that they yield the correct results. This is a very important ingredient in large-scale web applications. ASP.NET MVC facilitates testing of controllers and action methods in the following ways:

- You don't need to actually run the application in a web server to test controllers and action methods.

- You have access to the actual ActionResult object returned by action methods, to ensure that you received the expected result.

- You can simulate HTTP parameters and even pass a whole object into action methods to simulate a genuine HTTP request. To test an action method, you just call the action method and supply the required parameters with values that conform to your test.

Testing Action Methods That Return a View

When testing the result of an action method that returns a view, you can inspect the ViewResult object of the action method. With relatively small and simple views, you could go all the way to validate the generated HTML and ensure that it is the result you would expect, but, for even a simple view that has minimal processing, this could be quite a complex task.

Instead, you could examine some of the properties from the ViewResult object to ensure that you are getting the correct result. For example, you could examine that the Name property of the ViewResult object matches the name of the expected view, or, with a strongly typed view, that the type of the view model is the correct one.

Let's create a new test class in our test project to test action methods in the PetController class:

1. Create a folder in the test project and name it Controllers.

2. Right-click the Controllers folder and choose Add ➤ Unit Test.

3. Rename the class to PetControllerTest.

4. Rename the method to Index_NoInputs_ReturnsDefaultViewResult(). This name indicates that the action method being tested is Index(), that we are assuming it will return the default view, and that the expected result is a ViewResult object.

5. Add the HaveYouSeenMe, HaveYouSeenMe.Controllers, and System.Web.Mvc namespaces to the file:

    ```
    using HaveYouSeenMe;
    using HaveYouSeenMe.Controllers;
    using System.Web.Mvc;
    ```

The class should look like the one in listing 11-11.

Listing 11-11. PetControllerTest Class for Testing the PetController Class

```
using System;
using Microsoft.VisualStudio.TestTools.UnitTesting;
using HaveYouSeenMe;
using HaveYouSeenMe.Controllers;
using System.Web.Mvc;

namespace HaveYouSeenMe.Tests.Controllers
{
    [TestClass]
    public class PetControllerTests
    {
        [TestMethod]
        public void Index_NoInputs_ReturnsDefaultViewResult()
        {
            // Arrange
            PetController controller = new PetController();

            // Act
            ViewResult result = (ViewResult)controller.Index();

            // Assert
            Assert.IsNotNull(result);
```

```
            Assert.AreEqual("", result.ViewName);
            Assert.IsNull(result.Model);
    }


    }
}
```

In the unit test shown in Listing 11-11, we are creating an instance of the PetController class (Arrange) and executing the Index() action method (Act). We are also expecting a ViewResult object from the execution. To validate that the ViewResult object is correct, we are testing for three things:

1. That there is actually a result object (in other words, Index() didn't return null).

2. That the view name is an empty string. The default view should not have a name, as it is specified by the return View() statement in the Index() action method. To test for an actual view name, we would need to change the action method to return something like return View("Index").

3. That the ViewResult object returned from Index() doesn't specify a view model object (that is, result.Model is null).

After compiling the solution and running the tests, you should get the results shown in Figure 11-13.

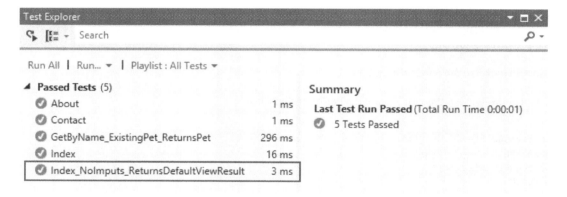

Figure 11-13. *Results of the first unit test*

Testing View Model Objects

Action methods that return a view result can also pass information to views in the form of view model objects or by using ViewData, ViewBag, or TempData, as you saw in Chapter 5. An example of a unit test using ViewBag is the one for the Index() action method from the HomeController class. An example of an action method that populates the view model is the Display() action method, shown in Listing 11-12.

Listing 11-12. Display() Action Method in the PetController Class

```
public ActionResult Display()
{
    var name = (string)RouteData.Values["id"];
    var pm = new PetManagement();
    var model = pm.GetByName(name);
```

```
    if (model == null)
        return RedirectToAction("NotFound");

    return View(model);
}
```

Because of the dependency on the database, explained earlier in the chapter, we need to make our controller class also loosely coupled. To do this, we need to modify the PetController class to use a variable of type IRepository, similarly to what we did for the PetManagement class. This will help us modify the action method to use the proper repository.

1. Add to the PetController class the private variable and two constructors, as follows:

    ```
    private IRepository _repository;

    public PetController()
    {
        _repository = new EFRepository();
    }

    public PetController(IRepository repository)
    {
        _repository = repository;
    }
    ```

2. Modify the Display() action method to use the _repository variable when creating the PetManagement object:

    ```
    var pm = new PetManagement(_repository);
    ```

Let's create a unit test for our Display() action method. The objective of the test is to ensure that we are getting a valid view model object when an existing pet name is requested. To test this behavior, we are going to assert that the view model exists (is not null), that it is of type HaveYouSeenMe.Models.Pet, and that the value in the PetName property matches the name of the pet we requested. The unit test is presented in Listing 11-13. Note in the code that, as we did before, we are creating a mock object to simulate the repository and configure it to return an object when called with the pet name "Fido".

Listing 11-13. Unit Test to Test the View Model Object Returned for a View

```
[TestMethod]
public void Display_ExistingPet_ReturnView()
{
    // Arrange
    Mock<IRepository> _repository = new Mock<IRepository>();
    _repository.Setup(x => x.GetPetByName(It.Is<string>(y => y == "Fido")))
                .Returns(new Models.Pet { PetName = "Fido" });
    PetController controller = new PetController(_repository.Object);
    string petName = "Fido";
    RouteData routeData = new RouteData();
    routeData.Values.Add("id", petName);
    ControllerContext context = new ControllerContext { RouteData = routeData };
    controller.ControllerContext = context;
```

```
// Act
ViewResult result = (ViewResult)controller.Display();

// Assert
Assert.IsNotNull(result);
Assert.AreEqual("", result.ViewName);
Assert.IsNotNull(result.Model);
Assert.IsInstanceOfType(result.Model, typeof(HaveYouSeenMe.Models.Pet));
Assert.AreEqual(petName, ((HaveYouSeenMe.Models.Pet)result.Model).PetName);
}
```

The action method checks the URL to obtain the name of the pet being requested. This check is done by examining the RouteData dictionary. For example, a request made to /Pet/Display/Fido will be handled by the Display() method in the PetController class, and the {id} segment will be saved in the RouteData dictionary with the value Fido.

In the unit test, we need to simulate the request. To simulate the request, we can call the action method directly simply by instantiating the PetController class. All that is left is to make the PetController object aware of the information in the RouteData dictionary. To do that we need to create a RouteData dictionary object and add an entry for the id key with value Fido. Then we set the RouteData property of a ControllerContext object with the new RouteData object we created. This object gives the controller all the information it needs to process the request. The information in the ControllerContext includes the request itself, the base controller, the routed data, the HTTP context, and the display mode. Finally, we set the ControllerContext property of the PetController object with the ControllerContext object we created. At this point, we are ready to call the Display() action method and see if it works as expected. After compiling the solution and running the tests, you should get a result indicating that the test passed.

Testing Redirections

The Display() action method in the PetController class also handles the case where the pet requested is not found in the system. When this condition is met, the result is a redirection to a different action method (using the RedirectToAction() method), which in turn returns a view named NotFound.

To test the redirection, we need to add a new unit test. Using the unit test presented in Listing 11-13 as a base, add a new unit test and name it Display_NonExistingPet_ReturnNotFoundView(). The name states that we are testing the Display() action method for the scenario where a pet name that is not in the database is requested, and that this method should return the NotFound view.

Because the Display() action method is doing a redirection instead of just returning a different ViewResult object, we cannot simply check the name of the view as we did before. In this case we need to test that the returned object is of type RedirectToRouteResult. This is the object type returned by the call to RedirectToAction(). Also, we need to ensure that the target of the redirection is the NotFound() action method. The unit test is shown in Listing 11-14.

Listing 11-14. Unit Test for Redirection

```
[TestMethod]
public void Display_NonExistingPet_ReturnNotFoundView()
{
    // Arrange
    string petName = "Barney";
    Mock<IRepository> _repository = new Mock<IRepository>();
    _repository.Setup(x => x.GetPetByName(It.Is<string>(y => y == "Fido")))
                .Returns(new Models.Pet { PetName = "Fido" });
    PetController controller = new PetController(_repository.Object);
```

```
RouteData routeData = new RouteData();
routeData.Values.Add("id", petName);
ControllerContext context = new ControllerContext { RouteData = routeData };
controller.ControllerContext = context;

// Act
var result = controller.Display() as RedirectToRouteResult;

// Assert
// The action method returned an action result
Assert.IsNotNull(result);
// The redirection actually happened
Assert.IsInstanceOfType(result, typeof(RedirectToRouteResult));
// It was redirected to the NotFound action method
Assert.AreEqual("NotFound", result.RouteValues["action"]);
}
```

Notice that the Arrange section in Listing 11-14 is quite similar to the Arrange section in Listing 11-13. The only difference is the name of the pet being requested. We can refactor the code to make it more maintainable. Let's start by creating a private variable of type PetController. This variable will be set in the PetControllerTests constructor with the mock object, as shown in Listing 11-15.

Listing 11-15. Constructor for the PetControllerTests Class

```
[TestClass]
public class PetControllerTests
{
    private PetController _controller;

    public PetControllerTests()
    {
        Mock<IRepository> _repository = new Mock<IRepository>();
        _repository.Setup(x => x.GetPetByName(It.Is<string>(y => y == "Fido")))
                   .Returns(new Models.Pet { PetName = "Fido" });
        _controller = new PetController(_repository.Object);
    }

    ...

}
```

Next, we create a private method to set up the ControllerContext object. Since the configuration is the same and the only difference is the name of the pet, the method will accept the pet name as a parameter, as shown in Listing 11-16.

Listing 11-16. Method to Configure the Controller Context

```
private void SetControllerContext(string petName)
{
    RouteData routeData = new RouteData();
    routeData.Values.Add("id", petName);
    ControllerContext context = new ControllerContext { RouteData = routeData, };
    _controller.ControllerContext = context;
}
```

Finally, we update the two unit tests to use the `SetControllerContext()` method with the corresponding pet name as a parameter. Listing 11-17 shows the modified version of the `Display_NonExistingPet_ReturnNotFoundView()` method.

Listing 11-17. Refactored Version of the Display_NonExistingPet_ReturnNotFoundView() Unit Test

```
[TestMethod]
public void Display_ExistingPet_ReturnView()
{
    // Arrange
    string petName = "Fido";
    SetControllerContext(petName);

    // Act
    ViewResult result = (ViewResult)_controller.Display();

    // Assert
    Assert.IsNotNull(result);
    Assert.AreEqual("", result.ViewName);
    Assert.IsNotNull(result.Model);
    Assert.IsInstanceOfType(result.Model, typeof(HaveYouSeenMe.Models.Pet));
    Assert.AreEqual(petName, ((Pet)result.Model).PetName);
}
```

Testing HTTP Status Codes

Testing action methods that return HTTP status codes is easy. When an action method returns specific HTTP status codes, it returns an `HttpStatusCodeResult` object. In your test, you can examine the returned object to assert that the code you are expecting is that defined in the object.

Imagine that we want to modify the `Display()` action method so that when a pet is not found, instead of redirecting to another action method to display a Not Found page, the action method would simply return an `HttpNotFound` object. The action method would look as shown in Listing 11-18.

Listing 11-18. Display() Action Method Returning an HttpNotFound Object When the Pet Is Not Found

```
public ActionResult Display()
{
    var name = (string)RouteData.Values["id"];
    var pm = new PetManagement(_repository);
    var model = pm.GetByName(name);

    if (model == null)
        return HttpNotFound("Pet Not Found...");

    return View(model);
}
```

If we were to actually modify the `Display()` action method as shown in Listing 11-18, we would need to change the unit test a bit. Instead of checking for a `RedirectToRouteResult` object, we would need to check for the `HttpStatusCodeResult` object. Then we would need to check the `StatusCode` property of the returned object to see if it is 404 (not found). The code in Listing 11-19 shows the revised unit test. Note that we would update the name of the unit test to be `Display_NonExistingPet_ReturnsHttp404()`, making it clear that we are testing the `Display()` action method for the scenario where a pet that is not in the database is requested, and that it should return an HTTP 404 status code.

Listing 11-19. Testing the Display() Action Method When It Returns an HTTP 404 Result

```
[TestMethod]
public void Display_NonExistingPet_ReturnsHttp404()
{
    // Arrange
    string petName = "Barney";
    SetControllerContext(petName);

    // Act
    var result = _controller.NotFoundError() as HttpStatusCodeResult;

    // Assert
    // The action method returned an action result
    Assert.IsNotNull(result);
    // The action result is an HttpStatusCodeResult object
    Assert.IsInstanceOfType(result, typeof(HttpStatusCodeResult));
    // The HTTP code is 404 (not found)
    Assert.AreEqual(404, result.StatusCode);
}
```

Testing Routes

Routing is an important part of your application, and you should test it to ensure requests are always routed to the correct controllers and action methods. Although testing routes is a simple process, there is a downside: we must make explicit use of MVC classes (HttpRequestBase, HttpContextBase, and HttpResponseBase) in our test code. All of these classes are needed to test routes. This means that our tests no longer obey the principle of isolation, but that's a price worth paying because it helps us to ensure that our routes work correctly.

To begin, create a new folder called Routes in the test project. Again, this is not required but will help you to keep your files organized. Then, right-click the new Routes folder and choose Add ➤ Unit Test. Rename the class to RoutesTest. Then, import the following namespaces:

```
using Moq;
using System.Web;
using System.Web.Routing;
using System.Web.Mvc;
```

Routes need to be created when the application starts. We do that in the Application_Start() event handler in the Global.asax.cs file. Because we are in the test project, we have to create the routes before we start testing them. The best place to do that is in the class constructor. Add a constructor method to the RoutesTest class to register routes as follows:

```
RouteCollection routes;

public RoutesTest()
{
    // Create the routes table
    RouteCollection routes = new RouteCollection();
    RouteConfig.RegisterRoutes(routes);
}
```

The class should look like the one presented in Listing 11-20.

Listing 11-20. RoutesTest Class in Routes/RoutesTest.cs

```
using System;
using System.Collections.Generic;
using System.Linq;
using System.Text;
using System.Threading.Tasks;
using Microsoft.VisualStudio.TestTools.UnitTesting;
using Moq;
using System.Web;
using System.Web.Routing;
using System.Web.Mvc;

namespace HaveYouSeenMe.Tests.Routes
{
    [TestClass]
    public class RoutesTest
    {
        public RoutesTest()
        {
            // Create the routes table
            RouteCollection routes = new RouteCollection();
            RouteConfig.RegisterRoutes(routes);
        }
    }
}
```

Testing Routing for Disabled URL Patterns

Chapter 10 showed you how routing can be disabled for specific URL patterns. For example:

```
routes.IgnoreRoute("{resource}.axd/{*pathInfo}");
```

Testing this type of route is particularly important. The routing engine will not process requests that match those URL patterns. We need to ensure that requests made to such resources are accurately identified so that they can be properly handled by Internet Information Services (IIS). Similarly, we need to ensure that no other resources are ignored with these routes; otherwise, they would not be handled appropriately.

To test routes, the most important task is to simulate a request. When using the application, a request is made via the browser. The user enters a URL such as /Pet/Display/Fido, and the request is then processed by the routing engine to determine which controller and action method will handle it. With unit tests, there is no browser, so we need to find a way to send a request to the routing engine. For this, mock objects come to the rescue.

We are going to create a mock object for the HttpContextBase class. This object will give us access to the HTTP-specific information about an individual HTTP request. We will configure the mock object so that when the request starts with the tilde notation (~), the object will make it relative to the root of the application. We do this by using the AppRelativeCurrentExecutionFilePath property. With this configuration, we can make requests such as ~/folder/page.aspx and the HttpContextBase object will convert it to /approot/folder/page.aspx. Next, we'll tell the mock object to return a file with extension .axd (e.g., Resource.axd), as shown in Listing 11-21. This is to simulate an HTTP request that will be matched to the URL pattern {resource}.axd/{*pathInfo} in the ignored route.

Listing 11-21. Unit Test for Disabled URL Pattern Processing .axd Files

```
[TestMethod]
public void IgnoreRoute_AXDResource_StopRoutingHandler()
{
    // Arrange
    // Create the mock object for the HttpContextBase object
    Mock<HttpContextBase> mockContextBase = new Mock<HttpContextBase>();
    // Simulate the request for a resource of type {something}.axd
    mockContextBase.Setup(x => x.Request.AppRelativeCurrentExecutionFilePath)
                    .Returns("~/Resource.axd");

    // Act
    // Get the route information based on the mock object
    RouteData routeData = routes.GetRouteData(mockContextBase.Object);

    // Assert
    // Make sure a route will process the resource
    Assert.IsNotNull(routeData);
    // Verify the type of route is of type StopRoutingHandler. This indicates
    // the request matches a URL pattern that won't use routing
    Assert.IsInstanceOfType(routeData.RouteHandler, typeof(StopRoutingHandler));
}
```

To be able to verify if the request was ignored by the routing engine, we call the GetRouteData() method using the mock object. This method returns an object of type RouteData. The reason to get this object is to examine its RouteHandler property, which indicates which type of handler will process the request. For our test, we need to verify that the type of handler is StopRoutingHandler. If this is the case, then we can be sure that the routing engine will not handle the request.

Testing Routes

When testing routes, the primary goal is to ensure that the routing engine will call the appropriate controller and action method to handle the request. For example, the code in Listing 11-22 shows the unit test for the request to ~/ (the home page). For the test to succeed, the controller and action method that handle the request should be HomeController and Index, respectively. Also, the default route includes an optional segment ({id}). The unit test should also verify the {id} segment is properly identified as optional.

Listing 11-22. Unit Testing the Route to the Home Page

```
[TestMethod]
public void DefaultRoute_HomePage_HomeControllerIndexActionOptionalId()
{
    // Arrange
    // Create the mock object for the HttpContextBase object
    Mock<HttpContextBase> mockContextBase = new Mock<HttpContextBase>();
    // Simulate the request for the home page
    mockContextBase.Setup(x => x.Request.AppRelativeCurrentExecutionFilePath)
                    .Returns("~/");
```

```
    // Act
    // Get the route information based on the mock object
    RouteData routeData = routes.GetRouteData(mockContextBase.Object);

    // Assert
    // Make sure a route will process the resource
    Assert.IsNotNull(routeData);
    // The controller is Home
    Assert.AreEqual("Home", routeData.Values["controller"]);
    // The action method is Index
    Assert.AreEqual("Index", routeData.Values["action"]);
    // The {id} segment is optional
    Assert.AreEqual(UrlParameter.Optional, routeData.Values["id"]);
}
```

Summary

This chapter introduced you to unit testing using Microsoft Test Framework. We examined the base concepts of unit testing, such as using the AAA pattern, isolation, and mocking. We also reviewed the application and prepared it to start writing unit tests. You discovered that there are many frameworks that help with unit testing, both free and commercial. Visual Studio 2012 offers the possibility to use many of those frameworks. You just have to install the one you want. We chose the one from Microsoft simply because it is already included and is very simple to use. Other popular frameworks include NUnit, MbUnit, and xUnit.net. For mock objects, we used Moq, which is a free library that can be easily downloaded from NuGet.

An important concept to keep in mind when writing unit tests is that each unit test should test only one behavior. Closely following this principle will help you to identify particular functionality issues. If you are testing a method that should behave differently under different conditions, you need to write a unit test for each of the behaviors, to ensure the method behaves correctly under all of the conditions.

The most important tasks when unit testing are testing the functionality of the application in the business models, testing controllers, and testing routes. All of these tasks are not complex, but you need to write your tests to make sure they all behave as expected. Testing the business models will ensure that the core functionality of the application (what the application is supposed to do) works fine. You need to make sure the code is built in such a way that dependencies on external sources can be clearly identified and are not tightly coupled to the business models; otherwise, if the test fails, you won't know where the problem is located. Testing controllers and routes is also key to the application, as they handle the HTTP requests from the users.

Once your tests succeed and you are happy with the result, you are ready to move ahead to the next and final chapter of the book, which deals with deploying the application to the production environment.

CHAPTER 12

■ ■ ■

Deploying the Application

In this chapter we are going to prepare the ASP.NET MVC 4 application for deployment and then deploy it. There are many deployment scenarios, most which require the development team to hand the application to the operations team so that they can make the application available to users. We are going to examine two scenarios where developers deploy the application directly: the first scenario involves deploying it to an in-house server (such as a company server), and the second scenario involves deploying it to a cloud-based service. For the cloud infrastructure, we are going to use Windows Azure.

Generally speaking, the deployment process is handled using Visual Studio. You can either generate the necessary files for deployment or directly deploy the application to the target server. As you will see in the chapter, Visual Studio includes the tools required to deploy the application. With Visual Studio you can target both of the deployment scenarios we are going to examine. In addition, you will see how to manually deploy the database and deploy it using Visual Studio.

The database is currently running as a LocalDB database. LocalDB is a new edition of SQL Server that is designed specifically for developers. It has certain limitations that make it unsuitable for production environments; for example, it has a maximum database size of 10GB, it allows local connections only through the Named Pipes protocol, and it can use only one CPU. For the purpose of development, it was fine to use a LocalDB database. LocalDB is easy to use and migrating it to a different edition of SQL Server such as SQL Server Web Edition or SQL Server Standard Edition is a simple process. Since LocalDB is, basically, another version of SQL Server, it is 100% compatible with other editions of SQL Server that are designed to handle the requirements of a production environment.

Preparing the Application for Deployment

Prior to deploying the application, we need to take care of the following simple housekeeping tasks, the purpose of which is to make sure the application will perform correctly in the target environment:

- Enable compile-time error checking for views
- Disable debugging and verbose errors
- Update settings in the Web.config file for production

Enabling Compile-Time Error Checking for Views

Views, by default, are not compiled until you actually run the application and make a request to each of them. This can lead to unexpected and annoying errors at runtime. To illustrate the problem, imagine that you are making a modification to the Login.cshtml view in the folder /Views/Account. Inadvertently, you change the LoginModel property UserName to userName, as shown in Figure 12-1.

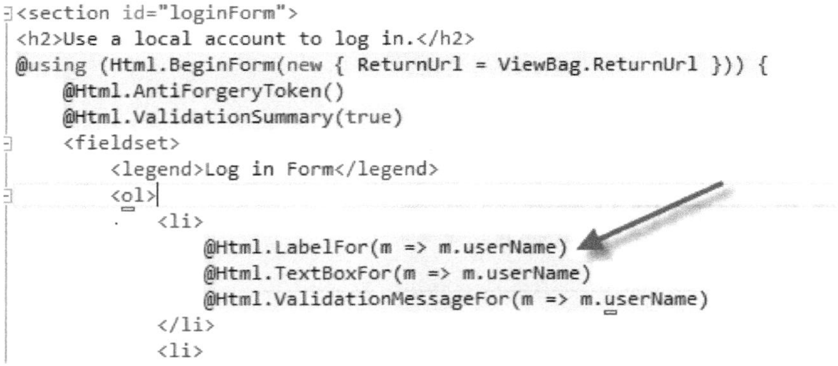

```
<section id="loginForm">
  <h2>Use a local account to log in.</h2>
  @using (Html.BeginForm(new { ReturnUrl = ViewBag.ReturnUrl })) {
      @Html.AntiForgeryToken()
      @Html.ValidationSummary(true)
      <fieldset>
          <legend>Log in Form</legend>
          <ol>
              <li>
                  @Html.LabelFor(m => m.userName)
                  @Html.TextBoxFor(m => m.userName)
                  @Html.ValidationMessageFor(m => m.userName)
              </li>
              <li>
```

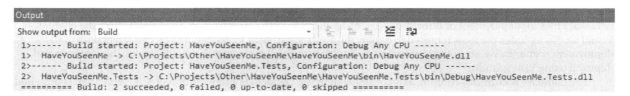

Figure 12-1. *Error introduced by changing the LoginModel property UserName to userName*

Then, you build the application and get a result similar to the one shown in Figure 12-2. As you can see, no errors were detected by the compiler.

```
Output
Show output from:  Build                                               ▼
1>------ Build started: Project: HaveYouSeenMe, Configuration: Debug Any CPU ------
1>  HaveYouSeenMe -> C:\Projects\Other\HaveYouSeenMe\HaveYouSeenMe\bin\HaveYouSeenMe.dll
2>------ Build started: Project: HaveYouSeenMe.Tests, Configuration: Debug Any CPU ------
2>  HaveYouSeenMe.Tests -> C:\Projects\Other\HaveYouSeenMe\HaveYouSeenMe.Tests\bin\Debug\HaveYouSeenMe.Tests.dll
========== Build: 2 succeeded, 0 failed, 0 up-to-date, 0 skipped ==========
```

Figure 12-2. *No errors detected by the compiler*

Since everything seems fine, you deploy the application, and that's when users start calling you to complain about an error. You then open the application in the browser and head to the login page to verify what the users are saying. Bam! You get an error similar to the one shown in Figure 12-3.

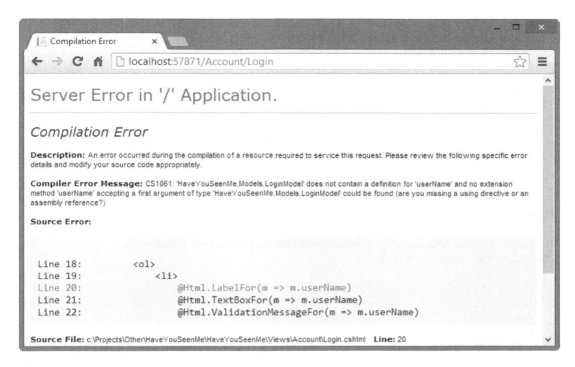

Figure 12-3. Runtime error caused in the login view

The error is classified as a compilation error, but it was not detected when the application was built. This could have been detected prior to deployment, but it wasn't. The reason is that the compiler ignores views when building the solution.

The good news is that there is a configuration setting to modify the behavior of the compiler so that it also compiles views when you build the application in Visual Studio. The bad news is that there's no direct way to change this setting. To change it, you need to edit the project file in a text editor (Notepad, for example). The following steps will guide you through the process of updating the project file:

1. If the project is loaded in Visual Studio, right-click the project name in the Solution Explorer window and choose the option Unload Project, as shown in Figure 12-4.

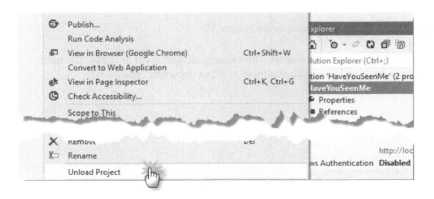

Figure 12-4. Unloading the project in Visual Studio

2.   Right-click the project name again, but this time choose the option Edit HaveYouSeenMe. csproj to edit the project file, as shown in Figure 12-5.

Figure 12-5. *Editing the project file*

3.   The project file is an XML file with all the properties for the project. Find the element `<MvcBuildViews>` (see Figure 12-6).

```
<?xml version="1.0" encoding="utf-8"?>
<Project ToolsVersion="4.0" DefaultTargets="Build" xmlns="http://schemas.microsoft.com/
  <Import Project="$(MSBuildExtensionsPath)\$(MSBuildToolsVersion)\Microsoft.Common.pro
  <PropertyGroup>
    <Configuration Condition=" '$(Configuration)' == '' ">Debug</Configuration>
    <Platform Condition=" '$(Platform)' == '' ">AnyCPU</Platform>
    <ProductVersion>
    </ProductVersion>
    <SchemaVersion>2.0</SchemaVersion>
    <ProjectGuid>{12B11DA1-9A24-4AC7-9218-63C69E4E0148}</ProjectGuid>
    <ProjectTypeGuids>{E3E379DF-F4C6-4180-9B81-6769533ABE47};{349c5851-65df-11da-9384-0
    <OutputType>Library</OutputType>
    <AppDesignerFolder>Properties</AppDesignerFolder>
    <RootNamespace>HaveYouSeenMe</RootNamespace>
    <AssemblyName>HaveYouSeenMe</AssemblyName>
    <TargetFrameworkVersion>v4.5</TargetFrameworkVersion>
    <MvcBuildViews>false</MvcBuildViews>
    <UseIISExpress>true</UseIISExpress>
    <IISExpressSSLPort />
```

Figure 12-6. *Element <MvcBuildViews> in the project file*

4.   The element `<MvcBuildViews>` is a Boolean. The value by default is set to `false`. To enable compile-time error checking, change the value to `true`, as shown in Figure 12-7.

```xml
<?xml version="1.0" encoding="utf-8"?>
<Project ToolsVersion="4.0" DefaultTargets="Build" xmlns="http://s
  <Import Project="$(MSBuildExtensionsPath)\$(MSBuildToolsVersion)
  <PropertyGroup>
    <Configuration Condition=" '$(Configuration)' == '' ">Debug</C
    <Platform Condition=" '$(Platform)' == '' ">AnyCPU</Platform>
    <ProductVersion>
    </ProductVersion>
    <SchemaVersion>2.0</SchemaVersion>
    <ProjectGuid>{12B11DA1-9A24-4AC7-9218-63C69E4E0148}</ProjectGu
    <ProjectTypeGuids>{E3E379DF-F4C6-4180-9B81-6769533ABE47};{349c
    <OutputType>Library</OutputType>
    <AppDesignerFolder>Properties</AppDesignerFolder>
    <RootNamespace>HaveYouSeenMe</RootNamespace>
    <AssemblyName>HaveYouSeenMe</AssemblyName>
    <TargetFrameworkVersion>v4.5</TargetFrameworkVersion>
    <MvcBuildViews>true</MvcBuildViews>
    <UseIISExpress>true</UseIISExpress>
    <IISExpressSSLPort />
    <IISExpressAnonymousAuthentication />
```

Figure 12-7. *Element <MvcBuildViews> set to true*

5. Save the project file, and then close it.

6. Finally, reload the project by right-clicking the project name and choosing the option Reload Project, as shown in Figure 12-8.

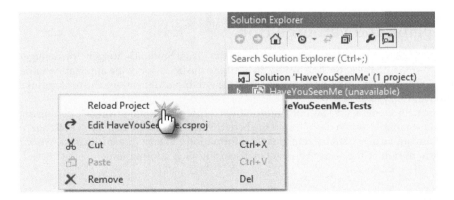

Figure 12-8. *Reloading the project*

Now, when you build the application again, you will see compilation errors, as shown in Figure 12-9.

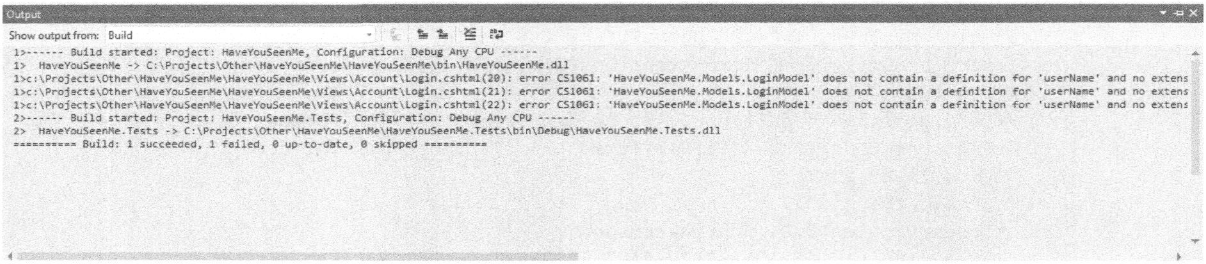

Figure 12-9. *Errors now detected in the view at compile time*

The error detail is listed in the third line of Figure 12-9, the complete text of which is as follows:

```
1>c:\Projects\Other\HaveYouSeenMe\HaveYouSeenMe\Views\Account\Login.cshtml(20): error CS1061:
'HaveYouSeenMe.Models.LoginModel' does not contain a definition for 'userName' and no extension
method 'userName' accepting a first argument of type 'HaveYouSeenMe.Models.LoginModel' could be
found (are you missing a using directive or an assembly reference?)
```

Now you can see errors in your views prior to running the application. At this point, you might be wondering why this setting is not enabled by default. The answer to that question is that checking views adds extra overhead to the compiler. In small applications like our sample application, it might not have much of an impact, but in large applications the impact could be significant. Please review the performance of the compiler before and after the configuration change to decide if you want to keep this setting enabled permanently for this project. If you decide to leave it permanently enabled, note that this is a project setting, not a Visual Studio setting. That means you will need to enable it on a project-by-project basis and evaluate for each project whether you want to leave it permanently enabled.

Disabling Debugging and Verbose Errors

During development, you'll find yourself making frequent use of the Visual Studio Debugger. The debugger allows you to run the application and step into the code, line by line, to examine the behavior of the application under different scenarios. Enabling the debugger in production however, is not a good thing. You will see the reasons for not enabling debugging in production and how to disable it.

Additionally, you normally want to have as much information as possible about errors happening in the application. The more information that can be collected the better. This information helps you to fix such errors. Unfortunately, allowing the public to see such detailed error information can lead to security risks. We will see how to disable this functionality to minimize the security impact of disclosing such information.

Disable Debugging

The debugger is allowed to integrate with your application by default based on a configuration setting controlled by a variable in the application's Web.config file. When deploying the application, you need to disable the debugging setting. The reason for this is that the application behaves differently when debugging is enabled; for example:

- Some optimizations are disabled so that the debugger can step through the code.

- Debug symbols are generated during compilation to aid the debugger. This normally slows down the compilation.

- Views are compiled as requested instead of in batch (where all views are compiled prior to running the application).

- Request timeouts are disabled so that developers can spend enough time reviewing the application between requests.

- Bundles are not minified or combined. The files in the bundles are sent to the browser in sequence rather than in parallel. Remember that bundled files are sent to the browser at the same time (in parallel) to reduce the number of requests and improve the load time of pages.

- Browser caching behaves differently. For example, when the debugger is disabled, images and scripts downloaded from the WebResources.axd handler are cached (saved) the first time and subsequent requests use the cached version. When the debugger is enabled, images and scripts from WebResources.axd are not cached and will be loaded every time they are requested.

To disable debugging, prior to deploying your application, find the <compilation> element in the application's Web.config file and either remove the debug parameter or change its value to false. For example:

```
<?xml version="1.0" encoding="utf-8"?>
<configuration>
...
  <system.web>
    <compilation debug="false" targetFramework="4.5" />
...
  </system.web>
...
</configuration>
```

Disable Verbose Errors

As you have seen throughout the previous chapters, when errors happen, a generic page is shown with the error details. The details in the page normally include the type of the exception and the file where it happened, and sometimes you even get the line number in the file where the error happened and much more information.

During development, all these details are useful. In production, however, they pose a security threat. An attacker can gather very useful information about the application from error messages, and such information is usually the first stepping stone to carrying out an attack. Error messages in ASP.NET MVC can give out the following information:

- The language it was developed in, such as C# or Visual Basic.NET

- The stack trace of the program that failed

- The version numbers for the .NET Framework and ASP.NET

- Development class names and object structures

In many cases, the information in the stack trace can be used maliciously. Stack traces are call chains of line-numbered source code that usually result from unhandled exceptions. Unhandled exceptions are circumstances in which something happens (e.g., the application has received user input that it did not expect, a database is suddenly not available, a file is not found, etc.) that the application doesn't know how to deal with. An attacker can leverage the conditions that cause these errors in order to gain unauthorized access to the system.

To disable disclosure of such extensive error information, you need to set the <customErrors> element in the Web.config file. If the mode property is set to Off, then all the information about the error (as described in this section) will be shown to the user. A better setting for this property is RemoteOnly, which will give remote users just an error message but will allow local users (e.g., developers) to see full error details when the application is run from the server (using http://localhost). For example:

```xml
<?xml version="1.0" encoding="utf-8"?>
<configuration>
...
  <system.web>
    <customErrors mode="RemoteOnly" />
...
  </system.web>
...
</configuration>
```

Updating Settings in Web.config for Production

The Web.config file can contain settings that control the application's behavior. During the development phase, developers often store in the configuration file information that later needs to be updated or cleaned up when the application is deployed. The following are some of the settings that you need to review prior to production:

- *Connection strings*: Make sure the only connection strings that are included are those that will be used, and make sure they have the correct configuration for the production environment. For example, you might be using a connection string for a LocalDB database when developing the application, but in production it will be a different edition of SQL Server.

- *Application settings*: The keys in the <AppSettings> dictionary often need to be updated once in production. For example, the application might access a remote service such as a payment gateway (e.g., Authorize.NET). For development, you would have a test URL for processing payments, but in production you would use a different URL to the payment gateway's production system.

- *Timeout settings*: You can configure several timeouts in Web.config, such as the database connection timeout and the execution timeout. Make sure they are set correctly for the production environment.

Deploying to an In-House Server

Now that we've discussed some general issues related to preparing an application for deployment, let's turn our attention to the task of actually deploying our application to a production environment. In our first scenario, we are going to deploy the application to an in-house server. This scenario assumes it is a server in the network to which we have access as administrators. The scenario also assumes we have access to an in-house SQL Server instance where the database will run. In many situations, the server is sufficiently robust (has enough CPU power, RAM, and disk space) for the web application and database to run in the same server.

Deploying the Database

The task of deploying a database is normally left to the database administrator (DBA). In Chapter 3 we created two script files, one with the definition of the tables for the application (Listing 3-2) and the other with modifications to add new columns to the UserProfile table (Listing 3-3). For easy reference, Listing 12-1 shows a combined view of the two database scripts from Chapter 3.

Listing 12-1. Combined View of Database Scripts from Chapter 3

```sql
CREATE TABLE [dbo].[Setting]
(
    [Id] INT NOT NULL IDENTITY(1,1),
    [Key] VARCHAR(50) NOT NULL,
    [Value] VARCHAR(500) NULL,
    CONSTRAINT [PK_Setting] PRIMARY KEY ([Id])
);

CREATE TABLE [dbo].[PetType]
(
    [PetTypeID] INT NOT NULL IDENTITY(1,1),
    [PetTypeDescription] VARCHAR(50) NULL,
    CONSTRAINT [PK_PetType] PRIMARY KEY ([PetTypeID])
);

CREATE TABLE [dbo].[Status]
(
    [StatusID] INT NOT NULL IDENTITY(1,1),
    [Description] VARCHAR (50) NOT NULL,
    CONSTRAINT [PK_Status] PRIMARY KEY ([StatusID])
);

CREATE TABLE [dbo].[Pet]
(
    [PetID] INT NOT NULL IDENTITY(1,1),
    [PetName] VARCHAR(100) NOT NULL,
    [PetAgeYears] INT NULL,
    [PetAgeMonths] INT NULL,
    [StatusID] INT NOT NULL,
    [LastSeenOn] DATE NULL,
    [LastSeenWhere] VARCHAR(500) NULL,
    [Notes] VARCHAR(1500) NULL,
    [UserId] INT NOT NULL,
    CONSTRAINT [PK_Pet] PRIMARY KEY ([PetID]),
    CONSTRAINT [FK_Pet_Status] FOREIGN KEY ([StatusID])
        REFERENCES [Status] ([StatusID]),
    CONSTRAINT [FK_Pet_User] FOREIGN KEY ([UserId])
        REFERENCES [UserProfile] ([UserId])
);

CREATE TABLE [dbo].[PetPhoto]
(
    [PhotoID] INT NOT NULL IDENTITY(1,1),
    [PetID] INT NOT NULL,
    [Photo] VARCHAR(500) NOT NULL
    CONSTRAINT [DF_PhotoFile] DEFAULT '/content/pets/no-image.png',
    [Notes] VARCHAR(500) NULL,
    CONSTRAINT [PK_PetPhoto] PRIMARY KEY ([PhotoID]),
    CONSTRAINT [FK_PetPhoto_Pet] FOREIGN KEY ([PetID])
        REFERENCES [Pet] ([PetID])
);
```

```
CREATE TABLE [dbo].[Message]
(
    [MessageID] INT NOT NULL,
    [UserId] INT NOT NULL,
    [MessageDate] DATETIME NOT NULL,
    [From] VARCHAR(150) NOT NULL,
    [Email] VARCHAR(150) NOT NULL,
    [Subject] VARCHAR(150) NULL,
    [Message] VARCHAR(1500) NOT NULL,
    CONSTRAINT [PK_Message] PRIMARY KEY ([MessageID]),
    CONSTRAINT [FK_Message_User] FOREIGN KEY ([UserId])
        REFERENCES [UserProfile] ([UserId])
);

ALTER TABLE [dbo].[UserProfile]
ADD
    [FirstName] VARCHAR(150) NOT NULL,
    [LastName] VARCHAR(150) NOT NULL,
    [Email] VARCHAR(150) NOT NULL;
```

In addition to those scripts, we need to create a few more. The additional scripts are for the tables required to run SimpleMembership, which is the system we are using for managing users and roles in our sample application. SimpleMembership uses several database tables to store the information:

- UserProfile

- webpages_Membership

- webpages_OAuthMembership

- webpages_Roles

- webpages_UsersInRoles

These tables are normally created by the application automatically when an operation from the AccountController class is executed (e.g., browsing to the login page). This method of creating the tables should not be used when deploying to production. These are some of the reasons for not using this approach:

- Tables could be created with specific settings for size growth.

- If for any reason the tables cannot be created from the application, an exception will be thrown and the application simply won't work. This defeats the goal of enabling users to have the best experience possible with the application.

- To ensure that you (or the DBA) have complete control of the objects created in the database.

Since only five tables are needed for SimpleMembership, we are going to generate the scripts manually from Visual Studio. The following steps will guide you through the process:

1. Open Visual Studio and open the HaveYouSeenMe web application.

2. Open the Server Explorer window and open the database connection the application uses. (We have been using DefaultConnection in our sample application).

3. Expand Tables.

4. Right-click the UserProfile table and choose Open Table Definition, as shown in Figure 12-10.

Figure 12-10. Opening the UserProfile table definition in Visual Studio

5. Choose File ➤ Save dbo.UserProfile.sql As (see Figure 12-11) to save the table definition to a script file.

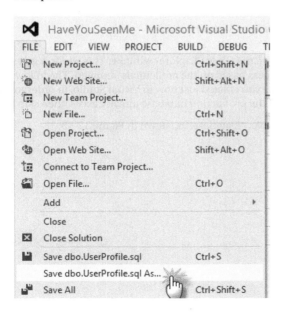

Figure 12-11. Saving the script file for the UserProfile table

6. Repeat steps 4 and 5 for the other four tables: `webpages_Membership`, `webpages_OAuthMembership`, `webpages_Roles`, and `webpages_UsersInRoles`.

Now we are ready to deploy the database to a server with SQL Server. The tool we are going to use is SQL Server Management Studio. This tool is normally installed in the server where SQL Server is installed but can also be installed separately in client computers to remotely manage the database. You can install SQL Server Management Studio either from the SQL Server installation CDs or by downloading SQL Server from the Microsoft Download Center web site. With either option, you will need to choose to install the client tools only.

Open SQL Server Management Studio and connect to the production server. The connection settings will vary, and you may have to get them from the DBA. Figure 12-12 shows the Connect to Server dialog with typical settings using Windows Authentication (which is normally preferred over SQL Server Authentication, for security reasons). In the Server name box, enter the name or IP address of the computer where SQL Server is running.

Figure 12-12. *SQL Server Connection settings using Windows Authentication*

Once you are connected to the server, you should see the Object Explorer window. This window gives you access to all the areas of SQL Server you have permission to access based on the credentials supplied. The following steps will guide you through the process of running the scripts you created just now in Visual Studio, in order to create the `SimpleMembership` tables in the production database. If the production database already exists, then skip to step 4.

1. Right-click the Databases node and choose New Database, as shown in Figure 12-13.

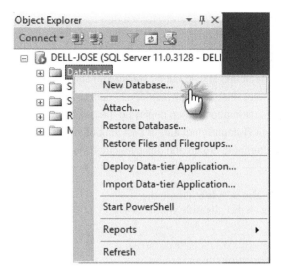

Figure 12-13. *Creating a new database*

2. In the New Database dialog, set the name of the database to be **HaveYouSeenMe**, as shown in Figure 12-14.

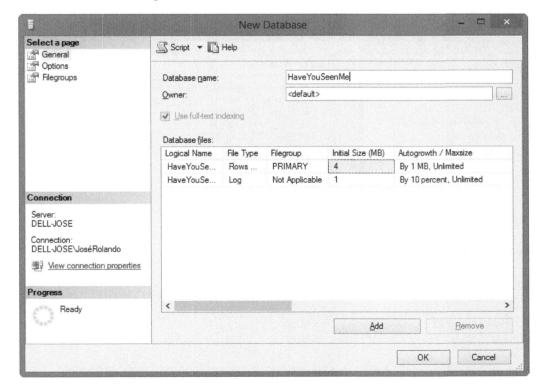

Figure 12-14. *New Database dialog*

3. Leave the rest of the settings with their default values and click "OK". You now have a new database, ready to be used.

■ **Caution** The steps outlined are for a very simple database deployment and should not be considered suitable for all cases. Under normal circumstances, developers rarely deploy databases; instead, they hand the scripts to the DBA, who will then do this task. There are many performance and security considerations when deploying the database, and those considerations are outside the scope of the book. Consult your IT department and/or DBA about the settings and established procedures to deploy databases prior to making any attempt to create and deploy a database.

Now that the database has been created, you need to run the scripts to create the SimpleMembership tables in the database. The remaining steps will guide you through the process of running the scripts:

4. Expand the Databases node and select (just once) the new HaveYouSeenMe database. This will make sure that this is the database in use when opening the script files.

5. Press Ctrl+O to open a file (or choose File ➤ Open ➤ File).

6. Find and open the script generated for the table UserProfile earlier in this chapter.

7. Click the "Execute" button, as shown in Figure 12-15 (or press F5).

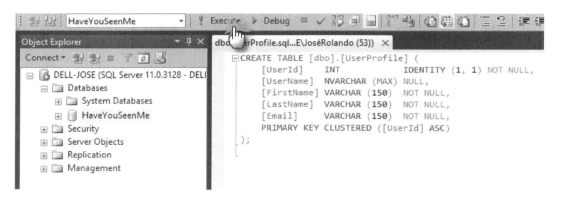

Figure 12-15. *Executing the script in SQL Server Management Studio*

You should get a message similar to the one shown in Figure 12-16.

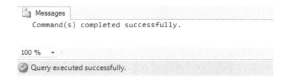

Figure 12-16. *Success message after executing the script*

8. Repeat steps 6 and 7 for the rest of the scripts generated earlier in the chapter. The script for the UserProfile table (dbo.UserProfile.sql) includes the new columns added to the UserProfile table so we won't need to run script 3-3 anymore.

9. Now repeat steps 6 and 7 for the script created for Listing 3-2.

Alternatively, you can use the Package/Publish SQL section of the project configuration options in Visual Studio to deploy the database at the same time you deploy the application. To use this option, open the project properties window by right-clicking the project in the Solution Explorer window and select Properties at the bottom. Then click the Package/Publish SQL option in the menu on the left, as shown in Figure 12-17.

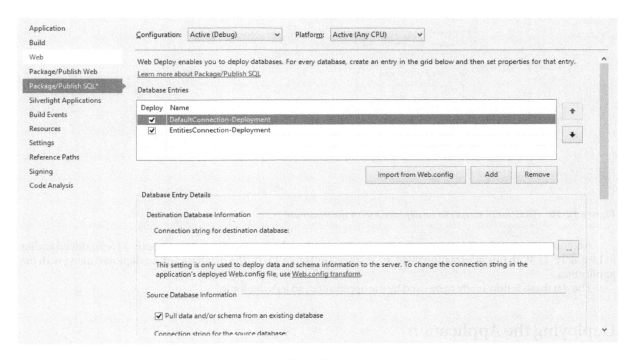

Figure 12-17. *Package/Publish SQL options in the web application properties*

Click the "Import from Web.config" button so that Visual Studio reads the connection strings in the Web.config file and adds them to the Database Entries section. This action will enable the options in the Database Entry Details section on the same page. The first box, under Destination Database Information, allows you to enter the connection string that should be used to deploy the database and additional scripts.

The options under Source Database Information, shown in Figure 12-18, allow you to pull the schema (and optionally data) from an existing database used in development. Note that Visual Studio automatically filled in the information for the existing LocalDB database we are using for development. What is going to happen is that the deployment process will read the definition of all the tables, views, stored procedures, and so forth from that database and will re-create them in the destination (production) database.

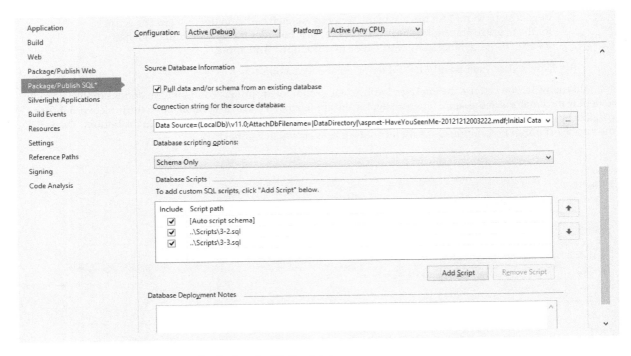

Figure 12-18. *Additional scripts to be deployed with the database*

Additionally, you can add your own custom scripts, such as the ones we created in Chapter 3 (reproduced earlier in Listing 12-1). With this information filled in, as shown in Figure 12-18, the database will be deployed along with the application.

The database is now ready to be used by the application, so let's deploy it.

Deploying the Application

To deploy the application to an Internet Information Services (IIS) web server, we need to have an available web site already created in the server where the application will run. To illustrate the deployment process, we are going to use the same development computer as if it were the production server.

The following instructions guide you through the steps to create the web site in IIS:

1. Open the Internet Information Services (IIS) Manager program by running the file
    inetmgr.exe or by choosing Start ➤ Administrative Tools ➤ Internet Information Services
    (IIS) Manager.

2. The IIS Manager window is divided into three sections, as shown in Figure 12-19.
    The left pane is the navigation pane. You can connect to different servers from this
    pane. The center pane gives you access to all the features for the selected element
    in the navigation pane. The right pane has shortcuts to common actions to perform
    on the selected element.

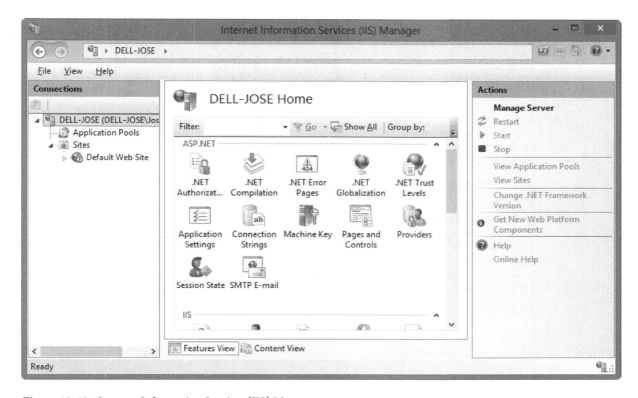

Figure 12-19. *Internet Information Services (IIS) Manager*

3. In the navigation pane, right-click the Sites node and choose Add Website, as shown in Figure 12-20. This will open the Add Website dialog.

Figure 12-20. *Adding a new web site in IIS*

4. Complete the Add Website dialog as follows:

   a. In the Site name field, enter **Have You Seen Me**.

   b. In the Application pool field, a new application pool named the same as the web site is created by default. Leave the default. An application pool basically defines the security boundaries under which the application is executed. This means that the application is executed under the security credentials defined for the application pool.

243

If the credentials are insufficient for executing an action, then the application cannot execute the action (e.g., access to files in a folder where the application pool has no permissions). Additionally, an application running in an application pool cannot access other applications running in different application pools. This is particularly important because if an application misbehaves, it won't affect other applications. More information on application pools can be found at `http://bit.ly/IISAppPool`.

c. In the Physical path field, type the path to the dedicated folder into which the application will be copied on the production server. Optionally, you can browse for the folder, or create a new folder, by clicking the ellipsis button on the right to open the browse window.

d. In the Binding section, leave the Type and IP Address fields with the default values.

e. In the Port field, modify the port to be **8080**. You will normally use port 80, but the Default Web Site has already been configured to use port 80, so we need to use a different port. In order to have two web sites using the same port (80, for example), you need to define a domain name for the web site (e.g., `haveyouseenme.org`) in the Host name box. This way you can access the web site with the domain name without having to use a specific port (e.g., you would use `http://haveyouseenme.org` instead of `http://servername:8080`).

f. Leave the Host name box empty.

5. Click "OK."

6. IIS Manager creates the web site, ready for us to deploy our web application into it (see Figure 12-21).

Figure 12-21. *The new web site has been created*

7. Open Visual Studio as an administrator. Right-click the Visual Studio icon and choose "Run as administrator." If you have the User Account Control feature enabled, you might get a confirmation dialog. Click "Yes" to continue. This step is important because running Visual Studio as an administrator will give you more privileges to perform certain actions.

8. In Visual Studio, right-click the project name in the Solution Explorer window and choose Publish, as shown in Figure 12-22. This opens the Publish Web wizard.

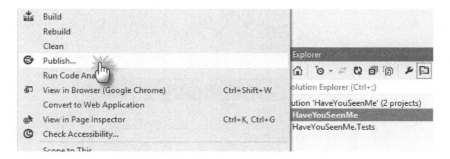

Figure 12-22. *Opening the Publish Web wizard*

9. The first page of the Publish Web wizard is Profile (shown in Figure 12-23), which gives you
    the option to select or import a publish profile. A *publish profile* is a group of settings
    that instructs Visual Studio on how to deploy the application.

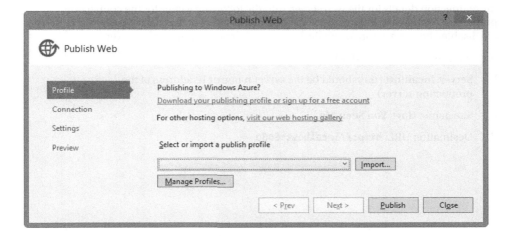

Figure 12-23. *Profile page of the Publish Web wizard*

10. Create a new profile by selecting "New" from the drop-down list under "Select or import
    a publish profile," as shown in Figure 12-24. This option opens the New Profile dialog,
    which asks for the profile name. Type **In-House Deployment** and click "OK."

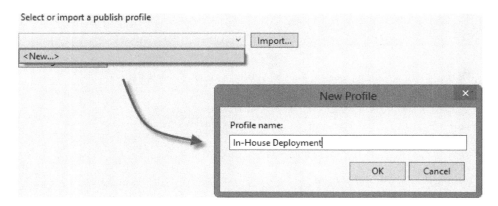

Figure 12-24. *Adding a new publish profile*

11. Now that the profile has been created, the next step of the Publish Web wizard is to define the connection details for the web server. Add the following values for the connection properties, as shown in Figure 12-25 (the Username, Password, and Save Password options are disabled because we are using the same development computer as server):

    a. Publish method: **Web Deploy**

    b. Server: **localhost** (this should be the server name or IP address of the production server)

    c. Site name: **Have You Seen Me**

    d. Destination URL: `http://localhost:8080`

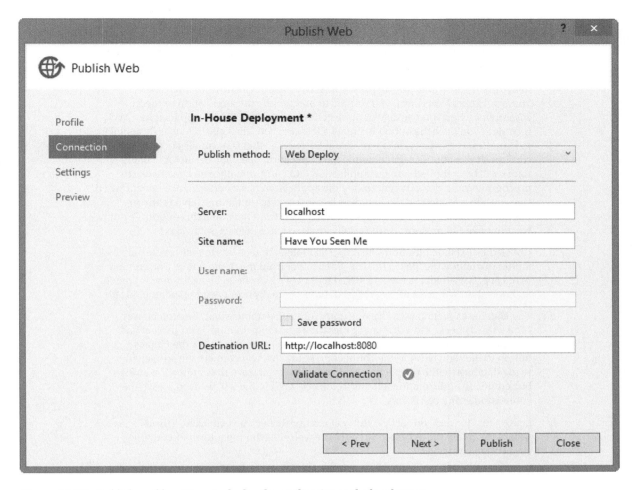

Figure 12-25. *Publish profile settings to deploy the application to the local server*

12. Click the "Validate Connection" button to make sure that you entered the settings correctly. If the settings are correct, you should see a green and white check mark icon next to the button, as shown in Figure 12-25. If everything is okay, then click the "Next" button.

13. The next step of the Publish Web wizard is to add the settings for the deployment. Complete the Settings page as follows (see Figure 12-26):

a. In the Configuration drop-down list, choose Release (if it was not previously selected). Configuration options are basically groups of settings for the application. You can create your own, but by default Visual Studio includes two, Debug and Release. With configuration options, you can define how the application will run (for example, whether debugging will be enabled, whether tracing will be enabled, etc.). The built-in Release configuration includes some of the settings described earlier in the "Preparing the Application for Deployment" section (e.g., disabling the debug mode).

b. Leave the "Remove additional files at destination" check box at its default, unchecked. Checking this box deletes files on the destination server that have no matching files in the web application on your computer. Since this is the first time we are going to deploy the application, there is no need to check this box.

c. Leave the "Precompile during publishing" check box at its default, unchecked. You would check this box if you wanted to precompile the application or merge assemblies when you package or publish the project. In ASP.NET applications (MVC included) you have the option to create a folder called App_Code, which is designed to contain server-side code (C# or Visual Basic.NET) that is normally compiled at runtime. If you choose to precompile the application, the code in the App_Code folder will be compiled into the application DLL. Additionally, you can choose to precompile your views. Precompiling the application has a performance benefit when the web site is loaded for the first time because this compilation step has already happened. Additional settings are available if you want to enable this option. For now, we don't need to precompile the application, so leave the box unchecked.

d. Check the "Exclude files from the App_Data folder" check box to instruct Visual Studio to exclude the files in the App_Data folder from the deployment. The content of the App_Data folder is the LocalDB database we have been using for development, and now that we have a SQL Server database, we really don't need to include this file.

e. The Databases section includes one entry for each database that the project uses. (The wizard checks the Web.config file to read this information.) Our project has only one (DefaultConnection), so only one is shown. You can click the ellipsis button to the right to build the connection string that will connect the application to the database in the production environment. If you leave the connection string box empty, the information already in the Web.config file will be used. Leave the connection string box empty.

f. Leave the "Use this connection string at runtime" check box checked. This tells the wizard to update the Web.config file in the web site with the information in the connection string box.

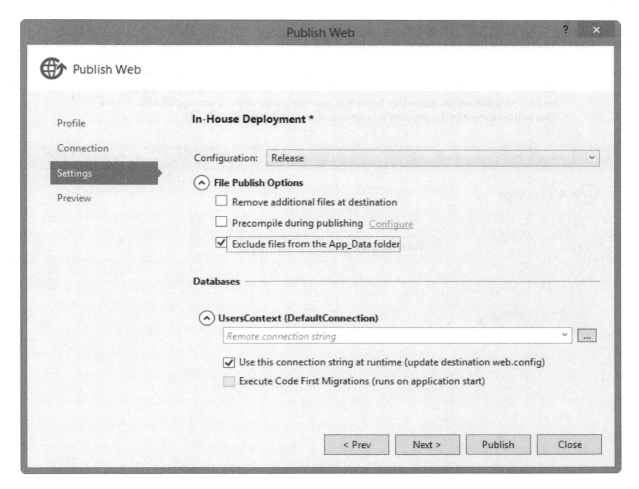

Figure 12-26. *Publish settings*

■ **Note** The "Execute Code First Migrations (runs on application start)" check box is unavailable because of the Entity Framework (EF) option we chose in Chapter 6 when creating the data model for our application. Recall that there are two options to create the data model: *database first*, when the database already exists, and *code first*, if the database will be built using the entities in the EF model. Since we had already created the database in Chapter 3, we used the database-first approach. If we had chosen the code-first approach, this check box would have been checked by default, which tells the application to use the Code First Migrations tool to deploy the database and updates to the database schema directly to the database when the application starts for the first time.

---

14. Click the "Next" button.

15. The last page of the Publish Web wizard (as shown in Figure 12-27) is an option to preview the outcome of the publishing process. Click the Start Preview button, the dialog will compile the application and compare the version in Visual Studio against the version in the server (if there is a version in the server, of course). The result is the list of files that will be copied to the server. Since this is the first time we are publishing our application, all the files will be shown in the preview window, as shown in Figure 12-28.

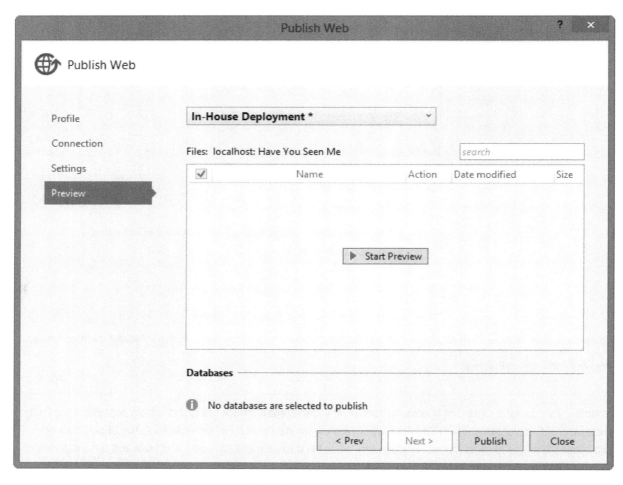

Figure 12-27. *Preview step in the Publish Web wizard*

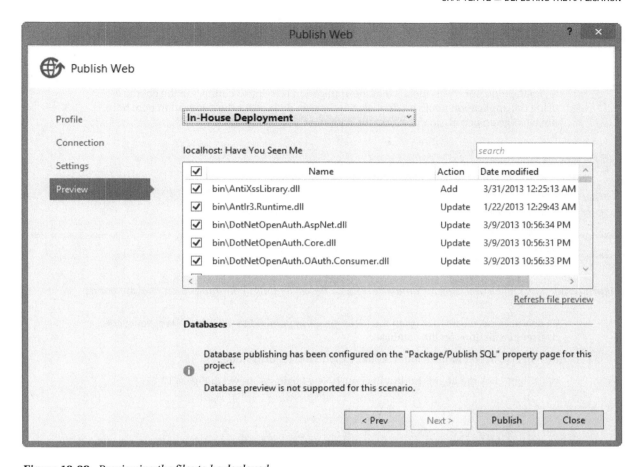

Figure 12-28. *Previewing the files to be deployed*

16. Click "Publish" to deploy the application. The Output window in Visual Studio will show the result of the publishing process, as shown in Figure 12-29.

```
Output
Show output from: Build                                          ▼ | ≝ | ≜ ≜ | ≍ | ᵃᵇ⃨
2>Adding file (Have You Seen Me\Views\Home\Contact.cshtml).
2>Adding file (Have You Seen Me\Views\Home\Index.cshtml).
2>Adding directory (Have You Seen Me\Views\Shared).
2>Adding file (Have You Seen Me\Views\Shared\Error.cshtml).
2>Adding file (Have You Seen Me\Views\Shared\_Layout.cshtml).
2>Adding file (Have You Seen Me\Views\Shared\_LoginPartial.cshtml).
2>Adding file (Have You Seen Me\Views\Web.config).
2>Adding file (Have You Seen Me\Views\_ViewStart.cshtml).
2>Adding file (Have You Seen Me\Web.config).
2>Adding ACL's for path (Have You Seen Me)
2>Adding ACL's for path (Have You Seen Me)
2>Publish is successfully deployed.
2>Site was published successfully http://localhost:8080/
========== Build: 1 succeeded, 0 failed, 0 up-to-date, 0 skipped ==========
========== Publish: 1 succeeded, 0 failed, 0 skipped ==========
```

Figure 12-29. *Output of the publish process*

17. At this point, Visual Studio has finished the deployment process. The application is now ready in the server and Visual Studio opens a browser window to the published web site.

18. You might get an error (as shown in Figure 12-30) when trying to access the new database. The reason for this error is that in IIS, web sites run under the security context provided by an application pool. This means that the application is trying to connect to the database using the application pool's credentials but the user defined for the application pool have not been given permission to access the database.

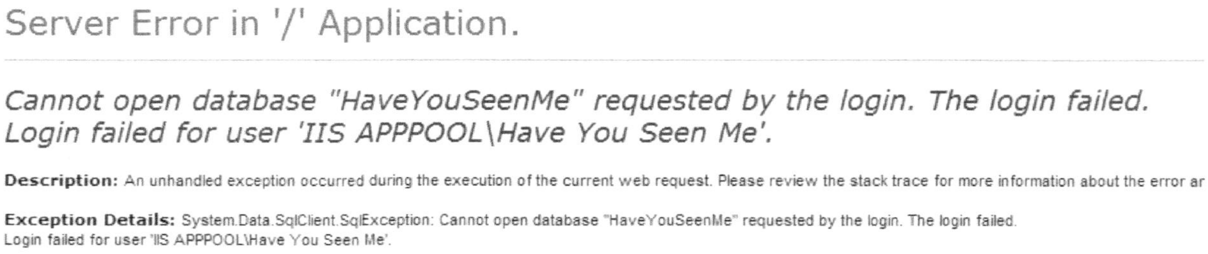

Server Error in '/' Application.
Cannot open database "HaveYouSeenMe" requested by the login. The login failed.
Login failed for user 'IIS APPPOOL\Have You Seen Me'.
Description: An unhandled exception occurred during the execution of the current web request. Please review the stack trace for more information about the error ar
Exception Details: System.Data.SqlClient.SqlException: Cannot open database "HaveYouSeenMe" requested by the login. The login failed.
Login failed for user 'IIS APPPOOL\Have You Seen Me'.

Figure 12-30. *Error when accessing the database because the credentials in the application pool are not set*

To fix this issue, we need to grant the IIS application named `IIS APPPOOL\Have You Seen Me` user permissions on the database:

a. In SQL Server Management Studio, expand the Security node.

b. Right-click the Logins node and choose New Login, as shown in Figure 12-31.

Object Explorer
Connect
DELL-JOSE (SQL Server 11.0.3128 - DELI
Databases
Security
Se
Cr
Server
Replic
Mana
New Login...
Filter
Start PowerShell
Reports
Refresh

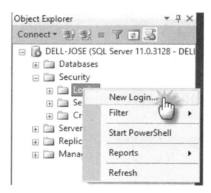

Figure 12-31. *Opening the New Login dialog*

c. In the New Login dialog, shown in Figure 12-32, type the login name **IIS APPPOOL\Have You Seen Me** and select the "Windows Authentication" radio button. At the bottom, set the default database to be `HaveYouSeenMe`.

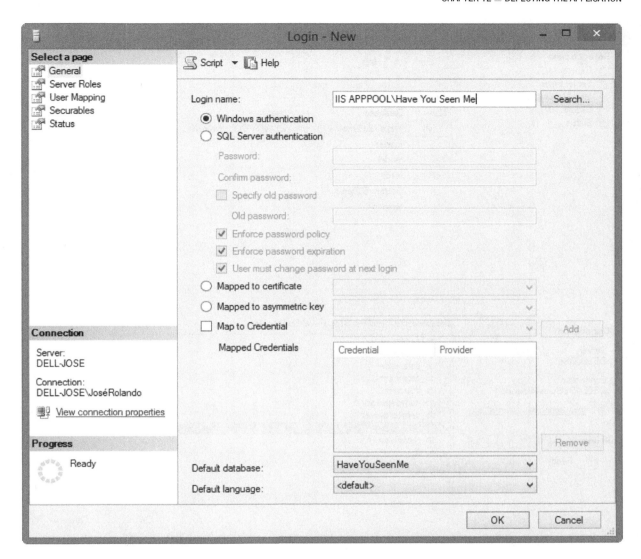

Figure 12-32. *Creating a new login for the web site*

d. Click the User Mapping option in the left pane of the dialog. This opens the settings to grant permissions on the database to the user. Select the database HaveYouSeenMe in the top section, and in the bottom section select db_owner and public as the roles for the new login in the database, as shown in Figure 12-33. The public role gives the user permission to connect to SQL Server and access the database. The db_owner role can perform all configuration and maintenance activities on the database, and can also drop the database. As mentioned before, you should follow the guidelines and security rules of your organization to give users proper permissions to the database. *You should not give db_owner privileges to an application user, but for the purpose of our deployment scenario, we will do it here.* Then click "OK."

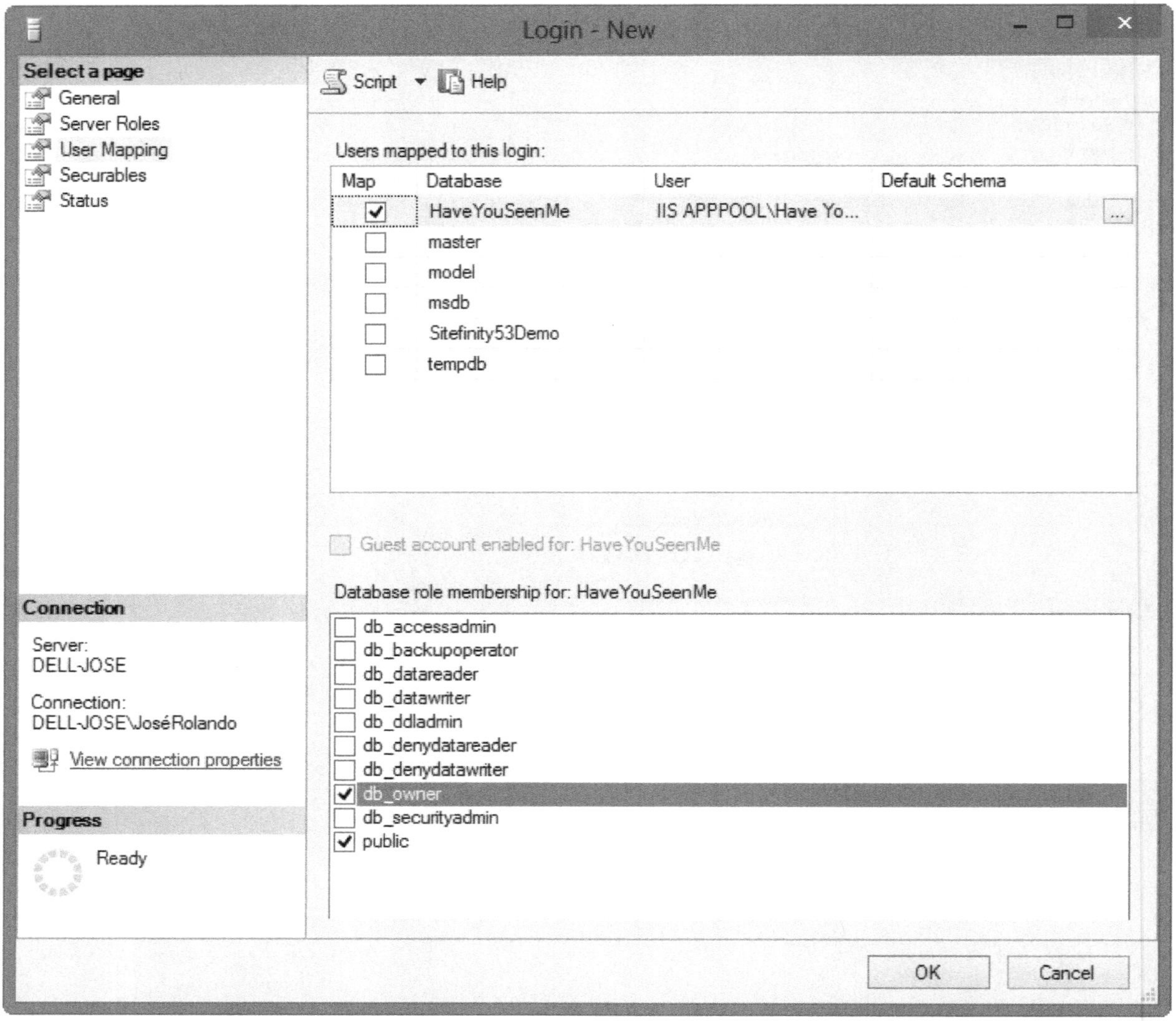

Figure 12-33. *Setting the roles in the database for the new login*

    e.   Refresh the page in the browser, and it should work.

With these steps, you have successfully deployed your application to an in-house server. Next we'll look at how to do this for a different scenario by deploying the application to a cloud web site in Windows Azure.

Deploying to Windows Azure

Windows Azure is the cloud platform from Microsoft. With Windows Azure you can host (at the time of this writing) up to ten web sites for free and scale up as needed. In addition to free web sites, you get a 90-day free trial of all other services from Windows Azure, including:

- *Infrastructure services*: Provide a scalable, on-demand infrastructure using virtual machines and virtual networks.

- *Mobile services*: Provide cloud storage for mobile apps; user authentication with Facebook, Twitter, Google, and Microsoft accounts; and notification hubs that allow apps to broadcast push notifications to Windows Phone, Windows Store, Android, and Apple iOS devices.

- *Cloud services*: Enable you to create highly available, scalable applications and services. Web applications run in a Platform as a Service (PaaS) environment that is automatically patched, upgraded, and maintained by Microsoft.

- *HDInsight*: A Big Data services service that allows you to store, process, and analyze large amounts of data using Apache Hadoop. Hadoop is a framework for distributed processing of large sets of data. The data is spread across multiple clusters of computers using simple programming models. You can find more information on Apache Hadoop at http://hadoop.apache.org and http://bit.ly/Azure-Hadoop.

- *Media services*: Enable you to create, manage, and distribute media on the cloud under the PaaS model.

To sign up for Windows Azure and get the 90-day free trial, you need to create an account by going to www.windowsazure.com and clicking the "Free Trial" icon in the top right corner of the page. Once your account is set up, you will gain access to the Windows Azure Management Portal. To access the Management Portal after you sign out, visit https://manage.windowsazure.com (see Figure 12-34).

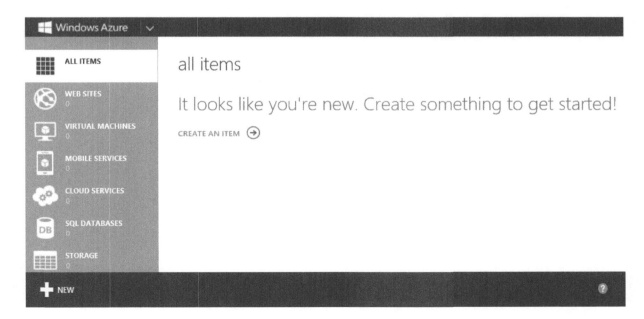

Figure 12-34. *Windows Azure Management Portal*

Setting Up a Web Site and Database in Windows Azure

We need to start by creating a web site that will host the application. At the bottom of the Windows Azure Management Portal, click the New link (with the big plus sign to its left). Choose Compute ➤ Web Site ➤ Custom Create, as shown in Figure 12-35. There's also a Quick Create option, but we are choosing the Custom Create option because it allows us to also create a new database.

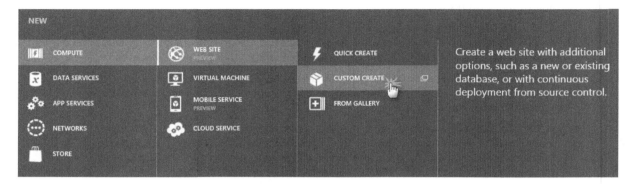

Figure 12-35. *Creating a new web site in the Windows Azure Management Portal*

One important aspect is that, while the web site is free (and will remain free beyond the 90-day trial), you have the option to create a free 20MB SQL Server database or purchase a larger database. For now, we will use the database allowance in the 90-day trial. You will need to consider the cost of a database when deploying your own applications. You can use the data management calculator at http://bit.ly/Azure-Calculator to estimate the cost of the database.

The first step of the New Website – Custom Create wizard is to define the URL for the web site and in which data center it will be hosted, as shown in Figure 12-36. All web sites in Windows Azure are created with a subdomain under the azurewebsites.net domain. The URL you choose will be used to access the web site. For our application, I'm going to use haveyouseenme.azurewebsites.net. You will need to use a different name.

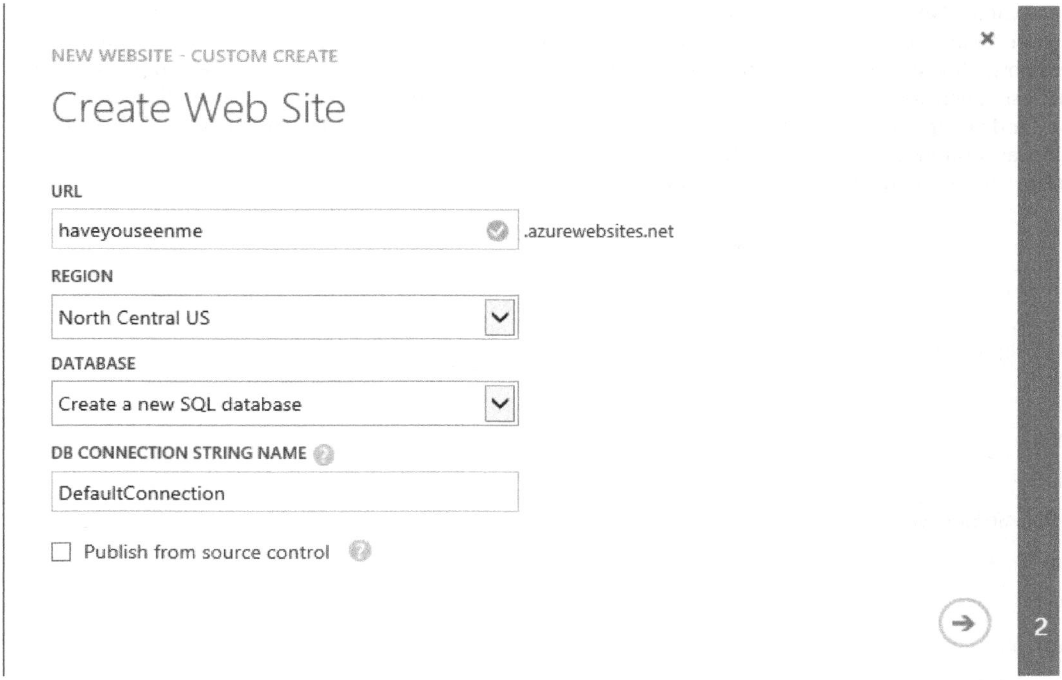

NEW WEBSITE - CUSTOM CREATE

Create Web Site

URL

| haveyouseenme | ✓ | .azurewebsites.net |

REGION

| North Central US | ∨ |

DATABASE

| Create a new SQL database | ∨ |

DB CONNECTION STRING NAME ❔

| DefaultConnection |

☐ Publish from source control ❔

Figure 12-36. *First step in creating a new web site with the Custom Create option*

■ **Note** Windows Azure offer three web site modes. The *Free mode* is the default mode when creating new web sites. The next one is *Shared mode*. Under the Free and Shared modes, web sites run in a multitenant environment with some caps for CPU, memory, and network usage. Finally, there is the *Reserved mode*. In Reserved mode, web sites are moved into a small virtual machine (VM) where they have dedicated CPU, memory, and network resources along with a higher cap for storage. Free web sites can only be accessed using the azurewebsites.net URL. If you want to use a custom domain, you will need to upgrade to a Shared or Reserved web site. Changing the web site mode is a per web site setting and can be done using the Windows Azure Management Portal. Click the Web Sites option in the left pane (shown previously in Figure 12-34), click the web site you want to modify in the list of web sites, and then click the Scale option at the top of the page. For more information on features and pricing, visit http://bit.ly/Azure-Websites.

In addition to specifying the domain name you need to define in which data center you want the the website to be created. Normally you would choose the one closest to you. After you selected the data center, tell the wizard to create a new SQL database (in the Database drop-down list box), and then define a connection string name in the bottom field. The connection string name allows your application to access the connection string programmatically at runtime. This way, you don't have to modify the connection strings you may have in your configuration file. The last option, the "Publish from source control" check box, enables you to specify whether you will be deploying through a source control system such as Team Foundation Service (TFS) or Git. For our application, we won't check this option. Click the right-arrow button to proceed.

The next step of the New Website – Custom Create wizard is to create the database, as shown in Figure 12-37. Give your database a name and choose whether it will be in a new server or an existing one. Since we don't have a database server now, choose "New SQL database server." In the following fields, define a username and password to access the database. Then you need to define in which data center you want the database to be located. To reduce network latency and ensure better performance, choose the same data center as the web site (in our case, North Central US). The last option, the Configure Advanced Database Settings check box, is use to specify whether you want to configure more settings on the database. Check this box and click the right-arrow button.

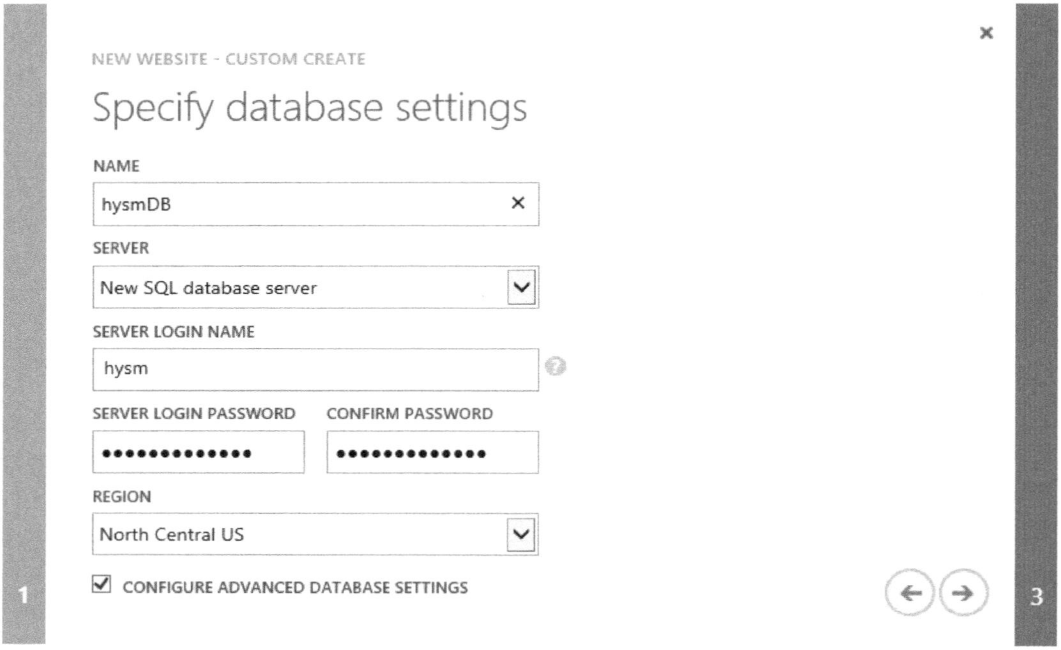

Figure 12-37. *Configuring the database in the New Website – Custom Create wizard*

The last step of the wizard is the "Advanced database settings" page (shown in Figure 12-38). In this step you define the edition of SQL Server to use for your database. The options available (at the time of this writing) are Web Edition and Business Edition. The difference between the two is that the Web Edition supports up to a 5GB database while the Business Edition supports up to a 150GB database. The price of the database is based on the actual size. More information on pricing can be found at http://bit.ly/Azure-Website-Database.

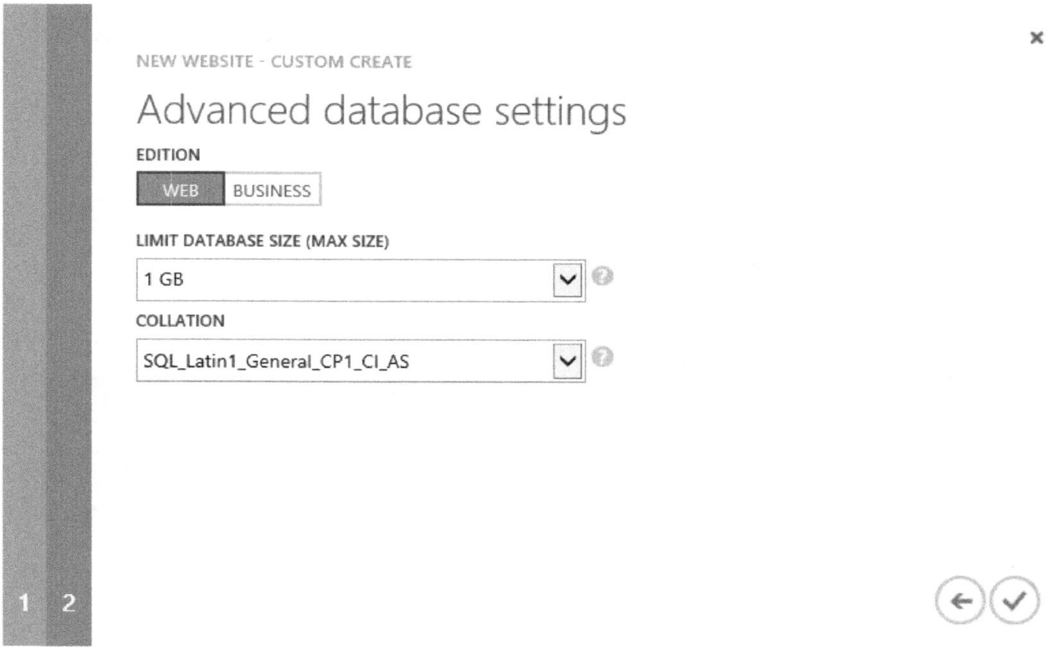

NEW WEBSITE - CUSTOM CREATE

Advanced database settings

EDITION

| WEB | BUSINESS |

LIMIT DATABASE SIZE (MAX SIZE)

1 GB

COLLATION

SQL_Latin1_General_CP1_CI_AS

Figure 12-38. *Advanced database settings when creating a database*

For our application, we are going to use Web Edition and limit the database size to 1GB. In the Collation field, define the collation for the database. *Collations* define rules for sorting and comparing data. The collation cannot be changed after database creation, so we need to make sure it fits the application needs. The default collation is SQL_Latin1_General_CP1_CI_AS. The settings of the default collation are as follows:

- Latin dictionary, which tells SQL Server to treat strings using basically ASCII characters
- Code page 1 (CP1), which defines the alphabet, punctuation, and symbols of the language
- Case-insensitive (CI), which means "ABC" is equal to "abc"
- Accent-sensitive (AS), which means "á" does not equal "å"

Click the finish button (the check mark icon) and the web site and database should be ready in a couple of minutes (see Figure 12-39). The task that takes the longest time is the provisioning of the database, but that only takes about one or two minutes.

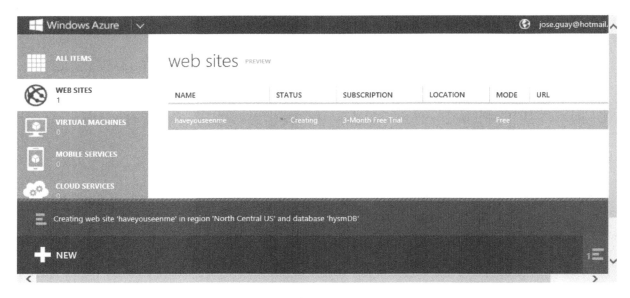

Figure 12-39. *Creating the haveyouseenme web site and database*

After the creation process is complete, you will see the status updated to Running, as shown in Figure 12-40, and the location and URL columns filled with the web site information.

Figure 12-40. *Web site created and running*

Deploying to Windows Azure Web Sites

The actual deployment process to a Windows Azure web site is very simple. You basically need to do two things:

- Obtain the web site publish profile file. The publish profile contains the URLs, user credentials, and database strings required to connect to and authenticate against each of the endpoints for which a publication method (FTP and/or Web Deploy) is enabled. The file is in XML file format. When you download the publish profile file, it is saved with the extension .PublishSettings and can be manually opened and examined using any text editor.

- Import the profile into the built-in publish mechanism in Visual Studio so that you can publish the web site to Windows Azure directly from within Visual Studio.

Obtain the Publish Profile File

To get the publish profile file after the web site is created in Azure, use the following steps:

1. Click the Web Sites category in the navigation pane on the left side of the Windows Azure Portal page (refer to Figure 12-40).

2. Click the web site name to go to the web site welcome page (shown in Figure 12-41).

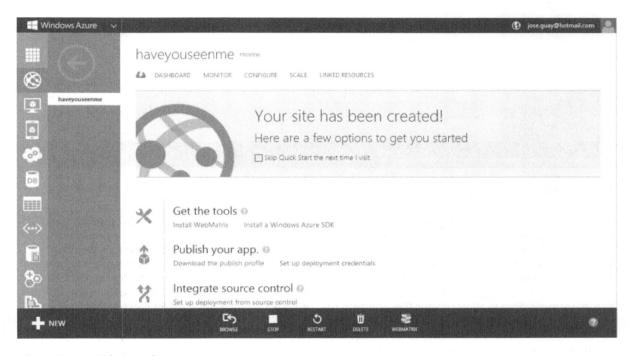

Figure 12-41. *Web site welcome page*

3. Click the Dashboard link at the top of the page. The Dashboard page will give you the current configuration information of the web site along with usage statistics and monitoring information.

4. On the Dashboard page, click the "Download the publish profile" link (see Figure 12-42) to get the publish profile file.

Figure 12-42. *Downloading the publish profile from the web site Dashboard page*

The content of the publish profile file is shown in Listing 12-2. Note that the content is in XML format. It has all the information needed to connect to Windows Azure, including the web site information and the database information. You can also see that the file actually includes two different profiles. The first profile uses Web Deploy and the second profile uses FTP. Both profiles serve the same purpose, which is to deploy the application to Azure. The main difference is the protocol they use: the Web Deploy profile uses HTTP and the FTP profile uses FTP. Having two profiles is an advantage because sometimes developers are only allowed to use FTP. This restriction is established by some organizations to allow copying files only with FTP, which is a protocol designed for files transfer. Having the two options facilitates the deployment process.

Listing 12-2. Content of the Publish Profile File

```xml
<?xml version="1.0" encoding="UTF-8"?>
<publishData>
    <publishProfile profileName="haveyouseenme - Web Deploy"
                    publishMethod="MSDeploy"
                    publishUrl="waws-prod-ch1-001.publish.azurewebsites.windows.net:443"
                    msdeploySite="haveyouseenme"
                    userName="$haveyouseenme"
                    userPWD="[not shown]"
                    destinationAppUrl="http://haveyouseenme.azurewebsites.net"
                    SQLServerDBConnectionString="[hidden]"
                    mySQLDBConnectionString=""
                    hostingProviderForumLink=""
                    controlPanelLink="http://windows.azure.com"
                    targetDatabaseEngineType="sqlazuredatabase"
                    targetServerVersion="Version100">
```

```
        <databases>
            <add name="DefaultConnection"
                connectionString="[hidden]"
                providerName="System.Data.SqlClient"
                type="Sql"
                targetDatabaseEngineType="sqlazuredatabase"
                targetServerVersion="Version100" />
        </databases>
    </publishProfile>
    <publishProfile profileName="haveyouseenme - FTP"
                    publishMethod="FTP"
                    publishUrl="ftp://waws-prod-ch1-001.ftp.azurewebsites.windows.net/
                                                              site/wwwroot"
                    ftpPassiveMode="True"
                    userName="haveyouseenme\$haveyouseenme"
                    userPWD="[hidden]"
                    destinationAppUrl="http://haveyouseenme.azurewebsites.net"
                    SQLServerDBConnectionString="[hidden]"
                    mySQLDBConnectionString=""
                    hostingProviderForumLink=""
                    controlPanelLink="http://windows.azure.com"
                    targetDatabaseEngineType="sqlazuredatabase"
                    targetServerVersion="Version100">
        <databases>
            <add name="DefaultConnection"
                connectionString="[hidden]"
                providerName="System.Data.SqlClient"
                type="Sql"
                targetDatabaseEngineType="sqlazuredatabase"
                targetServerVersion="Version100" />
        </databases>
    </publishProfile>
</publishData>
```

Import the Publish Profile File into Visual Studio

The following steps will guide you through the process of importing the publish profile into Visual Studio:

1. Open Visual Studio (if it is not open already) and open the web application.

2. As you did earlier in the chapter, right-click the project name in the Solution Explorer window and select the Publish option to open the Publish Web wizard.

3. This time, instead of manually creating a publish profile, click the "Import" button to the right of the profile drop-down list box, as shown in Figure 12-43.

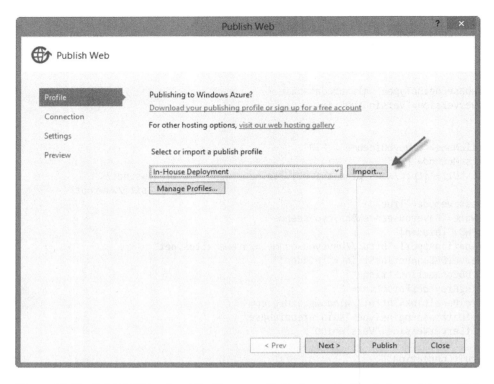

Figure 12-43. *Publish Web wizard Profile page with the Import button to import the publish profile*

4. Select the publish profile file and click "OK."

5. When the file is imported, the Publish Web wizard adds the two profiles (Web Deploy and FTP) to the profiles list. By default, the Connection page of the wizard shows the connection details of the first profile from the file (i.e. if the Web Deploy profile was first in the file then it is selected by default in the Publish method dropdow), as shown in Figure 12-44.

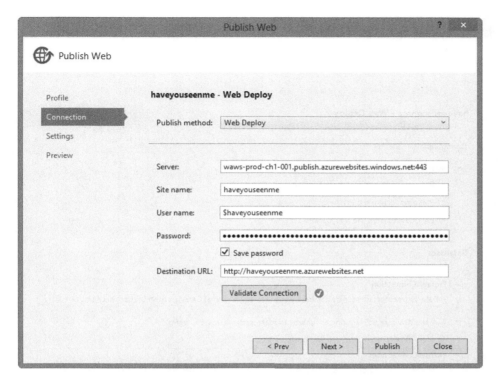

Figure 12-44. *Connection properties loaded from the publish profile*

As you did the first time through the wizard, click the "Validate Connection" button to ensure that you can connect to Windows Azure from your computer. If everything is okay, a green and white check mark icon appears next to the button. Then click "Next."

6. The next wizard page, Settings, shows the specific settings for the deployment. As before, the "Exclude files from the App_Data folder" check box should be checked to omit the contents of the App_Data folder. As shown in Figure 12-45, Visual Studio has already populated the information for the databases, including the information for the DefaultConnection connection string as well as the EntitiesConnection connection string for our EF data model and the UsersContext DbContext object. Click "Next."

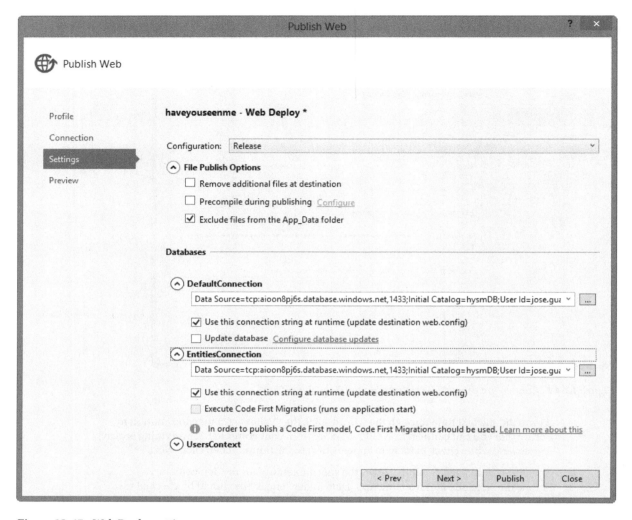

Figure 12-45. *Web Deploy settings*

7. On the Preview page, click the "Preview" button to review what will be updated in the web site. Since this is the first time the web application will be published to Windows Azure, the preview window lists all the files, as shown in Figure 12-46.

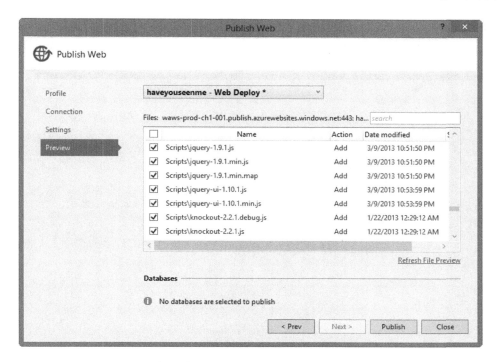

Figure 12-46. *Previewing the web application files that will be published*

8. Click the "Publish" button to publish the web application. If everything goes fine, you should see the published application in the browser, as shown in Figures 12-47 and 12-48.

```
Output
Show output from: Build                                          ▼  🔍  ⬒  ⬓  ⬐  ᵃᵇᶜ
2>Auuing TiTe (havcyouseenme\views\rec\riccurcupivau.cshtml).
2>Adding file (haveyouseenme\Views\Pet\View1.cshtml).
2>Updating file (haveyouseenme\Views\Shared\Error.cshtml).
2>Adding file (haveyouseenme\Views\Shared\ViewMasterPage1.Master).
2>Updating file (haveyouseenme\Views\Shared\_Layout.cshtml).
2>Updating file (haveyouseenme\Views\Shared\_LoginPartial.cshtml).
2>Updating file (haveyouseenme\Views\Web.config).
2>Updating file (haveyouseenme\Views\_ViewStart.cshtml).
2>Updating file (haveyouseenme\Web.config).
2>Adding ACL's for path (haveyouseenme)
2>Adding ACL's for path (haveyouseenme)
2>Publish is successfully deployed.
2>Site was published successfully http://haveyouseenme.azurewebsites.net/
========== Build: 1 succeeded, 0 failed, 0 up-to-date, 0 skipped ==========
========== Publish: 1 succeeded, 0 failed, 0 skipped ==========
|
```

Figure 12-47. *Publication to Windows Azure completed successfully*

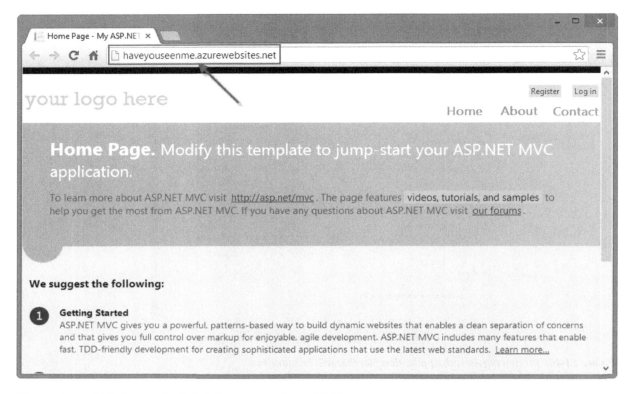

Figure 12-48. *Web site running in Windows Azure after publishing*

Using the Windows Azure SDK 2.0

The Windows Azure SDK is a set of tools and libraries that enables developers to manage and work with Windows Azure services from their client computers. With the Windows Azure SDK, developers could, for example, manage and configure settings on their Windows Azure web sites, including settings such as the target .NET Framework they use or whether or not they use PHP.

With the release of Windows Azure SDK 2.0, developers can now manage their Windows Azure accounts from within Visual Studio, which greatly facilitates the web site deployment process.

Install Windows Azure SDK 2.0

To install the Windows Azure SDK 2.0:

1. Visit the Windows Azure Developer Center at `http://bit.ly/AzureDev`.

2. In the Quick Links section on the right, click the "install the SDK" link.

3. Click the link for the version of Visual Studio you are using (2010 SP1 or 2012).

4. When prompted to download the WebPI installer file, save the file to your local disk.

5. Double-click the file to start the WebPI installation process.

6. Follow the steps in the WebPI wizard to install the Windows Azure SDK.

Link Your Windows Azure Account to Visual Studio

To use Visual Studio to manage Windows Azure services, you need to link your Windows Azure account to Visual Studio. The following steps will guide you through the process of linking your Windows Azure account to Visual Studio:

1. Open Visual Studio and open the web application.

2. Right-click the web application name in the Solution Explorer window and choose the Publish option. This opens the Publish Web wizard, as shown earlier in Figure 12-43.

3. Click the "Import" button. As you saw earlier, prior to installing the SDK, clicking this button opens a browse window where you select the publish profile for the web site. Having installed the SDK, clicking this button now opens the Import Publish Profile dialog, shown in Figure 12-49, which gives you two options, "Import from a Windows Azure web site" and "Import from a publish profile file." The second option is the traditional option (which you saw in the previous section) to browse for a publish profile web site already downloaded. The first option allows you to link Visual Studio to your Windows Azure account, so leave that selected.

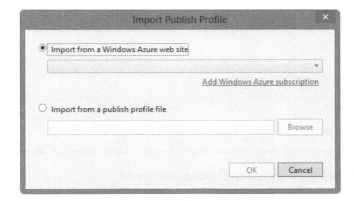

Figure 12-49. *New Import Publish Profile dialog*

4. Click the "Add Windows Azure subscription" link. This opens the Import Windows Azure Subscriptions dialog (shown in Figure 12-50), where you can browse for the subscription file (if you already downloaded it) or download the subscription file. The subscription file contains information about the current subscription to Windows Azure in your account. It provides Visual Studio with the information it needs to connect to your Windows Azure account and gain access to the services you have previously set up.

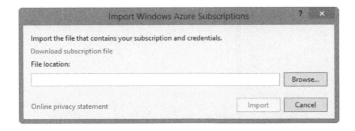

Figure 12-50. *Import Windows Azure Subscriptions dialog*

5. Click the "Download subscription file" link. This opens a browser window where you can connect to your Windows Azure account and download the subscription file. Once you log in, you will be taken to a page to download the subscription file, as shown in Figure 12-51.

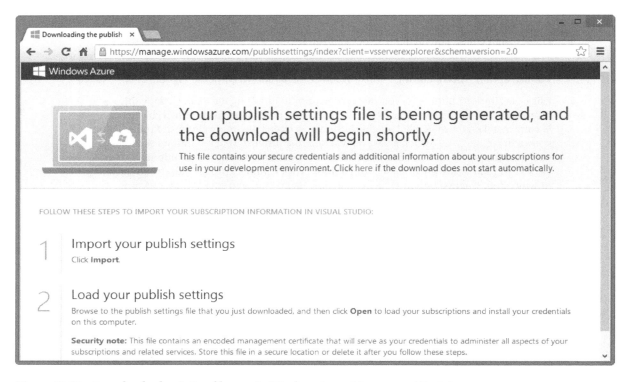

Figure 12-51. Download subscription file page in Windows Azure Management Portal

6. Save the subscription file, and then click the "Browse" button in the Import Windows Azure Subscription dialog to browse for it. Then click the "OK" button. This closes the dialog and returns you to the Import Publish Profile dialog, where the web site information will be available in the drop-down menu, as shown in Figure 12-52.

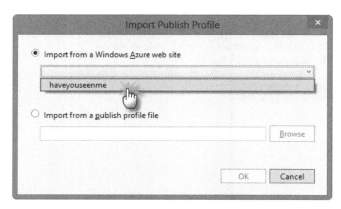

Figure 12-52. Windows Azure web site publish profile loaded from the subscription file

7. Select the publish profile from the drop-down list and click "OK."

At this point your web site publish profile is loaded and ready. You can use the steps outlined in the previous section to publish your web site.

Use Visual Studio to Manage Windows Azure Services

Now that Visual Studio is linked to your Windows Azure account, it has access to the web sites and all other services you may have, such as virtual machines, storage accounts, compute services, and more. The Server Explorer window now has access to all those services (see Figure 12-53).

Figure 12-53. Server Explorer window with access to Windows Azure services

Expand the Windows Azure Web Sites node to see your web sites. Right-click any web site to see the available options to manage that web site, as shown in Figure 12-54. You could, for example, view the web site settings (.NET Framework, PHP version, etc.), open the web site in the browser, or download the publish profile file.

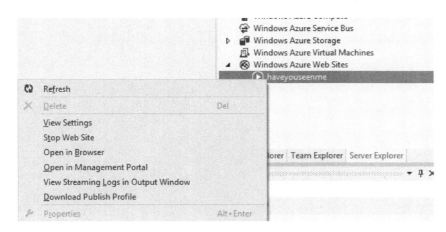

Figure 12-54. Administration options for Windows Azure web sites inside Visual Studio

Choose the View Settings option to make changes to the web site configuration in the same way as you would if you were in the Windows Azure Management Portal. Figure 12-55 shows the Configuration page, where you can change all aspects of the web site, such as the .NET Framework version, logging options, connection strings, and application settings. You can also stop and start the web site. Additionally, links are available that will take you to the web site page in the Windows Azure Management Portal.

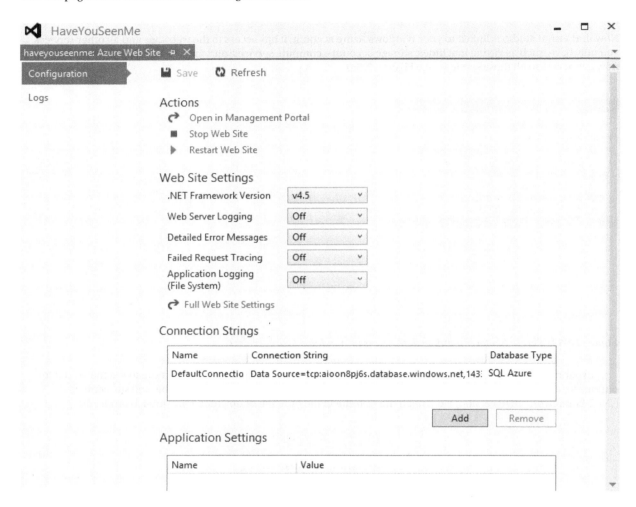

Figure 12-55. *Web site Configuration page in Visual Studio*

Summary

In this chapter you have seen the process of preparing the web application for deployment. The scenarios for deployment vary depending on the environment where the application will run. Many of those scenarios were not described because they involve handing the application and database to the operations team, which will then deploy them according to the policies and security standards in place. As you saw, other, simpler, scenarios can be handled by developers.

One of the scenarios involves creating the web site in IIS if the application will run in an in-house server. The application can then be published from Visual Studio directly to IIS. To deploy the database, we have created T-SQL scripts that can be run in any SQL Server database to create the databases and other objects that are needed for the application.

Another scenario we studied is to create a web site in the Windows Azure cloud platform. After creating the web site, you can download a publish profile file that can be imported in Visual Studio so all the connection and configuration information is already prepopulated. Deploying the application to a web site in Windows Azure is then a simple process, similar to the one examined in the in-house server scenario.

With the introduction of the Windows Azure SDK 2.0, the management tasks are now integrated into Visual Studio. Almost all the options to manage web sites are available so that you don't have to leave the development environment. With the SDK, the deployment task is also simplified, as the publishing profile can be directly downloaded and imported to Visual Studio.

As you saw in this chapter, the process of deploying a web application has improved significantly. The deployment process has been greatly simplified to the point that all the necessary tools are already integrated in Visual Studio. With just a few clicks you can have your application up and running in the production environment in no time. There are no significant differences between deploying applications to an in-house server or deploying them to the Windows Azure cloud platform. And best of all, you don't even have to leave Visual Studio now to deploy your applications.

Index

CPSIA information can be obtained at www.ICGtesting.com
Printed in the USA
LVOW01s0814191013

357677LV00007B/272/P